YEARNING FOR IMMORTALITY

YEARNING FOR IMMORTALITY

The European Invention of the Ancient Egyptian Afterlife

Rune Nyord

The University of Chicago Press CHICAGO AND LONDON

This book is freely available in an open-access edition thanks to the generous support of Emory University and the Andrew W. Mellon Foundation.

The University of Chicago Press, Chicago 60637
The University of Chicago Press, Ltd., London

Published 2025
Printed in the United States of America

34 33 32 31 30 29 28 27 26 25 1 2 3 4 5

ISBN-13: 978-0-226-83823-6 (cloth)
ISBN-13: 978-0-226-83825-0 (paper)
ISBN-13: 978-0-226-83824-3 (e-book)
DOI: https://doi.org/10.7208/chicago/9790226838243.001.0001

Library of Congress Cataloging-in-Publication Data

Names: Nyord, Rune, author.
Title: Yearning for immortality : the European invention of the ancient Egyptian afterlife / Rune Nyord.
Description: Chicago : The University of Chicago Press, 2025. | Includes bibliographical references and index.
Identifiers: LCCN 2024038396 | ISBN 9780226838236 (cloth) | ISBN 9780226838250 (paperback) | ISBN 9780226838243 (e-book)
Subjects: LCSH: Future life—Ancient Egyptian religion. | Eschatology, Egyptian. | Christianity and other religions—Egyptian. | Egyptology—History. | Egypt—Religion.
Classification: LCC BL2450.F83 N96 2025 | DDC 224/.207—dc23/eng/20240913
LC record available at https://lccn.loc.gov/2024038396

♾ This paper meets the requirements of ANSI/NISO Z39.48-1992 (Permanence of Paper).

For Henrijette and Leonora

Contents

Introduction

> We are therefore still in uncertainty respecting the actual intentions of the Egyptians, in thus preserving the body, and ornamenting their sepulchres at so great an expense; nor is there any decided proof that the resurrection of the body was a tenet of their religion. It is, however, highly probable that such was their belief, since no other satisfactory reason can be given for the great care of the body after death.
>
> (Wilkinson 1841, 2:445)

These are the words of English traveler John Gardner Wilkinson (1797–1875), who lived in Egypt for more than a decade during the 1820s and 1830s. He spent a substantial amount of his time in the decorated rock tombs on the west bank of modern-day Luxor, studying the wall scenes there with the aim of producing an ethnographic description of the "manners and customs" of the ancient Egyptians. Although this aim and the methods with which he pursued it prompted more interest in the outward aspects of the culture, Wilkinson also included lengthy discussions of religious topics. Among the questions he addressed was the motivation behind the famous elaborate embalming practices of the Egyptians, in the face of which he admits a certain frustration in the passage quoted above.

His line of argument is characteristic of early approaches to Egyptian mortuary religion, not just in the nineteenth century, but also well before that. This is true first in the sense that the question about

Egyptian religious "tenets" is worded as a matter of course in terms of a binary question of adherence or not to a specific Christian doctrine. An answer going beyond a simple yes or no is not anticipated. Second, Wilkinson's approach is characteristic in the deductive way the question is in turn answered. In the absence of "decided proof," it becomes a matter of what types of explanations of the empirical findings one can present. Together, these two premises lead Wilkinson to ultimately lean toward the solution that the Egyptians did in fact believe in the resurrection of the body. This is the third way the approach is representative: a certain tendency to affirm the conclusions predetermined by the way the question was posed.

This is also the approach behind the wording in the title of this book, taken from one of the letters of Benoît de Maillet, French consul general in Egypt in the late seventeenth and early eighteenth centuries. As I discuss further in chapter 4, Maillet regarded a "secret yearning for immortality" (*désir secrèt de l'immortalité,* Mascrier 1735, 45ff.) as a human universal, ultimately fulfilled by the Christian revelation. As such, it was only natural to assume that this was also the motivation underlying Egyptian burial practices. At one remove, the wording is also an apt characterization of European approaches through the centuries more generally, where a yearning to find an ancient quest for immortality is sometimes explicit and sometimes more "secret." But as I argue throughout the book, it remained a constant and stabilizing influence on thought about ancient Egyptian religion through the centuries.

Among the best-known ideas about the ancient Egyptian culture, both inside and outside academia, is that the ancient Egyptians went to extraordinary lengths in their funeral preparations. Even if the trope of their being "obsessed with death" has fallen into disfavor, the overall understanding of the Egyptians as bent on a quest for eternal life remains. Indeed, the evidence seems overwhelming: corpses mummified to preserve the body for eternity, servant figurines intended to come to life to see to material needs in the afterlife, funerary texts with vivid descriptions of the beyond, and so on. On closer scrutiny, however, it turns out that this evidence does not consist solely of the actions or interpretations by the ancient Egyptians themselves: each of the phenomena is tightly interwoven with the interpretive framework traditionally deployed to make sense of them.

As an example, consider wooden figurines like those depicted in figure 1, which were frequently deposited in Egyptian tombs of the late third and early second millennia BCE. Many are depicted producing food or other necessities of life in the Nile Valley. It seems a very small interpretive step, effectively little more than a neutral description, to say that these were servants meant to care for the deceased in the afterlife. Of course, for this interpretation to work one needs to assume that the Egyptians were a rather superstitious lot, but that has become a standard assumption underlying contemporary approaches to the ancient culture. But if we sidestep the intuitive attraction of such ideas and instead ask where these ideas came from and how and why they came to seem so attractive, things begin to look more complicated.

The contemporary version of the interpretation of figurines' magically coming to life to perform their tasks can be traced back to the late nineteenth- and early twentieth-century German scholar Adolf Erman (see chapter 8). But why did it seem to him and his readers like the most straightforward explanation? As the recipient of a tradition shaped by intellectual developments taking place over centuries, Erman had come to expect, as most contemporary observers do, that the goal of ancient Egyptian funerary culture was to save the souls of the dead so they could achieve eternal life, often as the result of a postmortem divine judgment of each individual's ethical and religious merits.

The model, in other words, sounded (and sounds) remarkably Christian, while the specific practices one could observe through the texts, images, and archaeological evidence available naturally were distinctively pagan. However, the model was highly capacious, as shown by the ease with which specific grave goods such as funerary figurines could be interpreted. Given the assumption that the Egyptians were bent on a quest for eternal life, along with the empirical fact that food offerings were deposited and presented regularly after the funeral (as known from numerous texts and images), it stood to reason that the food was necessary for the general purpose of achieving eternal life. It was a small step to think that the physically minded Egyptians were

Fig. 1: Figurines in model granary from the tomb of Meketre (ca. 1980 BCE). Painted, plastered wood with linen and grain. Metropolitan Museum of Art, 20.3.11.

afraid of running out of food during their eternal afterlife, and for Erman this *Hungersgefahr*, or danger of hunger, became a key concept. Having arrived at this idea, it was another small step to posit some sort of "magical" belief by which the Egyptians thought the wooden figurines could fulfill this need. In other words, the chain of inference is entirely deductive, based on the initial premise that the Egyptians wanted eternal life along the lines of popular Christian beliefs.

As this is merely one example of the way specifics of Egyptian mortuary religion could (and can) be explained, it becomes of significant interest to examine how the underlying assumptions came about. How did ancient Egypt come to be inextricably associated with themes of eternal life, rebirth, and postmortem judgment well before detailed knowledge of Egyptian funerary culture, let alone the workings of the hieroglyphic script or the contents of indigenous texts, was available?

And how could these ideas remain largely unchanged as such knowledge was gradually gained?

The following chapters explore these questions by tracing the development of the modern framework of the ancient Egyptian afterlife. As a key aspect of ancient Egyptian religion, one might expect the historiography of ancient Egyptian mortuary religion to be well established in the literature, but this is not the case, likely for a combination of reasons. A key factor is that, with the notable exception of the story of deciphering the hieroglyphic script in the early nineteenth century, detailed Egyptological historiography rarely goes back further than the establishment of systematic excavation practices and the proliferation of Egyptological chairs at universities around Europe in the 1880s and 1890s. By this time the afterlife framework had already surfaced more or less in the form it has today, giving the impression that it is an obvious interpretation emerging more or less directly from the ancient evidence itself.

This impression is strengthened by the traditional teleological mode of writing the history of Egyptology, focusing on individuals and their contributions to the field's current practices and state of knowledge. While providing innovations in other areas, including an increasingly international understanding of the discipline, this remains the basic approach in the most recent works (e.g., Thompson 2015–18; Bednarski, Dodson, and Ikram 2021). Exceptions, where past Egyptology is understood as a cultural, political, and intellectual phenomenon with its own historicity rather than primarily as practices pointing forward to the present discipline, remain rare and tend to be written by historians rather than Egyptologists (e.g., Gange 2013; Carruthers 2022; Sheppard 2022). This approach thus helps historicize the phenomenon, but it tends to produce results less directly relevant to current Egyptological practices, and hence potentially of less direct relevance to contemporary readers whose primary interest (whether professional or not) is in ancient Egypt.

Given the aims of this book, a traditional teleological approach would be counterproductive in an area where the argument is precisely that a conventional and largely unquestioned conceptual framework is in fact inadequate and rests on significant but largely unrecognized interpolations. Instead, the question becomes why people at different times were interested in ancient Egypt in general and the ancient Egyptian afterlife in particular, what concepts were available and useful for advancing particular agendas, and how this background influenced the lasting interpretation of the ancient Egyptian afterlife. While the exploration will thus necessarily focus especially on the influential writers who played a formative role in developing the conceptual frameworks, it is also necessary to look outside the Egyptological hall of fame to get a better sense of the issues under debate as well as the roads not taken.

The exploration thus falls within the history of ideas rather than the history of Egyptology strictly speaking, though the two areas naturally overlap. If anything, the danger thus becomes rather a kind of "reverse teleology." One main focus will by necessity be the genealogy of the ideas that ended up forming the modern view, even if the aim is to question them rather than—as in more traditional approaches—to celebrate the historical individuals who engendered them. However, by examining the internal logic of these ideas in the cultural and intellectual milieus where they first arose, along with the reasons they remained attractive in other times and places, and by contrasting them to ideas once prevalent that would prove less long-lived, I aim to provide a nuanced and critical exploration of this small but increasingly central area of Western thought about ancient Egypt.

The traditional approach to the history of Egyptology is to delineate the beginning of the discipline with Jean-François Champollion's publication on the principles of hieroglyphic writing in 1822. The rationale for this is the central role written sources and philology have played in the development of the discipline and the corresponding idea of the decipherment as a fundamental turning point. As will be seen in the following chapters, this idea can certainly be nuanced, not least because more than half a century passed from the initial decipherment to the publication and translation of substantial Egyptian texts (only really available from the last decades of the nineteenth century) that would enable them to play a significant role in the exploration of Egyptian culture alongside art, architecture, and artifacts.

Apart from this possibility of nuancing the cutoff date, the idea of a decisive "birth of Egyptology" has sometimes led to even more problematic expectations. Thus, in a recent contribution Jan Assmann and Florian Ebeling set up a marked dichotomy between "reception" of ancient Egypt (before 1822) and "Egyptology" (after that date):

> For intellectual history, it makes sense to put an end to the history of reception with the establishment of scientific Egyptology. Something has changed dramatically with the decipherment of the hieroglyphs. The West had direct access to ancient Egypt, being able to read the original texts of this culture. From then on there was no need to make an interpretation of the accounts of the bible and the classical literature to understand ancient Egypt. The perspective changed from focusing on the inside and the hidden wisdom, allegories and philosophical interpretations to the outside, quantification, editions and translation. (Assmann and Ebeling 2020, 36)

Two important caveats: As noted above, the change brought on by Champollion's decipherment was at best much more gradual than indicated in the quotation, and Assmann and Ebeling themselves go on to acknowledge the continued existence of ideas listed here as characterizing "reception" even after the decipherment of hieroglyphs. But a more fundamental issue with the scenario presented is whether there ever could exist a disinterested, objective "Egyptology" corresponding to Assmann and Ebeling's ideal type, transcending the time and place of its practitioners (cf. Colla 2007, 62–63). This idea has been a central claim of the discipline of Egyptology as part of its legitimation as an academic discipline, as a central example of what Gieryn (1983) has termed "boundary-work." As such, there seems no reason for the historian of Egyptology to take this claim at face value, and it can more fruitfully be approached as a strategy in the ongoing work of delineating the academic discipline of Egyptology against competing interests in, and approaches to, ancient Egypt. As explored in the following chapters, the entanglement between (proto-)Egyptologists and their cultural and intellectual setting was by no means a thing of the past by 1822, nor indeed is it today.

As an alternative to this approach, Okasha El Daly (2005) has contended that there is no fundamental difference between post-1822 engagements with Egypt's ancient past and those that came before. Specifically, this idea is part of a larger argument to rehabilitate, and increase knowledge of among Western scholars, the writings of medieval Arabic scholars as an important part of the history of Egyptology. As seen in chapter 2, the latter point is well taken, especially in light of the traditional neglect of these sources—mainly because of their relative inaccessibility to the typical Egyptologist, but certainly helped along by the stark traditional dichotomy between "reception" and "Egyptology" making scholarship predating decipherment of the hieroglyphs something of a curio, or at least a marginal area of specialization, from the point of view of mainstream Egyptology.

However, El Daly's suggestion of extending the use of the term "Egyptology" to cover production of knowledge about Egypt's ancient past in any era runs the risk of anachronism. As I occasionally touch on in the following chapters, the idea that "Egyptology" should be its own discipline rather than a subfield of, for instance, history or archaeology arose in very specific circumstances (cf. Champion 2003; Gange 2013). The burgeoning ancient Egyptian philology played a key role in the self-understanding of this new discipline, as did the colonial background of major European powers' strategic and economic interests in contemporary Egypt, the religious aims of biblical archaeology and chronology, and so on. As such, there does seem to be good reason for singling out "Egyptology" as a specific colonial and postcolonial cultural phenomenon of the nineteenth century through the twenty-first. However, that does not mean we should take the creation narrative of that discipline at face value and devalue knowledge produced before 1822. In fact, one of the main results of the exploration presented here is that the academic discipline of "Egyptology" as it appeared in the nineteenth century operated—and in many ways continues to operate—within a framework already established well before there was widespread access to ancient Egyptian written sources, and in certain central respects even before the deciphering of hieroglyphs.

A different type of criticism against Egyptological historiography comes from outside the discipline itself, namely from historians of science interested in the history of Egyptology. In a useful discussion of recent approaches to the history of Egyptology, William Carruthers

(Carruthers 2014) criticizes a tendency, especially in Egyptologists' own writings on this topic, to hold historical persons and processes up against a "pure" and timeless ideal Egyptology that practitioners of the past can be praised for living up to or criticized for failing to achieve (cf., e.g., Shapin 2010 for the language of purity). By contrast, Carruthers emphasizes works that approach the discipline as "neither pure nor stable, but one whose practices and existence are historically and spatially contingent" (Carruthers 2014, 5). It is far too easy to dismiss this distinction as merely one of disciplinary aims and interests between those of Egyptologists (interested in how best to practice their discipline in the present) and historians (interested in understanding Egyptology as a sociocultural phenomenon of the past). Rather, as Carruthers points out, what is at stake is the central epistemological question of how Egyptology is construed as a discipline.

None of these approaches is in itself entirely suitable for a study like this one, yet each offers useful insights to incorporate. Traditional Egyptological historiography is useful for framing the research questions in terms of the present state of the field of Egyptology, yet problematic in viewing that as an end goal and pinnacle that past scholars each contribute to approaching incrementally. This book thus rejects the assumption that present-day Egyptology holds the best possible answers to the questions taken up, while retaining the historiographical framing of the question "How did we get here?" Because of the book's focus on ideas about the ancient Egyptian afterlife as a specialized domain of thought (albeit one with numerous connections to other ideas) over a span of several centuries, traditional historiography is further useful in its method of focusing on individual writers and the interconnectedness of their ideas. I will pay greater attention to their historically contingent reasons for being interested in ancient Egypt in the first place, however, than is the norm in such traditional approaches.

Mnemohistory in the sense proposed by Jan Assmann is useful in its stance that studying the "memory" of Egypt is distinct from studying ancient Egypt itself directly, so the former should not be studied as a question of perceived success in the latter. However, as seen above, positing Egyptology as wholly distinct from reception as a pure, objective discipline transcending historical contingencies and with direct access to ancient Egyptian realities is untenable. In this book I thus adopt the approach of bracketing out any "objective reality" of ancient Egypt that past understandings could be held up against, yet I reject the idea that this approach applies only for pre-1822 reception as distinct from objective, academic Egyptology.

Finally, complementing the approach of traditional historiography, I find ideas from the history and philosophy of science useful in their insistence on viewing scholars and ideas of the past *and* the present as historically contingent, influenced by, and influencing, multiple aspects of their surroundings (e.g., Latour 2005; Shapin 2010). On the other hand, a critical historiography in the sense developed here needs to be guided by the present Egyptological concern that the afterlife hypothesis has in fact turned out to be problematic, which necessitates a limited element of presentism or teleology in shaping research questions and evaluating sources, even while studying scholars of the past within their historical and conceptual settings.

In one sense it certainly might be possible to conceptualize a project like this book along traditional lines, arguing that Egyptologists of the past failed to live up to disciplinary best practices by relying on conventional wisdom instead of examining the sources in an unbiased way. But that would ignore that the ideas and models criticized here have in fact been regarded as constituting mainstream Egyptology for well over a century. Questioning that the Egyptians were "obsessed with death [or life]" or bent on a "quest for eternal life" will actually be an intervention into what Egyptology is, as a historical product bound to change with the societies it is part of.

To come to terms with this, the perspective of the history of science is more useful than a conventional review of the literature. In this respect it is less interesting to point out that, by modern standards people were "wrong" in the past (and that some of these ideas continue to the present day) than it is to elucidate why and in what circumstances such ideas and practices developed, and why some ultimately turned out to be more successful than others. On the one hand, it is certainly important to demonstrate that the intuitive teleological answer (that ideas were successful because they offered the best explanation for the data) needs to be rejected, but a simple negation of that teleology would be equally simplistic. Rather, past engagements with ancient Egypt need to be understood in their historical contexts with attention to what interests they served and what work they performed in broader discourses and practices taking place in the pertinent times and places. In the words of Carruthers (2014, 8), the aim should be to write disciplinary histories that take into account the discipline's "inherent instability" and understand the discipline within the wider worlds it forms part of, which in turn have their own "contingent instabilities."

In this way the question of the creation and entrenchment of the Egyptological "afterlife" hypothesis becomes relevant to a much wider group of people than just Egyptologists. By exploring the wider conditions under which it developed and the social, intellectual, and practical reasons for its success, it becomes easier to understand why we have needed the Egyptians to take on this particular role, and how they have helped undergird particular widely held notions concerning universal human attitudes toward death and dying.

Yet at the same time, surely it would be coy for an Egyptologist writing on this topic to leave entirely open the question of what consequences contemporary Egyptology might draw from the historical contingencies of the "afterlife" hypothesis. My argument should thus be understood in the same vein. Rather than setting up an ideal Egyptology that forebears in the discipline have failed to live up to, it is in a sense a matter of recalibrating the relationship between Egyptology and neighboring fields such as archaeology and anthropology—equally unstable, and perhaps generally quicker to incorporate conceptual change.

Method and Aims

This book examines European ideas about ancient Egyptian mortuary religion, especially as they were increasingly construed in terms of belief in a personal afterlife, in their development from being a relatively negligible topic to becoming not only one of the most prevalent features of this ancient culture, but also a paramount cross-cultural example of universal human attitudes to death. A number of loosely connected themes are treated more sporadically, mainly when they have a bearing on this core topic. This includes especially the exploration of, and speculation about, ancient Egyptian practices of embalming, which were often understood within the prevailing medical discourses of the time rather than as phenomena of cultural history, although thoughts arising from this domain of the Egyptians' intent to preserve dead bodies often figured into more religious interpretations. In this category also belong broader ideas about the fundamental nature of Egyptian religion and culture that in some cases notably shaped thinking about the Egyptian afterlife more specifically.

Given the vast span of time explored here, and the enormous number of authors touching in one way or another upon the mortuary religion of ancient Egypt (especially in the periods discussed in the later chapters), any attempt at complete coverage would be futile. Instead, several criteria have guided my decision on whether to discuss individual scholars, and in what level of detail. Thus a contribution chosen for discussion here will tend to stand out from any contemporary treatments by the depth or breadth of its discussion, its influence on contemporary or later scholars, its context or motivation illustrating the scope of engagements with the topic in a given time and place, the more general prominence of the author, or some combination of these.

This set of criteria leaves obvious room for expansion in future studies. Perhaps most notably, since the objective is to trace the genealogy of a hegemonic European mode of thinking, I have made no specific attempt to privilege historically marginalized voices, as worthy an endeavor as that is (cf. e.g., Quirke 2010; Sheppard 2013; Doyon 2018; Navratilova et al. 2023). The ideas explored here are overwhelmingly those of white, male, Western European, and Christian scholars, and a main point of this book is precisely that these features, especially the last mentioned, have significantly circumscribed the discourse and determined its remarkable homogeneity and diachronic stability. The demonstration of this trajectory in the present book thus represents an important step in the effort to decolonize ancient Egyptian mortuary religion in the sense of recentering indigenous and coeval concepts and models.

The notion that the epistemology, priorities, and practices of contemporary Egyptology remain shaped in fundamental ways by the nineteenth-century origins of the field is no longer controversial (e.g., Jurman 2022; Langer 2017, 2023; Matić 2018, 2023), and an increasing trend in existing scholarship (e.g., Podemann Sørensen 1996, 2013; Riggs 2014; Nyord 2018) indicates that this is not least the case in conventional interpretations of ancient Egyptian mortuary religion. The developments traced here certainly corroborate this understanding, while also showing the significant ultimate anchoring of contemporary ideas and explanations in even older, early modern, attempts to fit ancient Egypt into a European worldview. A particularly striking result of this deep history is what might be termed a concerted effort of conceptual colonization, where the interpretation of indigenous ancient Egyptian texts, images, and even terminology that became increasingly known through the nineteenth century was effectively overridden by preexisting European frameworks and concepts. While the precise aims—and even practical feasibility—of a more general decolonization of Egyptology are still being debated (e.g., Gertzen 2020; Jurman 2022), this book aims to contribute to an awareness of such interpretations, and deliberate efforts to unravel them.

A related issue is that despite the vast time span, a small number of influential instances of "rhetorical closure" (Pinch and Bijker 1984) in this domain means that the ideas about ancient Egyptian mortuary religion turn out to change remarkably slowly and for the most part incrementally, even when deployed for ostensibly very different purposes. This means that the typical approach of demonstrating how different ideas arose from different historical contexts is only partly pertinent. To tackle this problem, I adopt a method of close reading with attention to wording, argumentative structure, and sources of evidence to capture and demonstrate the often minute variation in the sources and tie them to the wider agendas of authors.

Because of the emphasis on conceptual frameworks that are often only implicit in the analyzed sources, the discussion stays as close as possible to the original terminology. For the same reason, where English translations are given, key terms in the original language are provided in brackets. One partial exception is where specific ancient sources are referred to outside the context of particular historical analyses. For readers' convenience these are provided with their modern designations instead of (or in addition to) historical names that are now obsolete,(e.g., "the tomb of Ramesses VI [KV 9])" instead of "the Catacomb of Metempsychosis," or "the Book of the Dead" instead of "the Funerary Ritual." Similarly, the increasingly contested label "mummy" is unavoidable as an emic category in quotations and paraphrases, though for referring to actual human remains outside historical interpretations, I have generally preferred designations such as "embalmed body" or "mummified body."

All sources are quoted in English translations. For Classical sources, I have consulted the text in the original languages but cite authoritative translations with a preference for bilingual editions also containing the text in the original language. Relevant issues of translation and interpretation are discussed at the introduction of each such source in chapter 1. For medieval and later sources in Danish, French, German, Italian, and Latin, unless otherwise stated the English translations are my own. Sources in other languages are quoted in English translations by others as indicated in the references, although I have consulted them in the original language whenever possible.

Structure

This book traces the history of European ideas about ancient Egyptian mortuary religion from the accounts of medieval travelers through the formation of the modern Egyptological paradigm in the late nineteenth century. The main argument confronts the traditional understanding of this process according to which increasingly accurate knowledge of the ancient sources led to an increasingly correct understanding of Egyptian mortuary religion, culminating in contemporary Egyptology. Instead, the book contends, a basic framework was formed as far back as the seventeenth century using available concepts derived from Christianity to understand why the Egyptians apparently sought to preserve dead bodies and expended copious amounts of time and energy on the preparation of tombs. While this basic framework could be deployed for numerous reasons in changing intellectual milieus (e.g., in debates about universal history, about the relation between Christianity and paganism, or about Catholic versus Protestant theology and practice), such usages tended in practice to align with, and in turn entrench, the understanding of Egyptian religion in Christian terms.

A foundational claim in the book is that the framework for understanding the ancient Egyptian afterlife that is currently accepted in Egyptology had largely crystalized by the last decades of the nineteenth century. This means that when reading the scholars of the new generation emerging at this time—exemplified in chapter 8 by writers like E. A. Wallis Budge and Adolf Erman—their overall framework and often even the specific vocabulary seems very familiar. This is not to claim that nothing interesting or significant has happened since then in the exploration of ancient Egyptian mortuary religion, but in terms of the underlying assumptions or paradigm for understanding and explaining empirical details, the late nineteenth-century framework has demonstrated remarkable success and longevity. In turn, this makes that period a natural cutoff point of the present examination, which aims to establish the genealogy of the currently accepted framework. As it happens, in 1885 the two central authors mentioned each published a monograph that can serve to illustrate both the range of interpretations and the many points of agreement between scholars of the 1880s and those of the early twenty-first century. While thus admittedly a little arbitrary, 1885 works well as the end date of the present book (cf. the similar end point in, e.g., Moser 2006).

The first chapter introduces and analyzes passages from the Bible and classical authors (Herodotus, Diodorus, Plutarch, and several others) that would serve as basic building blocks for reasoning about ancient Egyptian mortuary religion, especially once the classical texts became available to European scholars starting in the late fifteenth century. Given the disparate nature of the evidence (spanning effectively almost a millennium from classical Greece to late antiquity), I make no attempt to reconstruct *the* classical understanding of the topic. Rather, I introduce each source in its context and discuss major issues of interpretation. As elsewhere in the book, whether each source is "correct" by modern standards is largely sidestepped, and the different ways each source has been understood and deployed in concrete models and arguments are treated within their historical context in the following chapters.

Beginning in the late medieval period, chapter 2 traces early ideas about ancient Egyptian mortuary religion and related topics, centering on practices of mummification and the significance of the Egyptian pyramids and the motives behind them. The chapter examines the importance of the medicinal substance of *mumia* extracted from ancient Egyptian embalmed bodies and the ways ostensible curative efficacy and the observed preservation of the ancient bodies strengthened each other and led to the (intuitive, but strictly speaking fallacious) notion that the Egyptians mummified the dead to preserve their bodies. A major shift in understanding came about when the texts of a number of Greco-Roman authors became available in the late 1400s, including Herodotus, Diodorus, and the "Hermetic writings" understood at the time as preserving ancient Egyptian wisdom. These texts were used occasionally to reconstruct underlying ancient Egyptian beliefs in the transmigration of souls, where the soul was incarnated in a sequence of bodies of different species, leading to discussions about the proper theological understanding of the relation between body and soul. Despite the exotic detail of the transmigration of souls, the basic vocabulary and conceptual apparatus available to scholars was that offered by Christianity. Although toward the end of the period covered by this chapter Egypt became increasingly deployed in theological debates such as those resulting from the Reformation, the main challenge throughout this period was finding explanations for why the Egyptians embalmed bodies and built tombs, especially pyramids.

The second half of the seventeenth century, treated in chapter 3, saw a new effort to move beyond the largely descriptive treatments of the previous centuries as Egypt was increasingly deployed as part of grand diachronic syntheses where each civilization offered certain lessons of value to the early modern observer. The tenor could be vastly different, from Athanasius Kircher's idea of Egypt as a site of mixture of authentic monotheistic traditions with superstition and magic, to Jacques-Bénigne Bossuet's emphasis on Egypt as a profoundly just society that could be an example for European absolute monarchs. Correspondingly, interpretations of Egyptian mortuary religion split into two fundamentally different approaches, one "othering," emphasizing exotic details such as the transmigration of souls (albeit still using a vocabulary of body and soul, eternity, immortality, etc.), and the other emphasizing righteousness secured through judgment, which by analogy with Christianity became increasingly understood as taking place in the beyond rather than as a ritual performed by living humans (as described by Diodorus). Because of the shared vocabulary and concepts, it was possible to combine these ideas in quite different ways depending on the purposes for which ancient Egypt was deployed in a given model of universal history.

A continuation of the debates about universal history of more direct relevance to European Christians concerned the relation between the religion of the ancient Egyptians and that of the Jews, which plays a significant role in chapter 4. This question has been explored in detail by Jan Assmann in particular, but the specific role of, and implications for, the understanding of Egyptian mortuary religion has not always been fully appreciated. On some occasions, moreover, it has been distorted by retrospective understandings (i.e., taking one's point of departure in the extent to which seventeenth- and eighteenth-century scholars arrived at "correct" understandings of ancient Egypt). Accordingly, chapter 4 explores the ways scholars used Egyptian mortuary religion as part of arguments for or against a continuity between Jewish and Egyptian religion during the first half of the eighteenth century. Another phenomenon during this period is the increasingly prevalent notion of Egyptian mysteries and initiation, inspired in the first instance by the ancient author Apuleius, but becoming highly prevalent in eighteenth-century Freemasonry and related intellectual movements. For this reason, the chapter discusses in some detail Jean Terrasson's novel *Séthos*, which developed this idea in a manner that would prove highly influential not just for Freemasonry but also for scholarship on, and reception of, ancient Egypt more generally.

The second half of the eighteenth century, the topic of chapter 5, saw travelers inspired by Enlightenment ideals increasingly emphasizing the precise documentation of monuments, providing scholars back in Europe with a much more detailed sense of ancient Egyptian culture than had been available earlier. A similar aim for "objectivity" also led to interpretations largely sidestepping contemporary theological concerns, as in the case of the Danish scholar Georg Zoëga. Published in his magnum opus coinciding with Napoleon's occupation of Egypt, Zoëga's lengthy discussion of ancient Egyptian mortuary religion is analyzed in detail as a prime example of new ways of engaging empirically with ancient Egyptian monuments that would continue into the nineteenth century. Characteristically, since Zoëga's interests were largely without theological investment (despite the religious backdrop offered by the pope's patronage of his work), he tended toward an additive approach, where the different, sometimes apparently contradictory ideas of the ancient authors are joined in a complex sequential model for the fate of the souls of the dead, which in turn is related to ancient Egyptian iconography known through publications and collections.

Chapter 6 discusses the intellectual ramifications of Napoleon's invasion of Egypt in 1798 and the resulting publication of the monumental *Description de l'Égypte,* which have generally tended to be downplayed in recent scholarship, pointing to the presence of similar interests and stances before the invasion or the limited influence of the published work outside the French-speaking world. However, as far as Egyptian mortuary religion is concerned, the *Description* laid out an interpretation that would prove seminal for the next several decades, especially in its anchoring of ideas about postmortem judgment (now understood primarily as happening in the transcendent afterlife, in contrast to Diodorus's description), and transmigration of souls in concrete images found in Egyptian tombs, which were themselves made available through the plates of the *Description*. The new, authoritative interpretation was also able to take in influential eighteenth-century ideas about initiatory journeys, on the one hand, and an increasingly anthropocentric concept of the Christian afterlife on the other, by positing that the imagery found in funerary papyri showed the journey of the soul to the place in the beyond where judgment was to take place. This chapter analyzes the background of these ideas as laid out in the *Description* and tracks their widespread, though not universal, acceptance during the following decade leading up to Champollion's deciphering the hieroglyphic script in 1822.

As far as the understanding of ancient Egyptian religion was concerned, the effect of the deciphering of hieroglyphs, discussed in chapter 7, was much slower than is often assumed. Champollion was unrivaled in his ability to read hieroglyphic inscriptions, lending significant authority to his interpretations. This is seen, for example, in his reading of a scene of the weighing of the heart (which had by then come to be accepted as an illustration of a sort of Egyptian Last Judgment) in his published letters, which became highly influential. Here Champollion offered a detailed analysis of the iconography and inscriptions of the scene that gave the traditional interpretation as a postmortem judgment on a Christian model an authority lasting to the present. The result of this and other intellectual developments tracked in this chapter was that ideas about the transmigration of souls into new bodies became increasingly sidelined, first as speculation by elite priests (as in some of the major works of the 1830s and 1840s), and then eventually as a complete misunderstanding by Herodotus. The chapter argues that the idea became redundant as the (to nineteenth-century Christians) much more interesting, comprehensible, and relevant notion of an ethical postmortem judgment became increasingly entrenched and anchored in particular modes of reading the Egyptian funerary papyri.

The last chapter addresses the final crystallization of the modern understanding of the ancient Egyptian afterlife. As shown in the previous chapters, the notion of transmigration of souls had been sidelined and ultimately rejected, but the interpretation of funerary texts and imagery as depicting the travels of the soul had remained. In the meantime, new generations of scholars had built on Champollion's insights, and a growing body of texts translated in their entirety became available from the late 1860s onward. This chapter shows how religious texts, especially those that had come to be known as the Book of the Dead—and late in the nineteenth century also the inscriptions from royal pyramids of the Old Kingdom—were fitted into the existing overall expectations concerning ancient Egyptian beliefs about the afterlife. Given that a robust consensus had formed around an idea of the ancient Egyptians' concrete belief in a personal afterlife described literally in the funerary texts, it became easy to decontextualize sentences from such texts to show the exotic nature of Egyptian doctrines. In the absence of independent evidence of what the Egyptians might have believed about the afterlife, this approach was basically immune to falsification and thus has been able to continue to the present. At the same time, while explicitly Christian notions such as expiation were increasingly eschewed for indigenous terminology and ideas derived more or less directly from the funerary papyri, the overall framework of individual salvation and eternal life based on ethical judgment remained. The chapter ends with works by German Egyptologist Adolf Erman and British Egyptologist E. A. Wallis Budge that illustrate the completion of the modern framework by incorporating the newly available funerary texts to present a detailed description of Egyptian beliefs.

The conclusion follows the various strands of the developments analyzed in the book, bringing out the main trajectories and turning points. It also argues that given the historically contingent nature of the conventional model for the ancient Egyptian afterlife that I have demonstrated throughout, this model is in urgent need of rethinking. Although I have not taken up this task in earnest here, in closing I offer some preliminary notes on what this would look like.

ONE

Antiquity's Antiquity: Ancient Sources

Chronologically, it makes good sense to begin the exploration with ancient sources relating to Egyptian mortuary religion, though some cautions should be noted from the outset. First, apart from biblical passages, these sources generally began to be drawn on in Western scholarship only from the late fifteenth century CE, when the pertinent classical texts started to be published and translated. This means that, unlike the later history traced in this book, there is no unbroken tradition from the classical authors to the medieval reception. Second, in practice the label "classical" sources covers a vast time span ranging from classical Greece (e.g., Herodotus, Plato) to late antiquity (e.g., Porphyry, Hermetic Corpus) and encompassing authors of multiple cultural, philosophical, and religious backgrounds. Thus the extant sources cannot be meaningfully used to reconstruct a monolithic "classical" understanding of ancient Egyptian religion. Rather, I introduce these sources at this point to provide an overview of the basic building blocks that would delineate the conceptual framework for understanding ancient Egyptian mortuary religion from the Renaissance until the final decades of the nineteenth century.

I present the sources here in chronological order of their authorship, but as is detailed in the subsequent sections, they did not all become available or relevant to later scholars at the same time, nor did most such authors draw on the entire group of texts in their interpretations. Also note that this is not an exhaustive list of ancient sources drawn on in later discussions, but rather an introduction of the most influential and frequently cited that correspondingly are repeatedly referred to in the following chapters.

Joseph Story from Genesis

Apart from the authors from the Greco-Roman world to be discussed below, the other traditional main source of knowledge of, and interest in, ancient Egypt was the Bible, especially the main episodes involving Egypt in the narratives about Joseph and Moses in the Hebrew Bible, and the flight of the holy family to Egypt in the New Testament (cf. Amin 2013, 44–49). These narratives generally have little direct bearing on Egyptian mortuary religion except for the narrative in Genesis of Joseph embalming his father Jacob according to Egyptian tradition. This provided details on Egyptian burial practices within a well-known and authoritative story and as such became cited relatively frequently:

> And Joseph commanded his servants the physicians to embalm his father. And the physicians embalmed Israel. And forty days were fulfilled for him; for so are fulfilled the days of embalming. And the Egyptians wept for him threescore and ten days. (Gen. 50:2–3)

The main details provided here are thus the forty days of embalming and the seventy days of mourning, while the passage is silent on practical aspects like those described by Herodotus and Diodorus, as well as the conceptual background for the practices.

Herodotus of Halicarnassus (ca. 484 to 425 BCE)

The *Histories* of Herodotus (Godley 1926) contain accounts of the history and cultures of the ancient Mediterranean as a backdrop to the historical account of the Greco-Persian Wars of the first half of the fifth century BCE. For this reason one of the central topics the work examines as a whole concerns questions of identity, especially the nature and significance of being Greek or non-Greek (Hall 1989). Traditionally hailed as "the father of history," much has been written about the reliability of Herodotus and the sources he drew on in the different parts of the work (e.g., Luraghi 2006). For my purposes here, however, the main question is not so much how far his account of ancient Egyptian culture is "correct" by specific later standards such as those of the twenty-first century CE (as will be seen in the following chapters, opinions on this have differed widely); rather, it will be of interest to make some brief remarks on the overall backdrop to his treatment of Egyptian mortuary religion before turning to the most important and frequently cited passages.

Herodotus seems to have visited Egypt during the third quarter of the fifth century BCE, with a date between 449 and 430 BCE being perhaps most likely (Lloyd 1975, 61–68), though other authors doubt he was ever in the country at all (e.g., Nielsen 1997, 36–44). He makes frequent reference to local informants' being the source of his knowledge, occasionally explicitly identifying them as Egyptian priests, corresponding to a marked interest in religious concerns in connection with Egyptian culture. One of the recurring formative themes around which his discussion of Egypt is constructed is the great antiquity, even primordiality, of the culture, sometimes with the corollary idea that central features of Herodotus's native Greek culture were derivative of Egyptian or other barbarian models (Wees 2002, 324–28). In particular, Herodotus presented Egypt as a fertile source of Greek scientific ideas and religious beliefs and practices (Zographou 1995). At the same time, however, the more ethnographic parts of his discussion of Egypt are often structured by the theme of Egyptian culture as a direct opposite to, or reversal of, that of Greece (Lateiner 1989, 147–52).

Herodotus does not write much specifically about ancient Egyptian mortuary religion, but two passages in particular tend to be singled out in European scholarship from the late fifteenth century CE onward. In book 2, chapters 85–90, he offers a detailed and fairly technical description of the funerary preparations carried out by the Egyptians. The first of these chapters (85) describes the mourning performed at the death of a "man of note," involving women of the household daubing their heads with mud and roaming the streets lamenting with exposed bosoms, with the addition that men lament in a similar fashion. The following three chapters (86–88) introduce and detail the process of embalming, beginning with the embalmers' displaying those who bring a dead body painted wooden models so they can choose from three different methods of embalming varying in their degree of "perfection" and in price.

The best, and most expensive, method involves removing part of the brain through the nose using an iron hook and removing the intestines through a cut in the flank made with a stone knife, rinsing the cavity, and filling it with spices. Afterward the body is embalmed in saltpeter for seventy days, after which it is washed, wrapped, and anointed before being returned to the next of kin. The latter in turn are responsible for making "a hollow wooden figure like a man" (an anthropoid coffin) in which the body is placed, then kept in a "coffin chamber" (*oikēmati*, seemingly indicating a room in a house rather than a dedicated tomb) where it is placed erect against the wall.

The following chapter (87) describes the middle option. This involves filling the body with cedar oil by means of syringes inserted through the anus without cutting or removing the intestines. Following this, the procedure is presented as similar to the most expensive option with embalming for "the appointed days," after which the oil is drained. The corrosive effects of the cedar oil and saltpeter are such that "in the end nothing is left of the body but skin and bone" (*to derma mounon kai ta ostea*). The third manner of embalming (88) is described even more briefly: The body is cleansed with a purge and then embalmed for seventy days. In other words, the three methods differ solely in the preliminary treatment of the internal body parts: they all share the subsequent covering in saltpeter for seventy days.

The last two chapters dealing with the treatment of the dead offer additional observations, first (89) that important or beautiful women were passed over to the embalmers only after three or four days to deter them from having sexual intercourse with the corpse, and second (90) that a special set of observances was accorded to persons who had been carried off by a crocodile or drowned, in which case the townspeople of the place where the body is found become responsible for the burial "in a sacred coffin" (*en hirēsi thēkēsi*).

The entire passage of chapters 85–90 is kept in a generally descriptive language, and while it would provide much input in later explorations of practices of mummification, it was not immediately useful for explaining the purposes of the practices described. For this one must turn to a remark made in passing in chapter 123, which would be cited frequently until it was increasingly discredited in the mid- to late nineteenth century. The passage is brief and concise and deserves to be quoted in full:

> It is believed in Egypt that the rulers of the lower world are Demeter [Isis] and Dionysus [Osiris]. Moreover, the Egyptians were the first to teach that the human soul [*anthrōpou psychē*] is immortal [*athanatos*] and at the death of the body enters into some other living thing then coming to birth; and after passing through all creatures of land, sea, and air (which cycle it completes in three thousand years) it enters once more into a human body at birth. Some of the Greeks, early and late, have used this doctrine as if it were their own; I know their names, but do not here record them. (Godley 1926, 424–25)

Before moving on to how the passage can be interpreted, note that Herodotus's main reason for relating this belief in the context is to present it as a precursor to Greek ideas. As will be seen below, later authors plausibly understand Herodotus as referring here to philosophical ideas ascribed to the Orphics or Pythagoras (or both), who were credited with similar teachings about metempsychosis or transmigration of souls (cf. Bernabé 2013, 129–30). This creates some ambiguity in the passage about whether the specific ideas Herodotus describes come from Egyptian or Greek traditions. It is thus possible in principle that a relatively minor detail may have led Herodotus to reconstruct the connection to the better-known Greek framework, which might then have enabled him to supply the additional details given here assuming it was the same belief that was described. In the present connection it is not helpful to follow the conventional Egyptological verdict that the idea described here is "un-Egyptian" (Wilson 1970, 10), since this simply means it does not appear compatible with the understanding of ancient Egyptian mortuary religion that had developed by the twentieth century—an understanding that is itself based, as I will detail below, on specific conventional interpretations of both Herodotus and other pieces of available evidence.

The details of the passage are very specific, although some would seemingly need to be changed to fit into the frameworks developed by later authors. When a human being dies, the soul passes into an animal that is born at the same time. The inference from the following sentence must be that when that animal in turn dies, the soul passes on to an animal of a different species, and so on until the soul has inhabited every animal species after three thousand years. At the end of this cycle, the soul returns in the same way to a new human body being born. A number of details of this are unclear, but notably there does not seem to be any notion of reward or punishment, since each soul must go through every species. And since the second human body is said to be born at the same time as it is inhabited by the soul, Herodotus must have referred to being reincarnated in a new human body rather than (as later interpreters would understand it to explain the practice of mummification) returning to inhabit the original one.

Another open question relates to the word Herodotus used for the perishing of the original body: *kataphthinō*, "waste away, decay" (2, 123.2). While in the context it seems most reasonable to understand this as referring to the moment of death—and indeed this is by far the most common interpretation—the ambiguity of the word gave some later commentators the idea of connecting this passage with the practice of mummification (discussed entirely separately by Herodotus, as I noted above) to refer to the *decay* of the body. According to this reading, the soul would thus move on to a different body only once the original body had decayed (as opposed to immediately upon death), the implication being that mummification could be understood as staving off the onset of metempsychosis.

While these are the main passages pertaining to Egyptian mortuary religion, other details in Herodotus are occasionally brought to bear on related topics, especially those dealing with the construction of funerary monuments. As they tend to have a more marginal role and appear much more sporadically, such passages need not be discussed in detail here.

Plato (427/428 to 348/349 BCE)

Greek philosopher Plato wrote philosophical inquiries on a broad range of topics in the form of dialogues between his teacher Socrates and various other protagonists. Plato generally evaluates Egyptian wisdom positively (most clearly so in the description of Solon's visit to the country in the *Timaeus*), but he rarely provides details concerning Egyptian religion. However, in later tradition (mentioned, for example, by Cicero, *De finibus* V, 87), he was widely understood not only to have visited Egypt, but also to be part of a broader Pythagorean tradition drawing from Egyptian teachings in his own thought (Smith 2013). For this reason Plato came to be used by later scholars as often the most detailed and explicit source of such (broadly speaking) Egyptian ideas. In interpretations of ancient Egyptian mortuary religion, the teachings about the nature of the soul and its fate after death in particular (cf. Lorenz 2019) came to be interpreted as evidence of Egyptian religious beliefs. These ideas are described in most detail in passages of the two dialogues *Phaedo* and *Phaedrus*, to be discussed here, though other dialogues such as *Critias* and *Timaeus* have similar ideas and are sometimes cited instead or in addition by later scholars.

The dialogue *Phaedo* takes place during Socrates's last day alive, and as such circles naturally around questions of the fate of humans after death, as also indicated by its alternative title *On the Soul* (cf. Castagnoli 2019). The view of the soul that Socrates espouses in the dialogue is fundamentally dualist: Human beings consist of a body and a soul, the distinction between which corresponds to a broader ontological distinction between visible and invisible, mortal and divine, multiform and uniform, etc. (*Phaedo* 78b–80b; Emlyn-Jones and Preddy 2017, 374–85). During the course of this exposition, Socrates refers to Egyptian practices of embalming, understood to keep the body "practically intact for an incalculable [*amēchanos*] length of time" (*Phaedo* 80c–d; Emlyn-Jones and Preddy 2017, 384–85), his point being, however, that despite such practices, unlike the soul, it is impossible for the body to last forever. As noted above, though, it is not for such specific references to Egypt that Plato was mainly used, but rather for the traditional assumption that his system as a whole was ultimately derived from Egyptian religious philosophy and thus could be used to reconstruct it.

Against this ontological background, it becomes the goal for the human being to separate the soul from the body as completely as possible to allow the soul to "make for what is like it, the indivisible, the divine and immortal and wise, and on arriving there isn't its lot to be happy, being rid of wandering aimlessly, foolishness, fears, wild sexual passions and the other human evils, and, just as it's said of the initiated, does it not truly spend the rest of time among the gods?" (*Phaedo* 81a; Emlyn-Jones and Preddy 2017, 386–87). On the other hand, a soul that has not freed itself from such bodily concerns will depart "polluted [*memiasmenē*] and uncleansed [*akathartos*])," which in turn means it is "weighed down [*barynetai*] and dragged back [*helketai*] to the visible world" (*Phaedo* 81b–c; Emlyn-Jones and Preddy 2017, 386–89). Unable to leave the visible world, such souls remain near the tombs, where they can be seen, since they retain parts of the visible. Eventually the "desire for . . . the corporeal" that clings to such souls means they become imprisoned in new bodies, and more specifically bodies that fit their characteristics, so that violent and gluttonous souls, for example, "take the form of the family of asses and such animals" (*Phaedo* 81e–82a; Emlyn-Jones and Preddy 2017, 390–91). Only the philosopher is ultimately able to escape the body altogether, while souls that have practiced moderation and justice without philosophy pass into "a civic and cultivated family, such as of bees perhaps, or wasps, or ants, or back again to the very same one, the human race" (*Phaedo* 82c; Emlyn-Jones and Preddy 2017, 390–93).

Toward the end of the dialogue, Socrates relates a story (*mythos*) about the structure of the cosmos (*Phaedo* 110b–114c = Emlyn-Jones and Preddy 2017, 494–509). After describing the nature of the realm of the dead Tartarus, he details what happens when the souls of the dead arrive there:

> When the dead reach the place where the spirit [*daimōn*] brings each one, firstly they submit to judgment: those who have led good holy [*kalōs kai hosiōs*] lives, and those who have not. Now those who are considered to have led a moderate life make their way toward the Acheron, embark on rafts provided for them, and on these they arrive at the lake. There they dwell, are purified and are absolved of their wrongdoings by paying penalties, if anyone has done any wrong, and they win recognition for their good deeds, each according to his worth. But those who are judged to be incorrigible [*aniatos*] on account of the enormity of their wrongdoing, having committed either much great sacrilege or unjust killings and many lawless acts, or any other cases of this kind, their appropriate destiny flings them into

> Tartarus whence they never emerge. (*Phaedo* 113d–e; Emlyn-Jones and Preddy 2017, 506–9)

He goes on to detail the process of purifying souls depending on their specific transgressions, which correspond to areas in the topography of the realm of the dead as previously described. Strictly speaking, the myth thus presents a somewhat different model than the ideas described earlier that Socrates explicitly committed to (cf. Edmonds 2009, 159–220): Instead of the mechanistic system of souls' being weighed down and attracted to new kinds of bodies depending on the nature of their defilement, the mythic cosmology introduces the idea of judgment and sentencing, albeit without identifying who is responsible for these procedures. Nonetheless, the two models are compatible in that both differentiate the souls on ethical grounds. Given that some new bodies are additionally presented as more desirable than others, the fundamental idea of postmortem rewards or punishments based on behavior during life is also shared by the two models. In accordance with this loose fit between the two ideas, Socrates hedges that while one should not commit to all the details of the myth, he affirms that more broadly "either these things are so, or something like them, concerning our souls and their dwelling places, given that the soul is evidently something immortal [*athanatos*]" (*Phaedo* 114d = Emlyn-Jones and Preddy 2017, 510–511). While the precise relation between the two models is thus open to interpretation (cf., e.g., White 1989, 237–69; and for Neoplatonist interpretations Gertz 2011, 173–88), a reasonably unified set of ideas about the soul and its fate after death can emerge from reading the *Phaedo*, especially in terms of an association or at least compatibility between the ideas of metempsychosis (transmigration of souls or reincarnation) and afterlife judgment.

There is a long-standing discussion concerning whether the second dialogue to be discussed briefly here, the *Phaedrus*, was composed as a unified whole, because of its treatment of a wide range of seemingly disparate topics (including love, rhetoric, and writing) and its two halves with different formats (e.g., Werner 2012, 236–39). Nonetheless, ideas about the soul and its nature play an important role in the dialogue (e.g., Werner 2012, 54–68). One passage is particularly worth emphasizing for its exposition of Socrates's ideas about the soul, specifically as it is involved in chains of causality (*Phaedrus* 245c–49d; Emlyn-Jones and Preddy 2022, 408–425). Socrates's point of departure is another set of dichotomies between the soul and the material world: that the soul remains in self-directed motion, whereas anything that is moved by something else will at some point cease to move, a notion he connects with the ungenerated and immortal nature of the soul.

Having made this point, Socrates moves on to establish an analogy of the soul as a charioteer driving a pair of horses, one of good character and one of bad (*Phaedrus* 246b; Emlyn-Jones and Preddy 2022, 412–13). As in the discussion in the *Phaedo*, he describes how a soul can either be winged, and hence detached from any body or other earthly concerns, or can lose its wings, compelling it to attach itself to a body. The wings of the soul are nourished and grow thanks to divine qualities such as beauty, wisdom, and goodness, while the opposite qualities cause the wings to wither. In turn, the strength of the wings allows the soul to reach higher tiers of the cosmos and glimpse parts of the divine truth of the upper regions. The notion of the wings and their degree of growth and strength is thus fundamentally similar to the notion in the *Phaedo* of the soul's being weighed down by bodily concerns. This can be seen most clearly when Socrates turns to the differential fate of souls differing in this respect:

> And the law of Adrasteia is as follows: whichever soul has become a follower of a god and perceives something of what is true, remains without sorrow until the next circuit, and if it is always able to do this, is to remain unharmed always; but whenever it cannot see because it is unable to keep up, and experiencing some misfortune it is weighed down [*barynō*], filled with forgetfulness [*lēthē*] and incapacity [*kakia*], and in being weighed down it sheds its wings and falls to the ground: then the law is that this soul shall not be implanted in any wild creature in its first incarnation, but the one that has seen most shall be implanted in the seed which will become a man who loves wisdom, who loves beauty, some aspect of the Muses, or love; and the second in that of a law-abiding king, or one skilled in warfare, or government; the third in that of one engaged in state or domestic life, or in commerce; and the fourth in one who will become engaged in the hard work of physical training, or someone concerned with

> healing the body; the fifth will have the life of the seer, or someone concerned with mystic rites; fitting for the sixth will be the life of someone who is a poet, or some other of those engaged in imitation; the seventh a craftsman or a farmer; the eighth a sophist or a demagogue, the ninth a tyrant. (*Phaedrus* 248c–e; Emlyn-Jones and Preddy 2022, 418–21)

Here as well the result is a reincarnation of the soul into bodies that depend on the qualities of the soul, here presented as a gradation of types of persons. In the *Phaedrus* version of this idea, Socrates goes on to note that each soul returns to its point of departure after ten thousand years during which it regrows its wings—with the exception of the philosopher, who can gain wings and return after only three thousand years. In this version the connection between judgment and reincarnation is explicit, as Socrates states that the nonphilosophers, "when they have completed their first life [they] are put on trial [*krisis*], and some, after being tried, go to places of punishment below ground and pay their penalty, but others are raised up by Justice to some place in heaven and spend their time in a fashion worthy of the life they led in the form of a human being" (*Phaedrus* 249a–b; Emlyn-Jones and Preddy 2022, 422–23).

As in the *Phaedo*, the nature of the judgment and the identity of the judges are left unspecified. As exemplified by these passages, a reader of Plato understanding the ideas expressed by Socrates as deriving ultimately from ancient Egyptian religion and philosophy could obtain a relatively clear and specific understanding of the nature and fate of the soul. Being immortal, the soul passes from one body to another unless it has liberated itself from corporeal and earthly concerns far enough to escape. Moreover, the nature of the body into which the soul transmigrates depends on the qualities of the soul as exhibited by its behavior during its previous lives. Plato presents this as being directly connected to some kind of judgment (in the *Phaedo* myth said to take place in the realm of the dead), though the precise details concerning this remain vague, including the relation between judgment and the more "mechanical" aspects of the soul's ability to break free. Depending on the result of the judgment, the soul may receive rewards or punishments. A last central point introduced by the *Phaedrus* is that a temporal cycle governs the process of transmigration, with the soul needing to endure a certain period of incarnations.

Diodorus of Sicily (ca. 90 to ca. 30 BCE)

The Greek historian Diodorus of Sicily wrote the *Bibliothēkē* ("Library"), a self-styled universal history of the eastern Mediterranean world, beginning with the Trojan War and the legendary past preceding it and ending in the year 60 BCE (Duncan 2023, 464–73). Many of the earlier sources he based his work on are lost, though in places his dependency on Herodotus in particular is clear. He is traditionally often dismissed as a mere copyist of the works of other historians (though accordingly of value where these are not extant), but in recent decades research has tended to emphasize the importance and originality of Diodorus's own contributions (e.g., Sacks 1990; updated review in Hau, Meeus, and Sheridan 2018). At several places in the work he claims to have visited Egypt himself, very likely between 60 and 55 BCE as part of his wider travels in Europe and Asia (Sulimani 2011, 30–37). In the first five books in particular (including his discussion of Egypt), mythology, history, and geography are tightly interwoven, partly connected to a general tendency to interpret mythology euhemeristically, with the gods of mythology having originally been human beings (Sulimani 2011). Egypt takes a central place in the *Bibliothēkē* in several senses, including by being the topic of the very first book in the work, by being the most fully discussed in terms of the different cultural, historical, and geographical aspects of the country, and by recurring consistently in a number of the travel narratives throughout the work (Sulimani 2011, 169; Muntz 2017, 50–51).

Like Herodotus, Diodorus has two main passages that would especially inform later scholarship on Egyptian mortuary religion: book 1, chapters 71–72 and 91–96. The first of these (71–72) forms part of a more general discussion of Egyptian kings and deals specifically with the ceremonies carried out at the death of a king. Diodorus explicitly notes that he uses the elaborate rites as an illustration of how much Egyptian kings were loved by their subjects, "for the fact that the honour which they paid was to one who was insensible of it constituted an authentic testimony to its sincerity" (72.1, quotations from the English translation in Oldfather 1933; cf. the French bilingual edition Chamoux, Bertrac, and Vernière 1993). He goes on to describe how "all the inhabitants of Egypt" joined in mourning the dead king by rending their garments, closing the temples, and celebrating no festivals for seventy-two days. The following passage clearly depends on Herodotus when it describes how men and women put mud on their heads and expose their chests, adding that they are moving around in large groups singing chants in praise of the deceased. A range of food taboos are observed, and baths and other luxuries are avoided, as is sexual activity.

On the day of the funeral, the coffin containing the body is set up outside the tomb, and a tribunal passes judgment on the deeds of the deceased. Anyone is allowed to bring complaints about the dead king, while priests are tasked with offering the opposite perspective of praising him. The ultimate outcome is apparently decided (or at least reflected) by the general populace present, who shout approval or protest. Diodorus points out that this is more than an empty ceremony, as "in fact many kings have been deprived of the public burial customarily accorded to them." Again, Diodorus's primary interest in this custom lies in the incentive it gives kings to be just during their lifetimes, at the risk of the "eternal obloquy" (*blasphēmias eis hapanta ton aiōna*) of being deprived of a proper burial. A key concept here as well is that these rites' being carried out after the person dies ensures a certain purity of emotion and judgment unsullied by social pressures and the possibility of personal gain.

The second passage of interest here (91–96) forms part of a discussion of the religious practices of the Egyptians. Following Herodotus (cf. Burton 1972, 261–67), Diodorus categorizes embalming practices by three qualities, and while he offers no new details concerning the difference between them, he adds the price of each method that he has been told. This passage also repeats some of the practices described for the royal burial in chapters 71–72, including people's plastering themselves with mud, roaming the streets lamenting, and avoiding baths, wine, and "any other food worth mentioning" (91.1).

Diodorus goes on to describe the classes of embalming personnel: one who marks the place in the flank where the incision is to be made, one who makes the cut and subsequently is ritually driven away because of this act of violence, and a group of highly revered persons who extract the internal organs. In describing this, Diodorus provides several details not offered by the parallel narrative in Herodotus, such as washing each of the viscera after removal. The procedure is said to take "more than thirty days," and unlike Herodotus he characterizes the aim (or at least the effect) of the treatment, that of "not only preserving [the body] for a long time but also of giving it a fragrant odour" (91.6). The body that is returned to the family has "every member . . . so preserved intact that even the hair of the eyelids and brows remains, the entire appearance of the body is unchanged, and the cast of its shape recognizable" (91.6). This is the reason, according to Diodorus, why the Egyptians keep their ancestors' bodies in places where they can look at them face to face, from which they derive a "strange enjoyment."

Diodorus thus provides much of the motivation behind the Egyptian practices that was missing in Herodotus. Rather than the theological incentive one might have expected from Herodotus's description of metempsychosis, according to Diodorus the aim is more psychological in memorializing the deceased, and it is furthermore connected with distinct social practices of the surviving families' viewing the ancestors' bodies. Unlike Herodotus, he makes no mention of their being wrapped, which would seemingly have robbed the mummified bodies of the effect Diodorus attributes to them. This has led scholars (e.g., Burton 1972, 267) to speculate that he might in fact have had in mind the lifelike painted portrait masks coming into vogue in his time.

Echoing his description of kings, Diodorus (92) goes on to describe a ritual taking place just before the burial itself. Forty-two "judges" sit in a semicircle by a body of water referred to simply as "the lake" (*limnē*), and a special type of boat called a *baris*, intended to carry the coffin across, is launched. Before the coffin is loaded unto the *baris*, accusations against the deceased can be brought forward in a manner similar to that described for kings in chapters 71–72 (though the royal ritual is presented as taking place before the tomb itself). In this case it is explicitly the judges who determine the merits of the cases, and if they consider the deceased to have led an "evil life" (*bebiōkota kakōs*), he is denied burial. Otherwise the family and friends present "put their mourning aside and laud the deceased." The person's life and deeds are described, with emphasis on his righteousness, and the "gods of the lower world" are called on "to receive [the deceased] into the company of the righteous" (92.5). In another interesting turn of phrase, the deceased is said to be extolled as "one who is about to spend eternity in Hades among the righteous." The burial itself takes place in a specially dedicated tomb for those who can afford it, while others construct a room in their house where the coffin is stood upright against the wall (a detail paralleled in Herodotus, as noted above). Those bodies that are not allowed a burial are also kept in the relatives' home, possibly to be buried generations later once the charges or arears against them have been cleared (92.6).

The last chapter on this topic (93) begins by noting the related practice of putting up ancestors' bodies as security for loans. As he did for the royal practices, Diodorus here explicitly acknowledges the efficacy of these rules in instilling moral behavior "by means not only of their converse with the living, but also of their burial and affectionate care of the dead" (93.2). He contrasts the effectiveness of such actual social processes with the "fanciful tales and discredited legends" the Greeks told to give a sense of just rewards and punishments after death. This echoes a polemic idea related earlier in the passage (92.3), according to which the Egyptians considered that Orpheus had visited Egypt and witnessed funerary rituals like those described and invented his mythological account of Hades taking inspiration from the Egyptian practices, whereby Greek mythology and eschatology is at once paralleled and contrasted with social customs among the Egyptians.

While Diodorus thus exhibits a marked emphasis on social customs in this passage, it is worth examining his references to religious beliefs in more detail before moving on, since this aspect would become of predominant interest to later scholars drawing on his description. Although he explicitly disavows an interpretation (attributed to Orpheus) of the funerary proceedings as a description of otherworldly events (92.3), Diodorus uses formulations that could be seen as pointing in this general direction. This is particularly true in section 92.5, where he notes that the ritual calls "upon the gods of the lower world [*tous katō theous*] to receive [the deceased] into the company of the righteous" and referring to the worthy deceased as "one who is about to spend eternity [*aiōna*]) in Hades among the righteous [*eusebēs*]." Given that his explicit emphasis is on the ritual giving or denying of the right to burial, depending on how faithfully he recounts the actual wording of the incantation he cites (if any), it is possible that these expressions were used as conventional (Greek) phraseology for the fate of the blessed dead rather than being meant to reproduce ancient Egyptian ideas beyond that of joining the ancestors in the tomb or necropolis.

In the case of Diodorus as well, it is useful to bracket off for the moment the contemporary Egyptological understanding where this description is interpreted as a misunderstanding of the mythological theme of the weighing of the heart and judgment of the dead as related in the Book of the Dead, chapter 125 (e.g., Burton 1972, 268–70; Stadler 2001). Although Diodorus himself explicitly denies this interpretation of his description by contrasting the social, this-worldly rituals to their Greek misinterpretation as afterlife events, it is not impossible that he may have misunderstood this, for example based on tomb representations (as suggested, e.g., by Assmann 2005a, 85). More to the point, however—and as with Herodotus's narrative of metempsychosis—this current conventional understanding is itself the product of the development I will trace here, so assuming its pertinence from the outset would be counterproductive.

Another, much briefer discussion also caught the attention of later scholars on a number of occasions. Speaking of the different categories of edifices, Diodorus (51.2) contrasts the attention spent on dwellings of the living compared with funerary monuments. According to Diodorus, the Egyptians "consider the period of this life to be of no account whatever [*eutelē pantelōs*], but place the greatest value on the time after death [*meta tēn teleutēn*]) when they will be remembered for their virtue." Correspondingly, in a frequently cited evocative metaphor, he notes that they refer to dwellings of the living as "lodgings" (*katalyseis*), because they are occupied only for a short time, whereas they refer to tombs as "eternal homes" (*aidious oikous*) because "the dead spend endless eternity [*apeiron aiōna*] in Hades." For this reason they spend far more resources on the tombs than on houses of the living. While the contrast here between homes of the living being inhabited for a shorter time than tombs is logical and immediately understandable, the implicit connection between dwelling in the tomb and being in Hades is not further elaborated and thus remains open to interpretation.

A final passage, rarely cited by later scholars, is worth mentioning here because it is occasionally used to illustrate the increasingly popular understanding that the judgment of the dead took place in the underworld rather than (or sometimes in addition to) being a ritual before burial as Diodorus avows in the passage discussed above. The section in question comes from Diodorus's secondhand description of the "Tomb of Ozymandias" (the Ramesseum across the Nile from modern-day Luxor) in chapters 47–49 of book 1 (cf. Derchain 1965). The section of specific interest to later scholars of Egyptian mortuary religion comes from a description of the decoration of the "sacred library," likely located in the northwestern part of the complex outside the mortuary temple itself:

> Contiguous to this building are statues of all the gods of Egypt, to each of whom the king in like manner makes the offering appropriate to him, as though he were submitting proof before Osiris and his assessors in the underworld that to the end of his days he had lived a life of piety and justice towards both men and gods. (I, 49.3; Oldfather 1933, 172–75)

This enigmatic passage is part of a paraphrased description rather than Diodorus's own observations, so it does not become clear how Diodorus himself understands the mythological reference here. For later authors interested in Egyptian mortuary religion, it was not the description of the statues or their connection to mythology that would be of primary interest, but rather the specific notion that the king was thought to submit evidence (*eudeikymi*) to Osiris of having lived a just life. Oldfather's translation quoted above locates this "in the underworld," while the original text is more ambiguous, using the word "lower" (*katō*), which can certainly be used to refer to the Greek netherworld or realm of the dead. However, it seems to describe the origin or place of belonging of the "assessors" rather than the location of the act of submitting proof, as is probably the most likely interpretation of Oldfather's English translation (cf., e.g., Chamoux, Bertrac, and

Vernière 1993, 104, translating "infernal assessors" (*assesseurs infernaux*), or a nineteenth-century German translation as "judges of the dead" (*Totenrichtern*), in Wurm 1827, 82).

Plutarch of Chaeronea (ca. 45 to ca. 120 CE)

Middle Platonic philosopher Plutarch of Chaeronea wrote on a wide range of topics, and his attempts to systematize and interpret Plato's thoughts have earned him a place in the history of Western philosophy (Dillon 2014; Roskam 2017, 18–39). Plutarch's *Isis and Osiris* (forming part of the larger work *Moralia*) became a main source of knowledge on ancient Egyptian religion and mythology and as such forms an important backdrop to many discussions from the Renaissance to the nineteenth century—and indeed continues to be an important source for the complete narrative of the mythology surrounding Osiris (Richter 2001). As rich as it is on Egyptian mythology in general, only a few passages from this work and other writings of Plutarch deal specifically with Egyptian mortuary religion, and these are the ones singled out here.

Plutarch puts the Egyptian myths to use for his own philosophical project, in the course of which they become Hellenized to a significant degree (Manolaraki 2012, 252–54). It is especially his thoughts on the soul and its relation to bodies that form the backdrop of his passages that would be used to understand Egyptian mortuary religion. With his strong basis in Plato's thought, it is only natural that his overall system is dualistic, though in its more specific details his ideas have a considerable complexity, in particular by dividing the human soul into two parts, one divine in nature and one more closely connected with the body, and thus the origin of passions, vices, and such (Opsomer 2012). Unlike the case of Porphyry (see below), it is debated whether Plutarch derived his own ideals of vegetarianism and kindness to animals from an idea of metempsychosis (Newmyer 2014, 230–31), since he makes this explicit connection only in the context of ideas ascribed to the Egyptians, and it is sometimes difficult to draw precisely the distinction between Plutarch's own philosophy and Egyptian wisdom (e.g., Stadler 2017, 31–35).

In a passage of *Isis and Osiris*, Plutarch discusses various Egyptian practices of sacrifice. One detail (31; *Moralia* 363B–D) he emphasizes is that red animals were preferred for sacrifice because of the association of that color with Typhon (Seth). For this practice he gives the following rationale:

> For they regard as suitable for sacrifice not what is dear to the gods but the reverse, namely, such animals as have incarnate in them souls of unholy and unrighteous men who have been transformed into other bodies. . . . They think, as has been said, that the ass reaps the consequences of his resemblance because of his stupidity and his lascivious behaviour no less than because of his colour. (*Isis and Osiris* 31; Babbitt 1936, 74–77)

Later in the same work (chapter 72; *Moralia* 379F–380C; Babbitt 1936, 166–69), Plutarch refers to this notion again, now in the context of the alleged belief that the gods have transformed into animals, so that they are now present in the "bodies of ibises, dogs, and hawks." Plutarch is dismissive of this idea and likewise of the related notion that "as many of the souls of the dead as continue to exist are reborn into these animals only," though the wording does not make it clear whether "only" is the operative word in the passage, so that what is rejected is the specific idea that just the animals mentioned contain souls of the dead, or whether it is the entire idea of metempsychosis into animal bodies. Regardless of how we understand Plutarch's own degree of commitment to these ideas, he clearly ascribes them to the Egyptians, with the wording "as many as" (*hosos*) strongly implying that some souls may not "continue to exist" (*diamenō*), though this distinction is not elaborated.

Apart from the specific idea of metempsychosis, Plutarch further ascribes to the Egyptians a funerary practice that fits well with his own Middle Platonic understanding of the body and the soul. This idea is noted in passing in two works, both of which deploy the practice to establish a metaphor of the "pollution of the flesh" that Plutarch presents as resulting from eating meat:

> And, like the Egyptians who extract the viscera of the dead and cut them open in view of the sun, then throw them away as being the

> cause of every single sin that the man had committed, it would be well for us to excise our own gluttony and lust to kill and become pure for the remainder of our lives, since it is not so much our belly that drives us to the pollution of slaughter; it is itself polluted by our incontinence. (Plutarch, *On the Eating of Flesh II*, 1; *Moralia* 996E; Cherniss 1957, 562–65)

Plutarch has Solon make essentially the same argument in his *Dinner of the Seven Wise Men*:

> "Certainly," said Solon, "let us not show ourselves to be less discriminating than the Egyptians, who cut open the dead body and expose it to the sun, and then cast certain parts of it into the river, and perform their offices on the rest of the body, feeling that this part has now at last been made clean." (Plutarch, *Dinner of the Seven Wise Men* 16; *Moralia* 159B; Babbitt 1928, 420–21)

In light of the Platonic framework examined above, this idea is clear. The vices, and resulting pollution, of the body are seen as particularly concentrated in the internal organs, which are considered the motivator of meat eating in particular. The Egyptian practice of excising the viscera thus rhetorically becomes a metaphor for purification. Moreover, Plutarch implies that this is in fact the motivation for the Egyptian practice, so that the Platonic interpretation is ascribed to the Egyptians themselves. In terms of the concrete description of the Egyptian practice, Plutarch offers a few pieces of information not found in previous authors, notably that the internal organs are cut out "in view of the sun," and that they are subsequently discarded, more specifically, according to the second quoted passage, by throwing them into the river.

Porphyry of Tyre (ca. 234 to ca. 305 CE)

Porphyry of Tyre was part of the circle formed around the Neoplatonic philosopher Plotinus (204/5 to 270 CE) in Rome, whose biography he would later write (after 301 CE; Clark 2000, 5). His prolific work is very partially preserved in numerous fragments, many of which are the topic of ongoing debate (overview in Johnson 2013, 21–49). Like other thinkers in the Platonic tradition, Porphyry saw the body as a significant obstacle keeping human beings mired in the impermanent material world and thus barring the soul from its divine origin. To Porphyry, the way to liberate the soul was by virtue and intellectual contemplation (*theōria*), unlike his contemporary Iamblichus who espoused the necessity of ritual practices for this purpose (cf. Karamanolis 2014).

Like Plutarch, Porphyry uses the Egyptian practice of excising the viscera in a polemic against eating meat, and also like Plutarch he connects this practice to Egyptian ideas about the rationality, or even divinity, of animals (Simonetti 2019, 137–43). Although the main structure of these ideas is already known from Plutarch, Porphyry offers a number of additional details—said to derive from a lost work by the Egyptian Euphantos—that would make him the preferred source on this practice to later scholars. The first part of the description follows what is known from Plutarch, with the added detail that the removed entrails are put in a "box," the subsequent actions being related as follows:

> They take hold of the box and call the sun to witness, one of the embalmers speaking on behalf of the corpse. He says something like this, as Euphantos translated it from the language of his homeland: "O Lord Sun and all the gods who give life to humans, receive me and present me to the eternal gods to reside with them. The gods of whom my parents told me I have reverenced for all the time I lived under their rule, and I have always honoured those who begot my body. I have neither killed any other human being, nor stolen from any what he had entrusted me, nor done any other unpardonable act. And if during my life I have been at fault by eating or drinking something forbidden, I did not do it myself, but through these," showing the box which contains the belly. Having said this he throws it into the river, and embalms the rest of the body as being pure. In this way they thought that a speech for the defence was owed to the divinity about what they had eaten and drunk, and on account of this violence should be done. (Porphyry, *On Abstinence*, 4, 10; Clark 2000, 108. Original text in Patillon and Segonds 1995, 16–17)

The quoted speech provides significant new information on the indigenous understanding of the practice, and as an aside, the general wording and tenor of the prayer, and possibly even the details of the practices described (as argued by Lieven 2018), conform with present Egyptological knowledge from Egyptian texts. As with Plutarch, however, the related practice is explicitly situated within a Platonist interpretive framework so as to deploy it as an argument in a polemic. Also on the topic of the modern reception of the passage, the notion of the entrails as scapegoat as described here is another idea that has earned the predicate "un-Egyptian" in modern Egyptology because it does not fit with contemporary models (Assmann 2005a, 83).

In his *Life of Pythagoras*, Porphyry describes ideas very much along the lines of those Herodotus attributed to the Egyptians, as part of a long-standing Greek tradition according to which Pythagoras acquired his knowledge in Egypt and passed Egyptian wisdom on to the Greeks. Though Porphyry does not make this connection explicitly, he notes the following main features of Pythagoras's teaching:

> However, it became well known to everyone that he declared first that the soul is immortal, and second, transmigrant into other kinds of animals, and further, that all events recur at certain periods and nothing is absolutely new, and that all animate creatures should be thought of like race. (*Life of Pythagoras*, 19; Smith 1965, 113. Original text in Places 1982, 44–45)

Hermetic Corpus (ca. Second to Fourth Centuries CE)

The Hermetic corpus comprises texts of uncertain authorship most likely written from the second to the fourth century CE (Copenhaver 1992), although they were initially regarded as much older and as reflecting original pharaonic ideas (e.g., Campanelli 2019). Even after their late date became commonly accepted (Ebeling 2007, 91–100), it seemed clear that they drew on older sources of Egyptian mythology, and they were regarded as authoritative by mainstream Egyptological scholars as late as the final decades of the nineteenth century—although by then such evaluations were decidedly in the minority.

As a good example of the kind of knowledge applicable to ancient Egyptian mortuary religion the Hermetic writings provided, I will briefly examine the composition known as the *Korē Kosmou* (Maiden/Eye of the World) and related writings (Festugière and Nock 1954, 1–50; cf. Podemann Sørensen 2012). The text is structured as a dialogue between Horus and his mother Isis, who teaches her son about the workings of the cosmos. A detailed cosmogony lays out how types of souls were created through different mixtures of elemental substances. The souls of animal species are differentiated according to the souls' weight and degree of solidity (23). When one group of souls rebel against the order established by the creator, they are punished by being imprisoned in human bodies created for the purpose (24–25). To reward or punish the souls for their behavior, a system is created where when entering human bodies noble souls become kings, philosophers, and so on, while in animal bodies they become eagles, lions, and other suitable creatures (42).

This system is elaborated in separate excerpts following the *Korē Kosmou*, which detail the fate of the souls upon the death of their bodies. Different regions of the cosmos are dedicated to the categories of souls: the nobler the souls, the more elevated their destination (Excerpt XXVI, 1). Similarly, when they are incarnated, the souls enter bodies that suit the souls' qualities; for example, "those which are crafty enter reptile bodies, for reptiles never attack men face to face, but lie in ambush, and so strike them down" (6). Notably, the system is described in very mechanistic terms, like those found in parts of Plato's work. While the creator god may have established the system to reward and punish souls, no actual judgment of the souls is taking place. Rather, the souls appear to automatically seek out the places and bodies suitable for them depending on their qualities.

Servius (Late Fourth to Early Fifth Century CE)

Little is known about the late antique grammarian Maurus Servius Honoratus beyond his preserved commentaries on the works of Virgil (Marshall 1997; Fowler 2019). While otherwise not particularly concerned with ancient Egyptian culture, a single passage in the commentary on the *Aeneid* touches concisely on the motivations behind mummification, and so it became a rather central source in later scholarship. The passage in question concerns book 3 of the *Aeneid*, where Aeneas encounters the spirit of Polydorus, the prince of Troy who was murdered by the king of Thrace when he came to ask for help against the Greeks. Before leaving Thrace, Aeneas and his followers perform funeral rites for Polydorus, concluding with the lines, "We offer foaming bowls of warm milk and cups of victims' blood, lay the spirit at rest in the tomb, and with loud voice give the last call" (Fairclough 1999, 376–77). The words Servius comments on are *animamque sepulchro condimus*, literally "and we preserve the soul in the tomb" (*Aeneid* 3, 67–68; Fairclough 1999, 376).

In his commentary, Servius notes that the soul is thus thought to be restless until the proper funerary rituals have been carried out, citing the Stoic notion that the soul (*anima*) lasts as long as the body does (*tam diu durare dicunt, quam diu durat et corpus*, Stocker and Travis 1965, 32). This leads to the following observation on Egyptian practices:

> Whence the Egyptians, skilled in wisdom, stored preserved corpses for a longer time [*diutius*], surely so that the soul might last [*perduret*], be obligated [*obnoxia*] to the body, and not quickly pass over to the others. The Romans did the opposite, burning the corpses so that the soul would return at once to generality, that is to its nature. (Stocker and Travis 1965, 32; my translation)

In other words, the Egyptian embalming practice is explained as an effort to keep the soul with the body rather than letting it pass on. Servius makes no commitment to the permanence of this arrangement, nor does he tell why this should be desirable in the first place, noting simply that the soul can be kept for a significant period by preserving and keeping the body, leaving room for later scholars to fill in these gaps, for example, by assuming the body was meant to last forever to secure the soul's immortality, or that the existence near the soul was temporary, but pleasant, to explain the desirability of preserving the body. The relation between body and soul is further regarded as a cross-cultural universal, allowing the direct comparison between Egypt and Rome, with only the practical aims differing from one culture to another, not the conceptions of how the body and soul interact.

Conclusion

The knowledge that can be gleaned from ancient sources depends to a large extent on which sources are selected and how they are interpreted individually and harmonized mutually. The main areas touched on are the funerary rituals and especially the process of embalming, on the one hand, beliefs in souls and metempsychosis on the other, and the occasional intersection between these two areas as found in authors like Plutarch and Porphyry. The descriptions of funerary rituals in Herodotus and Diodorus could provide a sense of mourning practices as well as the different qualities of mummification. The description by Diodorus of a ritual judgment determining the right to burial in particular would attract much interest from later European scholars. A largely separate group of sources based on Herodotus and sometimes supplemented by the Platonic tradition indicated belief in a cycle of reincarnation, with or without a notion that souls were judged after death to determine rewards or punishments, as opposed to simply having to go through each animal species in turn or to the souls' being attracted mechanistically to particular types of compatible bodies. Writers like Plutarch and Porphyry on the one hand and Servius on the other offered different ways to bridge the apparent gap between such eschatological beliefs and the practice of mummification, understood either as an act of purification or as one of staving off decay to keep body and soul together longer.

The tendency and general reliability of each of the authors have been touched on occasionally in the discussion above, but as I noted, my primary interest here is the way later scholars used the passages, alone or in various combinations, to produce knowledge of ancient Egyptian mortuary religion.

TWO

Explaining the Remains: Medieval and Renaissance Sources

European interest in ancient Egypt during the Middle Ages was not quite as absent as has sometimes been assumed, but it did tend to be limited to particular domains and aspects (Burnett 2003; Thompson 2015–18, 1:43–55). Much of the European concern with Egypt related to establishing its place in medieval cosmography and geography. Correspondingly, interest in the ancient culture tended to focus on the connection with the biblical episodes of Joseph and Moses in the Hebrew Bible and the flight of Jesus, Mary, and Joseph in the New Testament. This interest occasionally intersected with the experiences and reports of travelers visiting Egypt, mostly as part of pilgrimages to the Holy Land, though other activities shaped by trade and the political reality of the Crusades also motivated European stays in the country (Kalfatovich 1992, 5–30; Amin 2013, 67–70). Meanwhile, among Arabic writers the interest often lay less in the inherent "Egyptianness" of the ancient monuments than in the practicalities of encounters with them. While generally not a main focus, these varying interests did occasionally connect in various ways with ancient Egyptian funerary culture.

Medieval Interpretations of Ancient Egyptian Tombs

A good illustration of the nature of such intersections is the understanding of the Great Pyramids in medieval European texts and images (cf. Khattab 1982, 99–101). A long tradition connected these salient monuments with the biblical story of Joseph, who built granaries during seven years of abundance to prepare for the following seven years of famine (Genesis 41). The idea may have been prevalent among Jews in Egypt, as the earliest written testimony seems to be a travel description from the fourth century CE (Egeria's travels as preserved by Peter the Deacon; e.g., Wilkinson 1971, 204n6). That this notion was transmitted as a linguistic concept, at least partly divorced from the actual appearance of the pyramids, is shown by the Hereford *Mappa mundi* (ca. 1300), where the "granaries of Joseph" (*orrea ioseph*) are depicted as the artist would have pictured a medieval hall rather than reproducing the characteristic shape of the pyramids as it might have been described by travelers (fig. 2) (Westrem 2001, 176–77 [416] and section 7).

The idea of the pyramids as Joseph's granaries naturally precluded any connection between these monuments and Egyptian funerary culture. Nonetheless their interpretation as funerary monuments was certainly present during this period as well, as exemplified by a passage from Sir John Mandeville (fl. fourteenth century AD):

> Some men say that they are graves of some great men in old time; but the common voice is there that they are the Barns of Joseph, and that find they in their chronicles. And soothly it is not likely that they should be graves, in als mickle as they are void within and have porches before them and gates. And also graves should not by reason be so high. (Letts 1953, 1:38)

Here the common opinion, and presumably the desire to fit these famous monuments into a comprehensible cultural framework, prevails despite awareness of the rival interpretation. The description of the pyramids as being hollow, having porches, and so on, shows that it can hardly have been based on personal observation. The last remark about the sensibility of having tall funerary monuments is thus the closest we get to an engagement with Egyptian funerary practices.

As noted by Mandeville's modern editor (Letts 1953, 3n2), much of this is in fact based directly on the earlier description by the pseudonymous author William of Boldensele (cf. Amin 2013, 152–63), whose details are more reliable, and indeed he comes down on the opposite side of the debate. In his 1336 account of his travel to the Holy

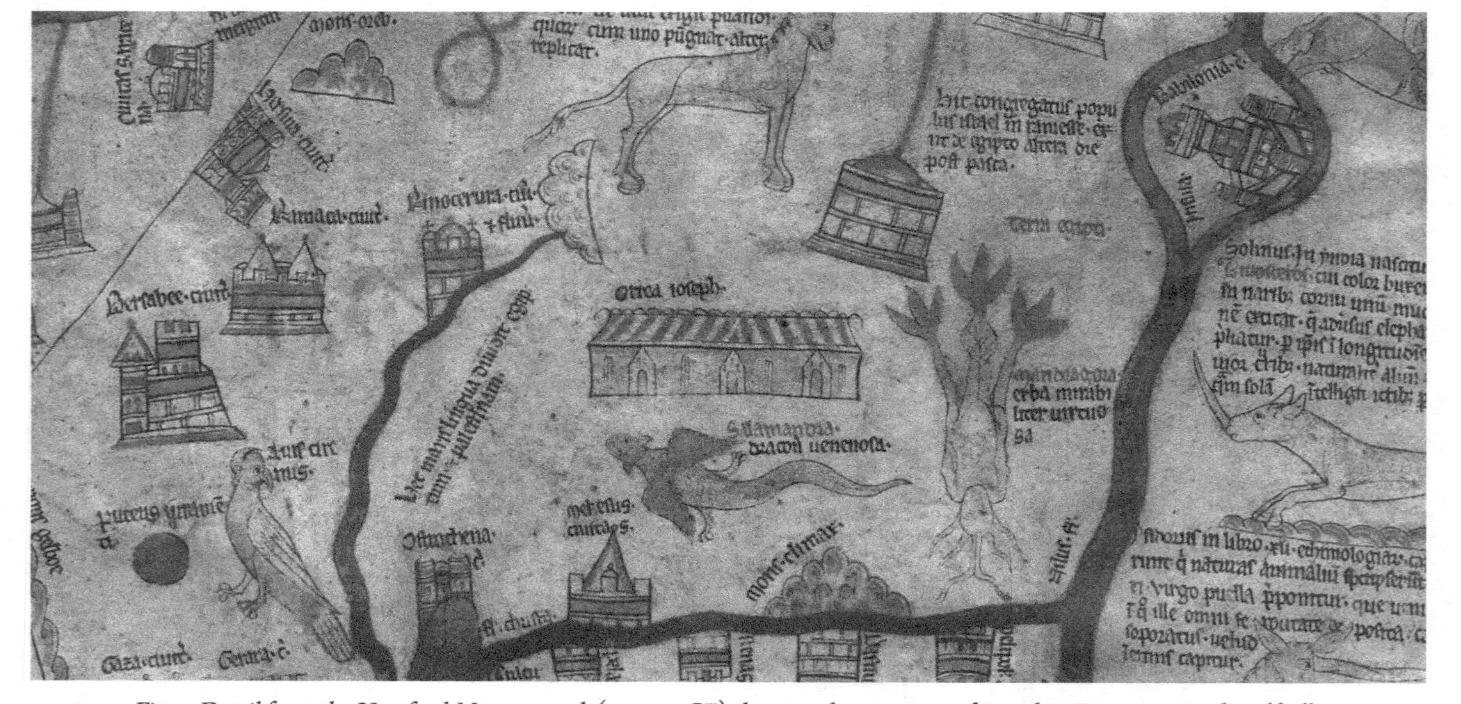

Fig. 2: Detail from the Hereford *Mappa mundi* (ca. 1300 CE) showing the granaries of Joseph in Egypt as a medieval hall.

Land, he wrote the following passage on the function of the Great Pyramids:

> Simple folk say that these great monuments were the granaries of Pharaoh and call them thus, which however is certainly not true, for there is no room to be found in these pyramids either for loading, unloading or storing of foodstuffs or grain, mainly because they are filled with very great stones connected closely to each other from top to bottom. Apart from a very small door remaining at some elevation from the ground and a dark, narrow passageway by which one descends to a certain room in them, there are no open spaces in them: That they were in fact monuments is demonstrated by the quoted verse [and] to one who sees many personally. (Graefe 1984, 571–73)

The idea of the pyramids being "monuments" is not explored further, and thus we get no sense of how von Boldensele understood their function more precisely. However, the use of observed details to critique conventional wisdom makes the discussion worth noting, while also showing why more detailed speculation about the function of the pyramids is hardly to be expected based on the sources available at this time. As noted by Charles Burnett (2003, 70), the "more educated could have known the true shape and purpose of the pyramids, from several classical and patristic sources. . . . , but the identification of the pyramids with tombs is rarely made."

Most of the European travelers to Egypt during this period visited the country as part of their pilgrimage to the Holy Land, which tended to focus their interest on places of biblical relevance (e.g., Carré 1932, 1:1–2; Khattab 1982; Amin 2013). A different and—because of the language barrier—largely independent perspective is offered by medieval Arabic writers. Here the scriptural connections often recede to give place to more practical considerations of what one might actually find when exploring Egyptian monuments (El Daly 2005, 95–107).

In a manuscript titled *Akhbār al-zamān* (History of time) dated roughly to the tenth century to the twelfth (El Daly 2005, 185), the funerary preparations performed for an Egyptian king are described in the following way:

> They anointed his body with preserving medicines and placed him in a sarcophagus of gold and made for him a *naos* plaited with gold and buried him in it with endless treasures and plenty of the Elixir of the Alchemical craft and gold. Then they inscribed on the tomb his date of death and placed on top talismans against harmful insects. (*Akhbār al-zamān*, 113; El Daly 2005, 99)

The passage contains a number of conjectures about the purpose of the evidence one might have observed on entering an Egyptian tomb, including that the inscription contains the date of death of the tomb's occupant, and that the amulets are intended to protect against insects (the latter idea perhaps deduced from the recognizable form of heart scarabs). But perhaps the most interesting notion for present purposes is the clear statement that the body was treated with "preserving medicines," which gives an indication that the author saw preservation of the body as a main purpose of mummification. No doubt this idea was related to the observation that mummified bodies were in fact preserved to an extent belying their evident great age. Thus Persian traveler ʿAlī ibn Abī Bakr al-Harawī (d. 1215) in his *Kitāb al-Ishārāt ila maʿrifat al-ziyārāt* (Guide to sites of pilgrimage) writes of mummified humans and animals that may be found in mountains in Upper Egypt that their "shroud is like the infant's garment; on it there are drugs in order that it does not disintegrate, so if you unwrap the shrouds from the animal you find that nothing has changed" (*al-Ishārāt*, 42; El Daly 2005, 100). In a similar way, the physician ʿAbd al-Laṭīf al-Baghdādī (d. 1231) relates in his description of his travels to Egypt the discovery of a mummified falcon he had been told about, on which he notes that "after an exhausting time unwinding its wrappings, [the discoverers] also found it intact, with not a feather missing" (al-Baghdādī, *al-Ifādah*, 1.4.69; Mackintosh-Smith 2021, 101; cf. also El Daly 2005, 101).

In the same work, al-Baghdādī presents some considerations concerning the many grave goods found in ancient tombs. He notes that judging from the sort of objects that had reportedly been found, it seems to have been "the ancient Egyptians' practice to bury a man with the tools of his trade and with his worldly wealth" (al-Baghdādī, *al-Ifādah*,

1.4.63; Mackintosh-Smith 2021, 97). He connects this custom to stories about contemporary practices among the Abyssinians:

> I have heard that there are certain Abyssinian communities who also follow this practice, and that they regard it as inauspicious to touch a dead man's possessions, or to make any use of them. A relative of ours moved to Abyssinia and made money there, including 200 *ūqiyyah*s of gold. When he died, the local people compelled an Egyptian who had been in his company to take the money—and so he did, with all due acknowledgment to them. (al-Baghdādī, *al-Ifādah,* 1.4.64; Mackintosh-Smith 2021, 97; cf. El Daly 2005, 100)

The explanation of ancient Egyptian burial practices thus does not evoke any particular notion of an afterlife. The reason for placing objects and valuables in the tomb is not about providing the deceased with these objects (at least that is not the explanation given), but rather is a way to dispose of things so strongly connected to the deceased that it would be inauspicious for others to keep them.

Mumia for Medicine

By far the most prevalent interest in ancient Egyptian burials from the late Middle Ages and well into the early modern period, however, related more specifically to the substance known in Arabic as *mūmiyā'* (the loanword *mumia* is attested in Latin from the eleventh century) and its use in healing practices, spanning Persian, Arabic, European, and Ottoman authors (e.g., El Daly 2005, 102–6; Bachour 2016; Pommerening 2010; Schmitz-Esser 2014, 616–27). While the Arabic term covers a range of materials of different origin, the substance that could be extracted from bodies in ancient Egyptian tombs came to be chief among them (Pommerening 2010).

The notion of "natural" *mūmiyā'*, referring to materials related to tar or bitumen, and its medical efficacy, had been established for centuries by the time the word was first associated with Egyptian bodies (Pommerening 2010, 193–95; Bachour 2016, 410–26). The earliest reference to *mūmiyā'* derived from tombs stems from the second half of the ninth century CE. In a work of which only fragments are preserved, Isḥāq ibn 'Imrān (d. 901) mentions a kind of *mūmiyā'* found in tombs when they are opened, speculating that it may have been placed there to prevent the body from being touched by worms (Bachour 2016, 427). This notion was transmitted to the Latin literature by the eleventh-century translator of Arabic texts on medicine into Latin, Constantinus Africanus (Pommerening 2010, 195; Bachour 2016, 427–28). Noting explicitly the difference between mumia as asphalt and the substance derived from Egyptian bodies, he writes:

> Some say that *mumia* is an asphalt; a particular type is also found in ancient tombs, however; this is the best. The ancients even used to rub the dead with it to prevent them from decaying right away [*cito putrescerent*] or producing worms [*vermes*]. (Bachour 2016, 428; trans. Pommerening 2010, 195)

As seen here, Constantinus Africanus presents the idea of mumia as a naturally occurring substance, the best quality of which can be obtained from ancient Egyptian corpses, because the ancients used to treat bodies with it. From this, it is a small conceptual step to ascribing a specific efficacy to the mummified remains themselves with which the "best" mumia was inextricably connected. Thus, the Salernite physician Matthaeus Silvaticus (ca. 1280–1342) writes in his influential *Pandects of Medicine*:

> *Mumia* is that which is found in the tombs of the embalmed—in which the [decomposition] fluids of the dead person are fixed with aloe and myrrh, through which these corpses were (then) prevented from decaying; and it is similar to sea pitch. (trans. Pommerening 2010, 196)

The "ingredients" of mumia are thus expanded to include vegetable substances as well, though mumia is no longer understood to denote those ingredients in themselves, but instead the specific substance that can be extracted from "tombs of the embalmed." As noted by Bachour (2016,

428–29), this crucial idea may in fact arise from a misunderstanding of the passage transmitted by Constantinus Africanus. The quoted passage also shows the cementing of the idea that the purpose of embalming was to preserve the corpse, in turn providing a plausible conceptual connection between the efficacy of the drug and its origin in ancient Egyptian mummification.

As has frequently been noted (e.g., Schmitz-Esser 2014, 616; Caciola 2016, 105), the origin of the concept of the efficacy of *mūmiyā'* is likely to be found in observations of the type noted above among the Arabic writers: The substance mummified bodies had been treated with had evidently allowed them to remain relatively lifelike through the millennia, in turn indicating that they contained a certain "life force" that could also benefit the living. This strong association can be seen especially clearly through the tradition of visualizing mumia in the late Middle Ages in Europe, where the substance is illustrated in medical handbooks in the form of an entire corpse (fig. 3), and later on in that of a skull (Camille 1999). In Europe, the use of mumia was conceptually and practically connected to other efficacious uses of parts of corpses, notably relics of saints and parts and substances extracted from executed criminals (Noble 2011; Schmitz-Esser 2014, 609–30; Caciola 2016, 104–7). Sometimes the corollary was made explicit that criminals and other undesirable members of society thus in fact benefited the nation more after their death through medical efficacy and knowledge obtained through dissection than they had during life, as was more obviously true also of ancient dead from faraway places (Noble 2011, 22–34).

The wide range of beneficial effects of mumia was described in various ways and differed somewhat between authors (El Daly 2005, 103; Schmitz-Esser 2014, 620–27; Bachour 2016, 434–39). A recurring idea is that mumia will heal broken bones and bruises and stop bleeding, connected logically to their apparent use in keeping ancient corpses intact, but many authors extend the effects of the substance significantly to healing other ailments as well, notably complaints of the head, as well as of the kidneys and bladder. The means of application shows a similar range of both internal and external treatments.

The heightened European engagement with ancient Egyptian mummified bodies came at a time of increasing interest among the elite in

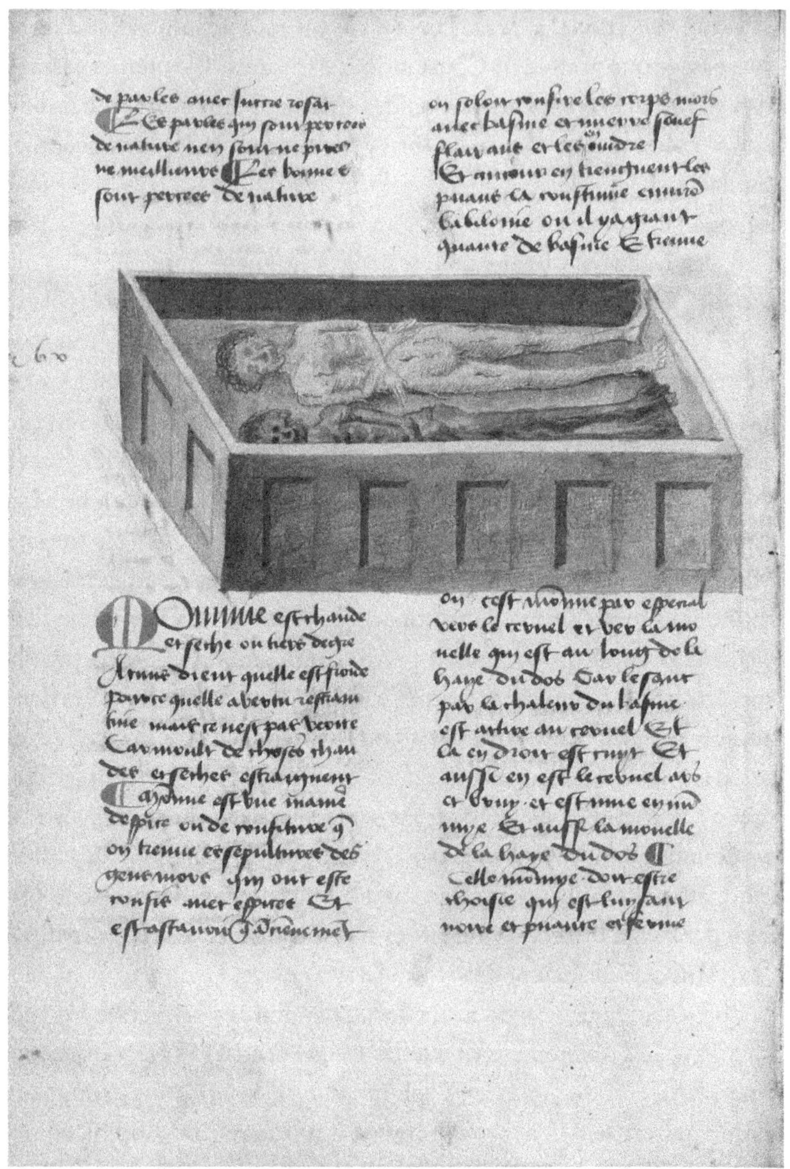

Fig. 3: Herbarium page (ca. 1470 CE) showing mumia as an ingredient in the form of mummified corpses. Matthaeus Platearius, *Livre des simples médecines*. Wellcome Collection MS.626, 159v.

practical embalming methods, spurred by long-distance travel, especially of the dangerous sort connected to the Crusades (Horrox 1999, 99–100; Schmitz-Esser 2014, 165–310), impelling the development of techniques for bringing the dead back to their homeland for burial. While not the main concern with Egyptian mumia, this framework did prompt an understanding of Egyptian mummification as basically similar in its aims to contemporaneous embalming methods aimed explicitly at preserving the corpse in a lifelike state. It should be noted, however, that actual treatments of dead bodies in medieval Europe were highly varied and sometimes contested, with ideas of long-term preservation, outward appearance, and even wholeness of the body not always going together (Bynum 1995; Tarlow 2011; Bynum 2012, esp. 239–98; Schmitz-Esser 2014, 165–310; Gray 2021, 111–17).

The desire for mumia continued into subsequent periods, but for now it will be useful to draw a few main conclusions concerning the early conceptions of mumia and its relation to ancient Egyptian burial practices. As I noted above, without access to the classical sources on mummification so popular in later scholarship, the medieval understanding of mumia and ancient Egyptian burials was largely deductive. Ancient bodies were seen to be well preserved as a result of the treatment they had undergone before burial. From this two things could be concluded. The more immediately relevant conclusion regarded the efficacy of the substances the ancient corpses had been treated with in preserving the integrity of human bodies. Another logical entailment, which tended to attract far less attention from most writers of the period, was that this preservation must in turn have been what the ancient Egyptians intended by their treatment of the corpses (implied by such wording as the *Akhbār al-zamān*'s "preserving medicines" quoted above). As there was generally little interest in such ethnographic aspects of the ancient culture, however, medieval authors for the most part did not go beyond simply noting or implying this intention, and there is no speculation about *why* the ancients might have wanted to treat bodies in this way. Because of the prevalence in later periods of the idea that the Egyptians aimed primarily at preserving the bodies of the dead, it is worth noting that as reasonable as this deduction seems at first, the logic is flawed concerning the aims of the ancient Egyptians. In principle there are no grounds for deducing intention from effect: that mummification could be seen to have *led* to preservation of bodies millennia later does not mean that preservation was necessarily the ancient Egyptians' *purpose* with the procedure (Riggs 2014, esp. 99–108).

In this connection it is worth briefly discussing the proposal by Egyptologist Okasha El Daly (2005, 106) that the belief in the efficacy of eating substances extracted from mummified bodies can be derived ultimately from ancient Egyptian ideas:

> This [the ancient Egyptian notion of the protective power of mummies] is surely what was in the minds of those who were excavating ancient Egyptian bodies for use as medicine, believing that they were endowed with powerful magical spells written among the wrappings, and that the magical effect would still be as powerful on those who consumed them. (El Daly 2005, 106)

As seen from the examples cited above, the additional sources cited by El Daly, and similar references characterizing the benefits of mumia, however, the idea of powerful spells or protective qualities was not at all prevalent in this period. If there was some acceptance of the efficacy of the ancient practices, it strongly tended to be conceptualized in terms of the power to preserve bodies rather than to a "magical effect" of the wrappings or inscriptions. Both in this regard and in El Daly's (El Daly 2005, 105) highly concrete interpretation of ancient Egyptian references to "cannibalism" (cf. Nyord 2009, 381–92), the continuities in this area between ancient and medieval concepts and practices thus appear to be overstated significantly (cf. Stephan 2017, 264–65 for a similar case). On the other hand, as seen above, there is considerable continuity between the medicinal use of mummified bodies and broader conceptions of the dead body in medieval and early modern Europe.

Classical Texts on Ancient Egypt

Beginning in the fifteenth century, the "rediscovery" and publication of texts from classical antiquity in the wake of the rise of the printing press gradually changed European understanding of ancient Egypt fundamentally. The increasing interest in, and access to, ancient Greek and Latin texts provided not only a new source of knowledge of ancient Egypt, but also a renewed impetus for studying ancient Egyptian culture (Curran 2007, 89–105). Rather than being primarily a matter of explaining salient traces of ancient Egyptian culture such as pyramids, obelisks, and not least mummified bodies, the new sources made the study of ancient Egypt also—and in some respects primarily—a textual and philological endeavor.

To begin with, much of the interest in ancient Egypt in this period was spurred by the discovery in 1419 of a manuscript of Horapollo's *Hieroglyphica* (Boas 1993; cf. Wildish 2018), which seemed to offer a key to understanding the ancient hieroglyphic script. The hieroglyphs came to be understood as a universal language of images bypassing the differences between human languages, an idea that proved highly appealing to Renaissance scholars (Curran 2003, 107–8). A further series of works by ancient Greek and Roman authors reporting on aspects of Egyptian history and culture were printed in the 1460s and 1470s. The Greek original of Plutarch's *Isis and Osiris* followed in 1509, and part of Diodorus Siculus's *Bibliotheca* in 1539; then the complete text was printed in 1559 (Dannenfeldt 1959, 8–9).

Another key discovery of the time was a manuscript of fourteen Hermetic dialogues; the Latin translation by Italian scholar Marsilio Ficino (1433–99) was first printed in 1471. Hermes Trismegistus was already known through the dialogue *Asclepius*, but the Hermetic writings now became a fundamental key to understanding ancient Egyptian religion. At the same time, however, the Hermetic corpus also raised vexed questions about the relationship between Christian revelation and Egyptian paganism, especially as long as the purported great (i.e., pre-Christian) antiquity of the texts was taken at face value (e.g., Grafton 1983). Regardless of such controversies, to most Renaissance scholars the Hermetic writings, along with the contemporary interpretations of Horapollo's *Hieroglyphica* read in the light of Plato and Neoplatonic authors, established Egypt as a primordial source of wisdom, but also of somewhat impenetrable secrets (Curran 2003).

At the same time, following a long tradition in Rome of appropriating

Egyptian symbols and monuments (Curran 2007, 27–87), Egypt came to be understood as a culture of great antiquity, so association with it could be a source of authority. This basic idea could be instantiated in very different ways, ranging from the forged "translations" of Annius of Viterbo (ca. 1432–1502; Stephens 2004; Grafton 2018), who interwove biblical, classical, Etruscan, and Egyptian myth to establish a genealogy worthy of respect for his native Viterbo, to the systematic (re)installation of Egyptian antiquities around the city of Rome by the Medici popes Leo X (1513–21) and Clement VII (1523–34)(Curran 2004).

The newly available classical texts offered entirely new interpretive possibilities not just for scholars, but also for travelers of the sixteenth century seeking to make sense of ancient Egyptian funerary practices (e.g., Carré 1932, 1:3–12). The Ottoman conquest of Egypt in 1517 further increased access to travelers from France in particular, thanks to the French-Ottoman alliance (Clément 1960, 2–3).

If this conceptual and historical background is relatively well known, for my purposes here it raises the question of what place ancient Egyptian funerary culture and mortuary religion had within European Renaissance thought. By the early fifteenth century CE, the idea of the pyramids as the granaries of Joseph had been largely abandoned, and they were almost universally understood as funerary monuments (Curran 2003, 103). This idea made it appropriate to incorporate the pyramid into mortuary monuments like the Chigi Chapel in the Basilica of Santa Maria del Popolo in Rome, commissioned by Agostino Chigi (1466–1520), though there were more local precursors, both ancient and medieval, that might have served as more immediate sources of inspiration (Shearman 1961, 133–34; Curran 2007, 27–49 and 65–87). The pyramid is generally understood in this connection as a "symbol of eternity" (e.g., Fischel 1948, 1:149), but one must admit that contemporary sources are not very explicit (cf., e.g., Giehlow 1915, 73–75), so that it is difficult to pinpoint its exact significance beyond the perceived appropriateness in a Christian mortuary setting. This would likely have precluded more specific associations to pagan religion, but it would be well in line with the general interest in hieroglyphs as pure ideational forms, as noted above, to the extent that the pyramid was understood as a specifically Egyptian form (e.g., Giehlow 1915, 113–29).

In the anonymous commentary appended to the study of Egyptian hieroglyphs (partly based on Horapollo's work) published by Pierio Valeriano (1477–1560), the form of the pyramid was interpreted along such Platonic lines as signifying "the nature of things and that formless substance which receives forms" (*rerum naturam & substantiam illam informem formas recipientem*) (Valerianus 1602 [1556], 640). Remarkably, Athanasius Kircher (1652–54, 2:110) would later use almost identical wording, while crediting and quoting an Arabic text by one Abenephius (a scholar cited repeatedly in Kircher's oeuvre but not known from elsewhere; cf. Stolzenberg 2013, 83–88) for the idea.

As an explicitly funerary understanding, the appendix to Valeriano's *Hieroglyphica* suggests that for the Egyptians the shape served to "outline the soul of a man, as they made the magnificent sepulchers of the kings and heroes under enormous pyramids to testify that, though the body was dissolved and rotten, the soul remained" (Valerianus 1602 [1556], 640). In laying out this interpretation, the commentator refers to Herodotus's notion of the transmigration of souls, which is connected more specifically to the cyclical return of the world to its pristine state after 36,000 years. This number is not explained further here, but it likely derives from medieval chronicler George Syncellus's concept of a cosmic cycle of 36,525 years (the time it takes for the Zodiac to return to its original position and also the total period covered by the thirty dynasties of Egypt in Syncellus's chronology; e.g., Adler 1983, 427).

In the early seventeenth century, a quite similar approach—though one largely bypassing Valeriano himself in favor of older, more authoritative sources–was taken by French Jesuit scholar Nicolas Caussin (1583–1651), who is explicit in his aim of aligning the symbolic meanings of ancient Egyptian hieroglyphs with a Christian rhetoric inspired by Clement of Alexandria's *Stromateis* (Campbell 1993, 48–56). Combining this theological background with the general Renaissance understanding of hieroglyphs as visual symbols bypassing ordinary human languages, Caussin arrives at an interpretation of hieroglyphic signs as "a model for the most faithful image of the divine language spoken in nature" (Campbell 1993, 50), giving a good example of how the hieroglyphs could be theorized in Christian theology. In practice, he accomplishes the marriage of these two different traditions by juxtaposing

Latin translations of Horapollo with commented passages from Clement (Caussin 1618).

Textual and Physical Studies of Ancient Egyptian Bodies

Often to some extent independent of the exploration of hieroglyphs, mummified bodies seen in Egypt or brought back by travelers attracted growing attention from scholars interested especially in verifying the methods of mummification as described in the newly available discussions by Herodotus and Diodorus. These developments somewhat shifted the balance during the sixteenth century in the understanding of mumia as not only a medicinal raw material, but also a substance originating in ancient Egyptian bodies as a result of culturally specific practices (e.g., Reetz 2019, 16–20).

In 1553 the French physician Pierre Belon published a three-part work on ancient Egypt, dealing respectively with Egyptian monuments and burial practices, mummification, and the materials used for preserving corpses, based in part on his own travels in the country from 1546 to 1549 (Belon 1553; cf. Carré 1932, 1:5–7; Reetz 2019, 29–33). The overall purpose of the work is to argue against the prevailing use of pulverized parts of Egyptian mummified bodies in medicine. This argument brings together a number of strands and especially forms the focus of the second book of the work *De medicato funere.* Here Belon argues that not only is the medical use of mumia unattested in authors of antiquity, but its efficacy can further be shown to be a misunderstanding due to medieval mistranslation (Reetz 2019, 30–32).

In the course of this argument, Belon touches briefly on the underlying religious motivation of the ancient Egyptians for the practice of mummification. Thus he notes that the bodies were "kept or preserved for eternity" (*ad aeternitatem custodita seu condita*), and that the Egyptians' reason for doing so was that they "expected the resurrection of the dead" (*mortuorum resurrectionem expectarent*) (Belon 1553, 24r). He does not cite Herodotus's passage on the transmigration of the soul, thereby avoiding the challenges in connecting this idea to practices of mummification. Instead, he cites a much more straightforward passage in book 7 of Pliny's *Natural History* referring briefly to "the vanity about preserving men's bodies and about Democritus's promise of coming back to life" (*Natural History* 7, 55), which Belon understands as directed at ideas originating with the Egyptians (Belon 1553, 24v). Ultimately, Belon's interests lie more in the practical matters of mummification, and he does not elaborate on the underlying Egyptian beliefs. It is worth noting that although he cites Pliny, the idea that the reason behind mummification is the notion of the soul returning to the body, which thus needs to be preserved for this reunion, is relatively intuitive and works equally well without any textual support. As such, it shows up occasionally in later authors as well, either by itself or as a complement to interpretations based on classical texts.

A more penetrating account of ancient Egyptian mummification and more general funerary practices was offered by the contemporary French explorer André Thevet in his 1556 travelogue (Thevet 1556, 155–57; cf. Carré 1932, 1:7–9). Thevet relates the custom of passing judgment on the deceased before burial based on Diodorus, also following that author in noting that this custom reinforced moral behavior in the population. He adds to this that some say the Egyptians held that a well-preserved body could offer an abode for the soul, likely based implicitly either on Servius or on a more deductive version of this idea along the same lines as Belon. After this account based on summaries of selected passages from classical authors and a suggestion that the word "mummy" (*Momie*) is derived from the cinnamon (*Cinamome*) used to treat them, Thevet (1556, 157–58) describes how during his stay in Egypt he accompanied a small group of physicians and merchants on a trip to find mummified bodies for medicinal use, where they encountered both human and numerous animal bodies, showing that the interest in, and demand for, mumia was alive and well in the sixteenth century (Dannenfeldt 1985). Somewhat similarly, Italian scholar Pietro della Valle (1586–1652; cf. Gurney 1986), who visited Egypt in 1615 as part of his travels in the East, describes how he organized a group to search for ancient mummified bodies, and he discusses the resulting find of decorated mummies and his interpretations of the iconography (drawing on Herodotus, Diodorus, and others) in significant detail, though largely without relating the mummies to any underlying ancient Egyptian ideas (Bull 1990, 53–63). Della Valle does, however, emphasize "how greatly the poor Egyptians exerted themselves to preserve their bodies, if it might be possible, along with their souls for eternity" (Bull 1990, 61). This suggests that, like Thevet, he had in mind either an explicit explanation derived from Servius where the survival of the soul depends on that of the body, or simply a more intuitive expectation of burial practices having the survival of the soul as their ultimate purpose.

Reforming the Egyptian Afterlife

The profound changes in religious thinking brought about by Reformation movements across Europe in the sixteenth century also had significant consequences for the ways Egyptian religion was understood. One of the major points of disagreement that had a direct effect on interpretations of Egyptian eschatology lay in the theological question of purgatory (e.g., Tarlow 2011, 21–26; Marshall 2015). Although purgatory was widely accepted before the Reformation (and by Catholics afterward) as a place of painful purification of sins not grave enough to lead to eternal damnation, reformed churches generally rejected the idea along with attendant practices such as indulgences that sought to shorten the stay there. The corollary of this change was the notion that deceased individuals were entirely responsible for their own postmortem fate (and/or needed to rely on divine grace for salvation) and that their survivors were not able to assist through prayers or alms. While this schism was not generally transferred directly to interpretations of Egyptian religion, when scholars did deploy notions of purgation or expiation as part of their interpretations of Egyptian postmortem fate, it was not infrequently tinted by scholars' own theological stance or background.

Egypt would also be deployed with more explicitly polemic aims in the religious conflicts in the wake of the Reformation. A striking example of this is offered by French historian Henri de Sponde (1568–1643; cf. Vidal 1929; Costa 2005, 185–89; Eurich 2008, 47–50), who followed his brother Jean (and indeed the king they served, Henry IV) in converting from Calvinism to Catholicism in 1595 (cf. Vidal 1929, 1–12; Daussy 2016, 86–87). Shortly thereafter he published a polemic book on "sacred cemeteries" (*cimitières sacrez*) (Sponde 1597), taking a strong stance in the religious debates in the wake of the French Wars of Religion. The book argued against the religious rights of Protestants, notably the right of burial in Catholic cemeteries (cf. Raeburn 2021, 170–73)—rights partially secured soon after the publication of the first edition of the book when King Henry IV promulgated the Edict of Nantes in 1798 (Thibaut-Payen 1977, 157–78; Bergin 2014, 43–63). With the official edict thus taking essentially the opposite side (although as a lasting solution it did recommend that Protestants and Catholics should have separate cemeteries), the book increased its relevance in certain quarters, and it was published in several expanded editions over the following years (the sixth and final edition appeared in 1600, by which time most provincial parliaments had ratified the edict), and eventually in an expanded Latin translation in 1638, addressing a more international readership during the Thirty Years War (cf., e.g., Vidal 1929, 170–76). In the book Sponde argues that owing to the sacred nature of cemeteries, Protestant Huguenots should not be allowed burial in Catholic cemeteries. To substantiate this, he demonstrates at some length how all peoples, divided into pagans, Muslims, Jews, Christians, and "heretics" (his designation for Protestants), have universally held cemeteries to be sacred and correspondingly not permitted persons of other faiths to be buried in them.

The Egyptians take pride of place in the book as the pagan "fathers of religion" (*peres de la Religion*; Sponde 1597, 27). Owing to their aptness for superstition, Sponde notes, their funerary preparations were "extreme," as shown both by the practice of mummification, intended to "safeguard them against corruption" (*les garentir de la corruption*; Sponde 1597, 27), and by the monumental tombs that he, following Diodorus, terms "eternal houses" (*maisons eternelles*; Sponde 1597, 27), as opposed to the temporary dwellings of the living. Sponde suggests that while pagan peoples would not have been able to appreciate this significance,

> the ceremony of burial has always been like a reflection of the Resurrection (*vn miroir de la Resurrection*), and was only instituted in

> consideration of a firm and certain hope that the immortal souls would one day take back the bodies that they had left for a time. (Sponde 1597, 39–40)

A new passage in the expanded 1600 edition notes more specifically that Christian practices of embalming were taken over from the Jews, who in turn derived them from the Egyptians, thus establishing a direct connection to the ancient culture (Sponde 1600, 63–64).

While the Egyptians are thus well suited for demonstrating the first of Sponde's theses, namely the cross-cultural importance of burial, they turn out to be less useful for the second and third ones: the exclusive nature of such burials to one particular religion and the exclusion of outsiders. For this reason his discussion of pagan religions in the second and third chapters skips directly to Greek and Roman practices (Sponde 1597, 60, 79; Sponde 1600, 116, 183). Ultimately the role of Egyptian burial practices in these early French versions of the work is primarily to establish the importance of funerary ceremonies among all peoples, among which the Egyptians take a special role as a pagan prototype.

The expanded Latin version of the book, however, draws considerably more on ancient Egyptian burial practices, devoting an entire chapter (Sponde 1638, 54–69) primarily to Egyptian mortuary religion, and fitting many additional details into the overall argument. While the French versions did not go into any detail about the motivations of the Egyptians, the new discussion begins by citing Herodotus for the idea that they believed the soul was immortal, and Sponde extrapolates from this that the body must have been regarded as the "abode" (*domicilium*) of the soul. Citing Plutarch's description of the ritual purification of the body by presenting the intestines before the sun as a source of impurity, Sponde notes that the Egyptians thus seem to have believed in the resurrection of the body (cf. Tarlow 2011, 33–38, for some contemporary Christian viewpoints on this), though only if the body was preserved intact, a notion for which he cites Servius's idea that the soul would last only as long as the body did (Sponde 1638, 54).

Following this outline of the motivations for preserving the body, he goes on to characterize Egyptian burial practices, citing a wide range of authors from classical writers to scholars closer to his own time like Thevet, Belon, and Valeriano—from the last of whom he takes the idea that the form of the pyramid is intended to signify the presence of the soul of the deceased (Sponde 1638, 57). After describing various specificities of Egyptian beliefs as related by ancient authors, Sponde returns to the deeper motivation behind the preservation of the body, which was touched on much more briefly in the earlier French editions. He enumerates various other ancient peoples who adopted similar practices "so that the whole structure of the bodies might be preserved [*conservaretur*] after death, hoping that sometime the bodies would be reclaimed by the souls and brought back to life [*reducerentur in vitam*]" (Sponde 1638, 63). The next step in the argument of the chapter is establishing the conceptual similarity between sleep and death, and showing that correspondingly dead bodies can be understood as resting and waiting for the soul to return, an idea that ancient Egypt is once again less useful for establishing than are Greece and Rome (Sponde 1638, 64–68). Specific Egyptian practices thus do not play a role in the rest of the chapter, but Sponde can conclude, as he did in the earlier, less detailed versions, that funerary rituals in general aim at safeguarding the body as it awaits resurrection, understanding the Egyptian practice of mummification as a particularly striking attempt at preservation. While this chapter of the first book is by far the most detailed discussion of ancient Egyptian mortuary religion in the work, a number of other sections have also been expanded with Egyptian illustrations. Thus, for example, the bans against burial related by Herodotus and Diodorus can also be turned to Sponde's purposes by showing the explicitly moral dimension of the right to burial (Sponde 1638, 366–68).

Although he cites not only Herodotus but also Hermes Trismegistus and Pythagoras (Sponde 1638, 68), Sponde makes no mention of the culturally specific belief in metempsychosis. This omission is entirely in line with his universalist aims. To make his argument about the cross-cultural significance and sanctity of funerary practices, he needs broadly similar conceptions of body and soul across the cultures he studies. Egyptian practices of mummification, especially as interpreted through Servius, are useful for constructing this cross-cultural model, while, by contrast, ideas of metempsychosis or other notions of a more temporary relevance of burial would be much less amenable to his aims. In practice this leads to a reconstruction of Egyptian mortuary religion on the model of contemporary Catholic concepts of bodily resurrection as underlying the more specific ideas of the soul's return to the body as related by, or deducible from, the classical sources.

It is noteworthy that despite this selectivity the book nonetheless presents one of the most detailed discussions of the topic of Egyptian mortuary religion (and indeed the beliefs and practices of many other cultures) available in the early seventeenth century. As such, it is occasionally cited simply as a repository of references to Egyptian practices by later authors with no apparent commitment to the general polemical argument concerning Catholic and Protestant cemeteries (e.g., Greenhill 1705, 240).

Another, more subtle, way Christian concerns started to surface is found in what begins as a relatively straightforward use of Herodotus to inform ancient Egyptian thinking about souls, found in English traveler George Sandys's travelogue describing his journey to the Holy Land starting in 1610 (Sandys 1615; cf. Haynes 1986). As part of a general description of the geography of Egypt and the achievements of its ancient culture, Sandys (1615, 104) notes briefly that "of all the Heathen, they were the first that taught the immortalitie of the soule, and the transmigration thereof into another body, either of man or beast, cleane or vncleane, as it had behaued it selfe in the former." In other words, Sandys follows a close paraphrase of Herodotus by adding an element of rewards and punishments not present in Herodotus, but in principle derivable from the later writings of Plato or the Hermetic corpus. That the idea of postmortem rewards and punishment is prevalent in his interpretations is even clearer a little earlier in the book where he credits the king Busiris with a number of social, intellectual, and moral improvements, including "emboldening and awing their minds with a being after death, happy or vnhappy, according to the good or bad committed in the present" (Sandys 1615, 103). The section in question is a significantly abbreviated paraphrase of fifth- to fourth-century BCE Greek orator Isocrates's *Busiris*, 15–26, but the part on postmortem rewards and punishments is an interpolation by Sandys himself. In extolling the great piety of the Egyptians, on which Sandys appears to base this, Isocrates writes that "each person believes that he will pay the penalty for his misdeeds immediately and that he will neither escape detection for the present nor will the punishment be deferred to his children's time" (*Busiris* 25–26; Hook 1945, 116–17). While in the context this clearly relates to divine retribution during life, as indicated by the word "immediately [*parachrēma*]," along with an earlier reference to "divine rewards and punishment" (*Busiris* 24; Hook 1945, 116–17), this passage could certainly have reminded a Christian primed to think in terms of rewards and punishments after death of the model of postmortem judgment, and indeed this is how Sandys presents the Egyptian beliefs.

With the question of the judgment's timing, Sandys touches on a long-standing discussion in Christian theology. From the perspective of modern popular Christianity, it seems obvious that the notion of postmortem judgment of ethical merits as found, for example, in Plato should be at least broadly compatible with Christian ideas. However, to the late medieval observer, this would have been much less obvious, because the prevalent Christian idea about judgment was a collective Last Judgment at the time of the Second Coming of the Messiah, rather than individual judgment of each person at the time of death. In a seminal study, Philippe Ariès has tracked this change in the timing (and hence to some extent the nature) of postmortem judgment as becoming prevalent during the fifteenth century (Ariès 1974, 33–39). In practice the two ideas continued to coexist, with Protestants often placing greater emphasis on the Last Judgment (because of their rejection of the doctrine of purgatory), although the individualist orientation of Protestant theology in many ways harmonized better with the notion of particular judgment at the time of death (Gittings 1999, 152–54; Tingle 2021, 36–38; cf. Tarlow 2011, 23). As the son of the archbishop of York, Sandys had a robust background in the Anglican Church (Haynes 1986, 13), and his book begins with a glowing dedication to King Charles I, though his precise position on Christian eschatology is not made clear. During his lifetime, Sandys will have experienced the concerted effort to eradicate the doctrines of purgatory and intercessory prayer from the English church, occasionally resulting in diverging interpretations of the role of judgment and resurrection in eschatology (Marshall 2002, 124–87). Regardless of the specificity of the correlation Sandys might have seen between his own beliefs and those ascribed to the ancient Egyptians, he would certainly have been aware of the idea of an individual judgment at the time of death and familiar with the notion that postmortem judgment of one sort or the other could serve as a motivator for ethical behavior—in ancient Egypt as in his contemporary England.

New Empirical Evidence

The Egyptian pyramids, and especially the three pyramids at Giza, also continued to attract attention, sometimes occasioning inquiries into the religious ideas that might have motivated the Egyptians to build them. Thus John Greaves (1602–52), professor of astronomy at the University of Oxford, made two trips to Egypt in 1638 and 1639 to study and measure the three great pyramids. The publication of his results not only contains this empirical examination but includes chapters discussing the background of the pyramids' construction, including one devoted to the underlying purpose (Greaves 1646, 43–66). He begins by ascertaining through references to classical and Arabic authors that the pyramids were intended as tombs. To explain the reasoning behind their construction, Greaves refers to the short commentary of Servius, according to which the Egyptians understood that the soul would continue to exist as long as the body could withstand decay. While to Servius this primarily explains the practice of mummification, Greaves extends this idea to include the construction of tombs to help secure the durability of the body:

> The same religion, and opinion continuing amongst the Ægyptians, *that so long as the body indured, so long the soule continued with it*, not as quickning, and animating it, but as an attendant, or guardian, and as it were unwilling to leave her former habitation: it is not to be doubted this incited the Kings there, together with their private ambition, and thirst after glory, to be at so vast expenses in the building of these *Pyramids*; and the Ægyptians of lower quality, to spare for no cost, in cutting those *hypogæa*, those caves, or dormitories, in the Libyan deserts. (Greaves 1646, 59; emphasis in the original)

On the more specific form of the pyramid, Greaves rejects the philosophical explanations offered by Valeriano, preferring instead to explain it by the Egyptians "apprehending this to be the most permament form of structure, as in truth it is . . . or else hereby they intended to represent some of their Gods" (Greaves 1646, 62). The first interpretation is also favored by the Roman traveler Pietro della Valle, mentioned above, who similarly estimates that the intention was to make a highly durable building rather than one of aesthetic beauty (Bull 1990, 51).

In constructing one of the latest and most encompassing treatments of Egyptian funerary practices in the Renaissance tradition of amassing and consolidating classical sources, Italian scholar Giovanni Nardi (1585?–1655?) arrived at his detailed study of the topic in a roundabout way in his 1647 commentary on Roman poet Lucretius's *De rerum natura* (The nature of things) (Nardi 1647; cf. La Brasca 1999). The last part of the lengthy poem deals with plagues, in particular the one ravaging Athens during the Peloponnesian War. For reasons that are not clearly articulated (cf., e.g., Butterfield 2015, 60; Reetz 2019, 61, for suggestions), and in fact probably mostly reflecting Nardi's own idiosyncratic interests, he appends to his commentary a detailed discussion of the nature of, and rationale behind, ancient Egyptian burial practices, drawing not only on classical authors, but also on firsthand knowledge of mummified bodies in his contemporary Florence (Śliwa 2007; Sutherland, Findlen, and Lelková 2018, 316–317). Although the book as a whole was largely unsuccessful as a contribution to the tradition of textual criticism of Lucretius, Nardi's treatment of ancient Egypt would have significant and direct influence on later scholars (Milanese 2016, 203–4), not least thanks to the plates illustrating a mummified body and other Egyptian artifacts (cf. Śliwa 2007). In line with more general developments of the mid-seventeenth century, the plates (fig. 4), reproduced for example with minor alterations by Athanasius Kircher (see chapter 3 below), allowed a broader audience to scrutinize these collection objects visually without physical access to them through what Shapin and Schaffer have termed "virtual witnessing" (Shapin and Schaffer 1985, 60–65; cf. Burke 2013 for seventeenth-century visualizations of antiquity more specifically).

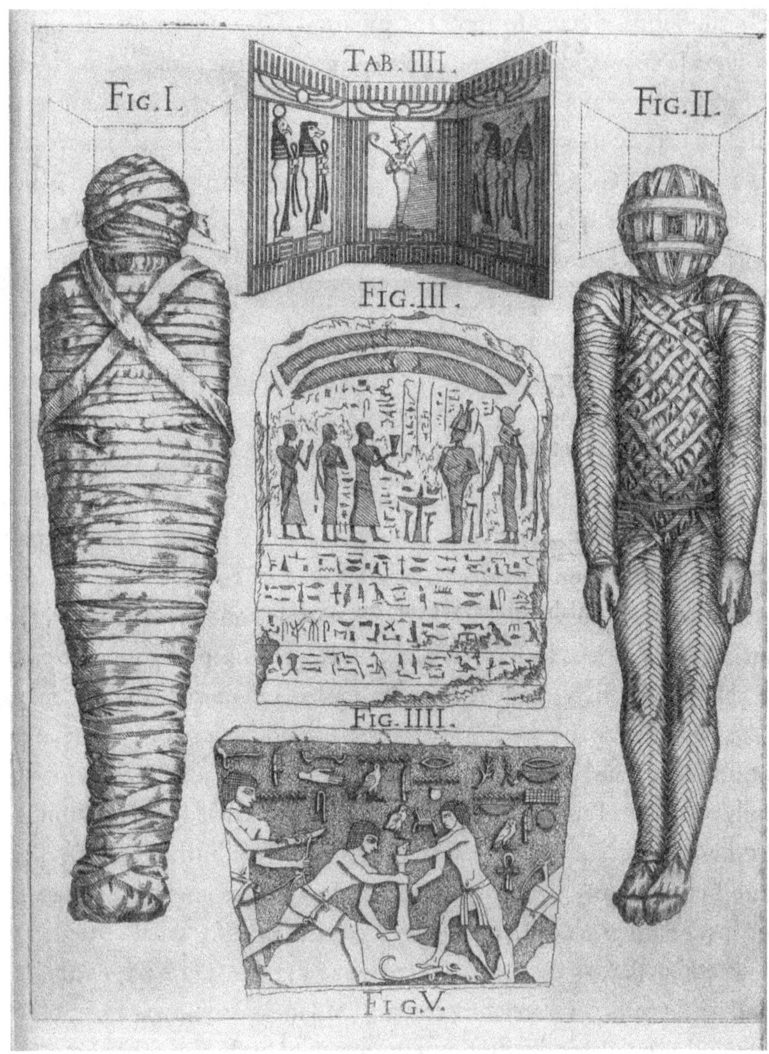

Fig. 4: Plate depicting Egyptian antiquities, including two mummified bodies. Giovanni Nardi, *Titi Lucretii cari de rervm natvra* (1647), plate 4. Bibliothèque nationale de France.

In his discussion of Egyptian burial practices, Nardi (1647, 627–41) takes as his point of departure Herodotus's description of the ancient Egyptian belief in metempsychosis. Without discussing the exact role of the body in this connection beyond a general Egyptian yearning for eternity and permanence, Nardi (1647, 628) notes that they sought to "keep putrefaction away from the corpse" (*putrilaginem . . . à cadauere arcebant*). He goes on to extract from various classical authors an overall distinction between sacred, royal, and private funerals, with the former concerning sacred animals such as the Apis bull, while the separation of royal and private funerals follows the way authors such as Diodorus treat the burial practices of these two groups separately (albeit with significant overlap).

In the last part of his discussion, Nardi (1647, 629–32) combines passages from Herodotus, Diodorus, Plutarch, and Porphyry to reconstruct in chronological order the rites leading up to the burial. He begins with the description of mourning from Diodorus, where family members daub themselves with mud and wander through the city in a disheveled state, then moves on to Herodotus's and Diodorus's details on the three types of mummification, beginning with the first and most expensive manner. To complement Herodotus and Diodorus, he introduces the description and citation of recited words from Porphyry (although it is Nicolas Caussin rather than Porphyry himself he credits for this information), where the intestines are removed as a kind of scapegoat for any dietary transgressions. By introducing this idea here, it thus becomes a seamless part of the most luxurious manner of mummification, following which he returns to information from Herodotus and Diodorus to describe the two less expensive modes. After discussing types of mummification, Nardi (1647, 631–32) ends by relating the information from Diodorus on the judgment of the deceased, sticking closely to the text and presenting this as a legal proceeding to determine whether the deceased may be buried.

Beyond the occasional remark or brief discussion of his own, Nardi largely keeps to presenting verbatim Latin translations of the authors he cites. Apart from collecting the relevant material, then, his main contribution lies in harmonizing several sources, as is especially apparent in the sequential ordering of the information gleaned from various authors into a coherent, chronological reconstruction of the ancient Egyptian funerary ritual (cf. his description of his method; Nardi 1647, 628). In terms of the underlying beliefs, he does not go much beyond Herodotus's description of the doctrine of metempsychosis, although he does indicate that this belief could logically lead to a quest for permanence and preservation, without clearly articulating how belief and practice relate to each other. Given his use of the Porphyry passage more rarely cited in this connection, he presumably did not see any contradiction, and possibly simply combined the idea of bodily permanence with the idea that certain body parts needed to be discarded to achieve purity.

Nardi's main idea of Egyptian burial practices, then, was that mummification sought to preserve the body, with the corollary that this was done to achieve immortality. As I noted above, this idea was mostly a foundational assumption rather than information that could be directly extracted from the classical sources, and as seen in the discussion of earlier authors, this idea likely developed partly from observation of mummified bodies, partly from the corollary notion of the preserving powers of the materials the Egyptians used (and hence of the embalmed bodies themselves), and partly from Christian expectations that burial practices should by definition aim for salvation and eternal life.

Conclusion

As is shown in the examples above, much of the engagement with ancient Egyptian mortuary religion through the middle of the seventeenth century was spurred by a desire to explain the remarkable things visitors to Egypt encountered (and occasionally brought back with them), including mummified bodies, obelisks, and pyramids. A consensus thus began to form, based on relatively straightforward readings of the newly available classical authors. Diodorus described the funerary rituals, including the notion of a ritual postmortem judgment by the survivors, even of the kings themselves, to ascertain their worthiness for burial. Herodotus related not just the details of the three qualities of mummification available, but also presented what might with a bit of creative elaboration be understood as a belief underlying and motivating such intricate burial practices: the notion of the transmigration of the soul. But the fact remained that Herodotus discussed these topics completely separately, making no explicit connection.

Servius's brief commentary, in which he presents the Egyptians as believing the soul would endure as long as the body survived, provided the missing link. This idea offered to Servius (and his much later readers) an excellent motivation for mummification, whose aim had much earlier come to be understood as preservation of the body under influence of the interest in mumia, and by extension tombs could be understood as having a similar purpose. This framework left considerable room for interpreting the precise nature and role of the soul. With the classical authors silent on the issue and no particularly pressing need to resolve it, the authors of this period tended either to leave the question open or to treat it briefly with a single deductive sentence or two, as seen, for example, in Greaves's notion that the soul served more as an attendant or guardian than as an animating force.

THREE

The Egyptian Afterlife in Universal History: 1650–1700

The split between heavily philological interpretations in the vein of Nardi on the one hand and more intuitive ideas about the possible reasons for "preserving" bodies on the other continued in the second half of the seventeenth century. The latter approach was particularly suitable in discussions that were not focused directly on the topic of Egyptian mortuary religion but touched on it for other purposes. Thus, for example, English polymath Thomas Browne (1605–82, cf. Todd and Murphy 2008) wrote his *Hydriotaphia: Urne-Buriall* (Browne 1658) in reaction to a recent find of Anglo-Saxon crematory urns in Norfolk. The text is a lengthy meditation on death and particularly on the vanity of hopes for permanence, with the Egyptians thus offering a particularly apt example of human folly in this regard (Schwyzer 2017). Thus Browne (1658, 78) notes that "[a] great part of Antiquity contented their hopes of subsistency with a transmigration of their souls," and a little later he observes more specifically on the contrast between the Egyptians' hopes of permanence and the treatment of ancient mummified bodies in his contemporary society (cf. Schwyzer 2005):

> Ægyptian ingenuity was more unsatisfied, contriving their bodies in sweet consistences, to attend the return of their souls. But all was vanity, feeding the winde, and folly. The Ægyptian Mummies, which *Cambyses* or time hath spared, avarice now consumeth. Mummie is become Merchandise, *Mizraim* cures wounds, and *Pharaoh* is sold for balsoms. (Browne 1658, 78–79; emphasis in the original)

Unlike Nardi's philological approach, to Browne the practice of mummification becomes the epitome of human vanity through a relatively simple dichotomy between the transitory nature of all earthly life and the human yearning for permanence. Browne's brief references can thus be situated in the intuitive tradition of understanding mummification as aiming to preserve the body, with a particular irony found not only in the general ravages of time, but particularly in the way these corpses had themselves become objects of consumption.

In a similar vein, a few years later in 1662, Silesian writer Andreas Gryphius (1616–64), better known as a poet and playwright of the German baroque, published a book devoted to the study of three embalmed bodies in a collection in Wrocław based in particular on the dissection of one of them that Gryphius took part in during the winter of 1658 (Reetz 2019). In the tradition of Pierre Belon, the discussion focuses largely on the technical aspects such as modes of mummification and the date of the mummified bodies. Gryphius does, however, begin the book by a dedication asserting the fundamental elements of Egyptian religion that made them mummify their dead (Reetz 2019, 80–81). Here he notes that souls lasted on (*perennare*), and that the objective of the funerary ritual was to enable bodies to house the soul when it returned to them. Consequently he labels the embalmed bodies as "these images triumphing over death" (*triumphales hasce de nece imagines*). It is not clear that he has in mind any specific beliefs such as metempsychosis, and he appears to fall in the tradition of the more intuitive notion of the soul returning to the body, with these concepts understood largely as used in Christian vernacular, as was the case with Browne. Once again this is very similar to the approach taken by Pierre Belon over a century earlier, and it shows a split between the medical approach to mummies in which the underlying beliefs are dealt with in an intuitive and cursory fashion as opposed to the more detailed scholarly engagements with classical texts. Because of the brevity and vagueness of the descriptions of Egyptian beliefs in the medical tradition, however, they remain largely compatible with many of the discussions based on classical texts. The general nature of Gryphius's thoughts on the purposes of mummification correspond well with the way he occasionally refers to mummified bodies in his wider poetic work of the 1650s, either in their medical use or as a figure of thought on death and afterlife (Reetz 2019, 195–200). In fact, Gryphius is explicit that his main interest in ancient Egyptian embalming and wrapping techniques lies in the relevance of this topic to a planned study of the crucifixion and burial of Jesus (Reetz 2019, 84–85).

A similarly brief and straightforward explanation is offered by French traveler Jean Thévenot (1633–67; Carré 1932, 1:24–29; Valence 2008, 7–18), who published detailed accounts of his two voyages to the East (Thévenot 1664, 1674, modern edition Valence 2008) reflecting in particular his interest in natural history and in geography. As part of his description of Egypt, he offers detailed chapters on pyramids and mummified bodies based on his visits to the cemeteries at Giza and Saqqara. After his description of the bodies he examined at Saqqara, he provides a brief explanation of the rationale for the Egyptians' expending so many resources on their tombs. Building implicitly on Diodorus's note on the difference between tombs and houses in ancient Egypt, Thévenot (1664, 262) notes, "one of their reasons was that their houses were only for dwelling in for the brief time that they lived, and their tombs were the palaces where their souls were going to dwell for several centuries." As he does not elaborate, it is not entirely clear what model for the soul's continued existence (if any) Thévenot has in mind here. Given that he is not speaking of "eternity," but only of "several centuries" (*plusieurs siecles*), he may in principle rely either on Herodotus's notion of metempsychosis over three thousand years or, perhaps more likely, on Servius's idea that the soul would remain with the body until the body was destroyed. Either way, for Thévenot as for most of his contemporaries, the question of Egyptian mortuary religion is largely a means to the end of explaining the practices resulting in mummification and monumental tombs.

Egypt in Universal History

The later seventeenth century saw a gradual departure from this relatively straightforward aim of explaining extant Egyptian monuments and mummified bodies, as scholars increasingly sought to deploy knowledge and interpretations of Egypt to grant its culture a place in universal history (Meyer-Zwiffelhoffer 1995; Assmann 1997a). Broadly speaking, the results of such projects depended on the contrasts and partial continuities individual scholars saw between ancient Egypt and their own contemporary society, usually mediated by the cultures of the Hebrews or classical antiquity or both (cf. Hodgen 1964).

An example that has been explored in detail by Jan Assmann (1997b, 55–79; 2014, 39–43) is that of English theologian and Hebraist John Spencer (1630–93). Spencer argued in favor of a wide-ranging continuity between the laws of the Egyptians and the ritual laws of the Torah, the gist of the argument being that while the moral laws of the Decalogue held eternal (and hence contemporary Christian) relevance, the political and ritual laws laid out by the Torah not only were temporary, but were in fact pagan in origin (Spencer 1685). This line of argument, where criticized religious beliefs or practices were traced back to an ancient Egyptian origin, would be deployed frequently during the following centuries. We can label its logic as a kind of reductio ad Aegyptum: by showing the ultimate origin of an idea or practice in ancient Egypt, its later, and especially contemporary, versions could be discredited. In particular, Assmann (1997b, 75–76) has called attention to the language of illness and corruption Spencer used in characterizing ancient Egyptian religion. Although he was not centrally interested in Egyptian mortuary religion, Spencer's work nonetheless provides a telling example of the contemporary stakes in claiming continuities or discontinuities between Christianity and the beliefs of ancient Egypt.

A much more direct engagement with Egyptian mortuary religion is found in the works of Jesuit polymath Athanasius Kircher (1602–80). The very different approach Kircher took as compared with that of his immediate predecessors and contemporaries can be explained by the much larger scope of his intellectual project. While he certainly spent copious amounts of time and energy on ancient Egypt and its hieroglyphs, ultimately his aims were much wider: in Stolzenberg's words a "project of intellectual history and reconstruction, which sought the philosophical and religious filiations of all the non-Christian peoples of the world" (Stolzenberg 2001a, 124). Kircher saw in the Egyptian tradition a mixture of original wisdom and corrupting influences, a conglomeration he attributed to the biblical Ham, who corrupted the pure teachings of Adam (passed on through Seth, Enoch, and Noah) with influences from the magic and superstition introduced by Cain (Marquet 1987; Stolzenberg 2001b). The Egyptian hieroglyphs were the secret means of transmitting the valuable parts of this tradition, which in this way were passed on to Greek sages such as Pythagoras and Orpheus, and ultimately to Plato. In making this distinction, Kircher drew on the central theological idea of an "ancient wisdom" (*prisca sapientia*), first used by church fathers such as Eusebius to rehabilitate parts of pagan philosophy that appeared to presage Christian concepts. During the Renaissance this idea had gained prominence with the discovery of the philosophy of the Middle Platonists and the Hermetic writings, ideas that could thus to some degree be incorporated into contemporary philosophy and theology (Curran 2007, 89–99).

This heterogeneous nature of Egyptian thought allowed Kircher significant leeway in sifting through the ideas he saw expressed not only in sources on Egypt, but also in those he regarded as derived from the same tradition, such as Platonism and Jewish Kabbalah. As Stolzenberg (2001b, 131) notes, he "adhered simultaneously to the pro-magic, Neoplatonist genealogy of knowledge stemming from Hermes Trismegistos and the anti-magic, biblically-based genealogy stemming from Ham." It is within this master narrative of two dueling traditions of pagan wisdom and pagan superstition that Kircher could carve out a central place for Egypt in a universal history that encompassed not just European history, but also relatively newly acquired knowledge of New World, Asian, and other African cultures. As aptly pointed out by Stolzenberg (2001b, 134–35), the overall narrative of competing traditions, one true and one false, followed the structure of Protestant ecclesiastic histories where, however, it is the Reformation that is presented as a return to the true, original teachings. In Kircher's Catholic version in service of Jesuit proselytizing aims, the notion that pagan religions contained kernels of the original truth that missionaries could pick up on could be turned to one's advantage in teaching and conversion (e.g., Arp 2010, 113–14; Pomplun 2010, 74–90).

To Kircher, then, the model of metempsychosis described by Hermes Trismegistus and Herodotus was at the core of ancient Egyptian mortuary religion, and he additionally saw it as forming the origin of similar ideas in a number of other traditions, which he could thus use to flesh out the underlying ideas in more detail. He offered three detailed, broadly similar discussions of the topic, one in the context of ancient Egyptian metaphysics and soul conceptions in his *Oedipus aegyptiacus* (Kircher 1652–54, 2:529–36), and two respectively in the same work (3:387–410) and the later and much briefer work *Sphinx mystagoga* (Kircher 1676, 1–19) in connection with his discussion and interpretation of Egyptian funerary practices, especially mummification (cf. also Reetz 2019, 51–59). The discussion here concentrates primarily on the last-mentioned, later and more focused discussion in *Sphinx mystagoga*.

From the outset, Kircher expands the idea described by Herodotus to include a sort of moral determination of the postmortem fate of the soul along the lines found in the Hermetic writings (which he regarded as the more original source), Plato, and others. Thus he describes the belief concisely in the following terms:

> Just as the so-called deities [*Numina*], thanks to the excellent virtues and benefits they conferred upon Egypt during life returned through the bodies of sacred animals by metempsychosis and earned divine honours when they were received into heaven, as they wickedly believed [*ut impiè credebant*], thus also after death everyone who had emulated the virtues of heroes during life went through a similar passage and were claimed to achieve similar honours. (Kircher 1676, 2)

In other words, Herodotus's description is expanded here to include the Platonic aspect of souls' achieving a fate after death befitting the nature of their existence on earth, rather than automatically moving through every species of animal over the course of three thousand years. In accordance with his overall scheme of universal history, Kircher goes on to trace similar ideas in other traditions, citing among others the Hebrew scholar Elias Levita (1469–1549), who argued that the consonants of the name of the biblical Adam (אדם, *ʾdm*) revealed his soul's triple incarnation as first Adam (אדם, *ʾdm*), then King David (דוד, *dwd*), and finally the Messiah (משיח, *msyḥ*), with the first consonant of each incarnation (*ʾ-d-m*) contained in the original name (Kircher 1676, 3). An example closer to ancient Egypt among the wide-ranging sources

Kircher drew on in this connection is a story related in Philostratus's third-century CE *Life of Apollonius* (Kircher 1676, 4). Toward the end of the fifth book of that work is a story of how the Pythagorean teacher Apollonius recognized a tame lion in Egypt as the reincarnation of King Amasis and recommended that it be honored in the temple of Leontopolis (Lion City) to reflect its royal origin and the miraculous transmigration of his soul (Conybeare 1912, 1:568–71).

According to the cross-cultural distribution of such ideas, Kircher concludes that the "stupid dogma of metempsychosis" (*stolidum Metempsycoseos dogma*) spread from Egypt throughout the East (Kircher 1676, 4). In the following chapter, Kircher turns to the more tangible matter of mummification, posing the question of "Why the Egyptians strove so much for incorruption" (Kircher 1676, 5–9). As indicated by this wording, the framework for understanding ancient practices of mummification is the by then well established idea that bodies were mummified to preserve them and avoid decay. He ends the chapter with a lengthy quotation of Giovanni Nardi's commentary on Lucretius's *De rerum natura* (Kircher 1676, 7–9; Nardi 1647, 629–32), which was also the original place of publication of the copper plates of mummies and tombs that Kircher reused in his *Oedipus aegyptiacus* and *Sphinx mystagoga* (Śliwa 2007, 156–60; cf. Sutherland, Findlen, and Lelková 2018, 315–17 for the relationship between the two scholars). As noted above, Nardi's understanding of Egyptian funerary practices, and of mummification in particular, largely consists of consolidating several classical sources into a chronological scheme taking account of the three modes of mummification discussed by Herodotus and Diodorus. Kircher does not comment further on the quotation and thus seemingly accepts Nardi's reconstruction. This gives us a clear indication of Kircher's main interest in the underlying esoteric beliefs in metempsychosis, of which he presents an innovative and wide-ranging discussion, while the more practical aspects of the funeral are quoted directly and at length from Nardi without elaboration. This is an instance of what Reetz (2019) calls a redefinition of the object of "mummy studies." Unlike predecessors in the genre like Pierre Belon and Andreas Gryphius, whose central interest in mummified bodies was medical and technical, Kircher approaches the embalmed body as "*aegyptiacum,*" aiming primarily to elucidate the conceptual and cultural background of the practice as it fits into his wider scheme of universal history.

As seen from the above, Kircher's construction of metempsychosis in ancient Egypt (whence it spread to many other pagan religions) is a deliberate antithesis to Christianity, emblematic of the superstitious layer of Egyptian thought as opposed to the secret, authentic teaching of monotheism. This makes it easy to take Herodotus at face value while supplementing his account with numerous other authors discussing similar ideas, whether or not they deal overtly with ancient Egyptian thought, thanks to Kircher's model of diffusion of Egyptian ideas to other cultures. In particular, Kircher can conclude that the teaching of the immortality of the soul in itself is part of the antediluvian *prisca theologia* (ancient theology) presaging Christian beliefs, while its concretely pagan implementation in the dogma of metempsychosis represents a corruption. In contrast to contemporary authors to be discussed below who have a more positive view of this aspect of Egyptian religion, Kircher has no need to introduce the idea of a moral judgment beyond that described by Plato or the Hermetic writings, since the general system is rejected and thus does not need the rehabilitation of an approximation to Christianity implied by other scholars.

Morality and the Afterlife

If Kircher thus largely follows Herodotus's description of ancient Egyptian metempsychosis, although augmenting it from additional sources, to other scholars of the period the efforts to create a particular position for Egypt in universal history could instead cast doubt on the veracity of the Greek historian's accounts. Thus, in his *True Intellectual System of the Universe* (1678), English philosopher Ralph Cudworth (1617–88) argues in favor of a primitive monotheism underlying the pagan religions of antiquity (cf. Assmann 1997b, 80–90; Assmann 2014, 43–53). Sharing many ideas with the Cambridge Platonists, Cudworth sets out to refute the arguments of "atheism," which include the charge that pagan societies like that of the Egyptians were fundamentally atheist. In this connection he notes that the Herodotus passage on metempsychosis shows that the Egyptians had a "higher kind of Philosophy also, concerning

Incorporeal Substances" (Cudworth 1678, 313; emphasis in the original) apart from their famed physiological and mathematical knowledge. However, he raises doubts that Herodotus had accurately understood the beliefs of the Egyptians in this regard. Notably, he refers to the Pythagoreans implicitly faulted by Herodotus for taking over the Egyptian doctrine (see chapter 1 above), presenting a slightly different model:

> That the Descent of Humane Souls into these Earthy Bodies, was first in way of Punishment, and that their sinking lower afterwards into the Bodies of Brutes, was only to some, a further Punishment for their further Degeneracy; but the Vertuous and Pious Souls should after this Life enjoy a state of Happiness, in *Celestial* or *Spiritual Bodies*. (Cudworth 1678, 313; emphasis in the original)

He goes on to note that this notion of reward and punishment is also present in Porphyry and the Hermetic writings. Cudworth even cites a similar notion among Indian Brahmins, "whether they received it from the Egyptians (as they did some other things) or no" (Cudworth 1678, 314). Finally he refers to a small part of the passage from Diodorus discussed in chapter 1 above, which he translates as the deceased's "being to live ever in the other World with the pious" (314). What is at stake for Cudworth in this discussion is that it demonstrates that the Egyptians believed in the "soul's incorporeity," and that this implies a belief in an incorporeal god—which in turn forms part of his larger argument supporting ancient Egyptian monotheism (Cudworth 1678, 314).

It is worth emphasizing that this conclusion regarding an incorporeal soul might equally well have been arrived at by taking Herodotus at face value. However, the added nuance of an ethical judgment of the souls followed by rewards or punishments clearly serves to further align the Egyptian beliefs with contemporary Christianity, corresponding with the overall argument in favor of Egyptian monotheism. Unlike scholars like Athanasius Kircher, the Cambridge Platonists did not see an inherent contradiction between Christianity and a limited form of metempsychosis, or at least a preexistence of souls (e.g., Walker 1964, 146–55). In fact, a notion that "those born in less than ideal circumstances beyond the boundaries of Christendom had been condemned to their plight by virtue of infractions committed in a previous existence" (Harrison 1993, 534) could be made the pivot of an argument against Calvinist notions of predestination (Harrison 1993, 531–35). Cudworth thus argues a moral relevance that not only helps make sense of Egyptian beliefs from a Christian point of view, but more specifically allows Egyptian beliefs to speak to universal human concerns in a way that would be more difficult without this moral dimension.

Arriving at a somewhat similar result from a rather different set of premises and purposes, a few years later French bishop and tutor to the dauphin, Jacques-Bénigne Bossuet (1627–1704), published his *Discourse on Universal History* (1681). The book was explicitly dedicated to the edification of the crown prince, and it emphasizes the moral lessons a future French absolute monarch might usefully draw from the episodes of religious world history it presents (Bossuet 1681). As such, the general tone in the part of the book that describes the character of ancient Egyptian society is highly laudatory, emphasizing the virtues and moral achievements that might inspire a Catholic ruler. Drawing on Diodorus, Bossuet extols the Egyptian laws as "simple, full of equity, and proper to unite citizens to one another" (*simples, pleines d'équité, & propre à unir entre eux les Citoyens*; Bossuet 1681, 443). Within the context of Egyptian laws, Bossuet emphasizes one as highly extraordinary: the risk that one might lose even one's good name after death, since everyone was subjected to a public judgment (Bossuet 1681, 446). For the details of this idea, Bossuet presents a close paraphrase of the passage from Diodorus on the ritual judgment before the funeral, further elaborating the point already found in Diodorus of the profound effect of this practice in instilling a moral sense in members of society. Bossuet links the practice of mummification to a similar transmission of morals and reverence for the laws when descendants were able to see their ancestors who had been honored in this way by society according to the rule of law (Bossuet 1681, 447).

Of particular relevance in the context of an instruction to the dauphin is the idea, also derived from Diodorus, that even kings were subject to such a public judgment after their death, and Bossuet notes that this practice was adopted from the Egyptians by the "People of God" (*Peuple de Dieu*)—the Israelites—as recorded in the scriptures: "It made the kings understand that if their majesty put them above human judgments during their life, they would return in the end when death had made them equal to other men" (Bossuet 1681, 450).

The implication of evoking the kings of Israel and the contrast between judgment during life and after death is clear, although it remains implicit: Through the practice described by Diodorus, the Egyptians in a sense presaged the Christian idea of postmortem judgment. While the king of France was naturally not subject to a public judgment after his death as Egyptian kings were, he was subject to a *divine* postmortem judgment and could no more rely on his earthly power to avoid this than the Egyptians could avoid their judgment. The parallel with contemporary Christianity is thus clear, even if it remains significantly more subtle than in Cudworth's notion of primitive monotheism. Indeed, Bossuet's use of Diodorus allows him to stay entirely true to the letter and intent of the ancient author while drawing clear contemporary implications that put the notion of postmortem judgment into an entirely different context.

Paralleling Hebrew and Egyptian practices had also been an integral part of the method of English historian and antiquarian John Marsham's (1602–85) *Chronicus Canon Aegyptiacus, Ebraicus, Graecus* (Marsham 1672; cf. Mosley 2021, 121–34), published just a few years earlier, and in fact Marsham's wider approach likely formed a partial inspiration for Bossuet's project (Mosley 2021, 127). The brief episode relevant to Egyptian mortuary religion to be discussed here is only a small part of the overall argument of the book, where Egypt is presented as the origin of a great many features of civilization later taken over by the Hebrews and Greeks. This positioning essentially reversed the traditional understanding of the Hebrews as the most ancient people and the origin of all other learning and languages, a notion that was increasingly questioned in the late seventeenth century by scholars such as the aforementioned John Spencer (1630–93), sparking considerable debate (Gascoigne 1991; Levitin 2013).

To establish the fundamental morals of the ancient Egyptians, Marsham took as his point of departure the passage from Porphyry's *On Abstinence* dealing with Egyptian funerary rites, quoting it in Latin translation. He labeled the recitation Porphyry cited the "Egyptians' funerary apology" (*funebris Ægyptiorum Apologia*; Marsham 1672, 151) and noted that the five acts referred to in the recitation (respecting the gods, honoring one's parents, not killing, not stealing, and not committing other dishonorable acts), correspond well to the commandments of the Decalogue (Marsham 1672, 150–51; cf. Assmann 2005a, 83–85; Levitin 2015, 162–63). In keeping with the overall stance of the book, this similarity is not merely superficial or universal but in fact shows that in Marsham's reconstruction Moses absorbed his wisdom from the ancient Egyptians (Mosley 2021, 126–27). Apart from Marsham's wider project, in terms of interpretations of Egyptian mortuary religion the main contribution is cementing the centrality of Porphyry's narrative as a basis for the ethical importance of Egyptian funerary practices, and further showing that Egyptian ritual rules can be paralleled to the Decalogue of the Hebrew Bible, with the implication of a divine postmortem judgment (and not just a social one as in Diodorus) on ethical grounds.

Despite their obvious differences, there are some commonalities between the examples discussed here of late seventeenth-century attempts to give Egypt, and more specifically Egyptian mortuary religion, a more or less central place in universal history. The project of constructing arguments around universal history being essentially a comparative endeavor, it is not surprising that in every case ancient Egypt is argued to exhibit certain commonalities with other cultures, and since usually the other cultures in question were better attested or understood, the comparison often involved a projection onto ancient Egypt of interpretations originating elsewhere.

This is most obviously the case with Kircher's reconstruction of a general pagan belief in metempsychosis and Marsham's similarly diffusionist idea of the Egyptian origin of parts of the Decalogue. Bossuet's model is more subtle, but as seen above the implicit understanding of Diodorus's postmortem judgment as a functional parallel to the Last Judgment in Christianity ends up adding new significance to the Egyptian practice in this case as well. As has frequently been remarked, Kircher's project was in many ways too idiosyncratic and his approach too outdated to be taken up in following generations (and to some extent even in his own). On the other hand, for all their differences, Bossuet and Marsham offered less esoteric ways of making sense of

Egyptian mortuary religion by emphasizing its moral dimension and its parallels to well-known interpretive frameworks. The lasting result was a more specific approximation between Egyptian religion and Christianity, establishing a crucial moral dimension that was largely missing in the classical authors.

Technical Inspiration

Contrasting with these theologically and politically motivated reconstructions, other scholars' interests in Egyptian mortuary religion were much more practical. As the culmination of the previous centuries' interest in ancient Egyptian methods of embalming, English physician Thomas Greenhill sought to put the insights gained to practical use in the embalming practices of his own society. As shown by the title of his 1705 book *Nekrokēdeia, or The Art of Embalming* (Greenhill 1705), his examination of "the Right of Burial, the funeral Ceremonies, and the several Ways of preserving dead Bodies in most Nations of the World" led him to propose "a better Method of Embalming than hath hitherto been discover'd" (Greenhill 1705, title page). Not surprisingly, Egypt takes on a prominent role in his cross-cultural study of embalming methods, and this culture forms an important point of reference in the first of the three books of the work surveying different funerary ceremonies and attitudes toward them. Regarding the Egyptians' motivations for embalming the body, Greenhill draws implicitly on the tradition originating in Servius when he states, departing from a quotation from Aristotle

> *That the Soul neither remembers nor loves the Body when Putrify'd;* which is agreeable to the Opinion of the *Egyptians*, who pleasantly conceited, that the Soul only left the Body when it was Corrupt and Putrify'd, as abhorring so loathsome an Habitation; whereas on the contrary, it never forsook it when it was preserv'd uncorrupt and entire. (Greenhill 1705, 106; emphasis in the original)

In line with Greenhill's wider aims of promoting the benefits of embalming among his contemporaries, his attitude toward the Egyptian practices described is wholly positive. Thus he goes on to point out explicitly, "Methinks so good an Example from Heathens might excite us to take more Care of our inanimate Part. . . . Now as we are all desirous of Immortality, so ought we likewise to be of Eternity" (Greenhill 1705, 106–7). To make this argument, it is clear that Greenhill needs to assume a strong analogy between ancient Egyptian and contemporary Christian beliefs in order to promote a similarity in practices. This is made easier by the conventional vocabulary used where, as seen above, Egyptian motivations are generally spoken of in terms of bodies and souls, rendering them immediately comparable.

If it might thus have been expedient to his argument to leave out the more exotic details and focus on such general similarities, nonetheless Greenhill includes a lengthy discussion of the landscape, climate, and culture of Egypt, drawing on a variety of sources not just classical, but especially also the travel description by Thévenot discussed above. Here Greenhill particularly needs to separate the "Magic" infusing embalming practices in the form of "painted Characters and Hieroglyphics" and "little Idols or Averruncal Gods" from the chemical and surgical techniques that his contemporaries would recognize as efficient and appropriate for preserving the body (Greenhill 1705, 176–77). More specifically, for the motivation behind practices of mummification, Greenhill returns to Servius—whose interpretation he knows through Greaves's *Pyramidographia* (Greenhill 1705, 237–40)—and adduces a number of other sources from Plato to Saint Augustine to support the idea of the survival of the soul in Egyptian thought.

Greenhill's discussion of ancient Egyptian embalming techniques more specifically takes as its point of departure the descriptions by Herodotus and Diodorus, quoted in full (Greenhill 1705, 240–46), after which he proceeds to compare these with the results of early modern "mummy studies" such as that of Gryphius and knowledge from other sources about the techniques and materials employed. Although he takes his main framework from Servius (by way of Greaves), in a few places he curiously calls this idea "metempsychosis" (Greenhill 1705, 238, 331), although he does not seem to actually entertain the notion that the souls transmigrated to new bodies. Rather, they would stay in the tomb as long as the body remained intact, even to the point of needing perpetually burning lamps, both to "animate the Defunct with perpetual Fire" (Greenhill 1705, 331), and also for more practical reasons:

> To the end that their Souls might not lye miserably imprison'd in darkness, and thereby any hurt befal them; but on the contrary, enjoy eternal light and be free from all evil, or that when the Soul should wander, it might not mistake its Residence, but be by the light of the *Lamp* guided and conduced to return to its former Habitation. (Greenhill 1705, 332; emphasis in the original)

For the rituals taking place on the day of the funeral, Greenhill makes oblique reference to the "Funeral-Oration" described by Porphyry, as well as to the discussion of the judgment after death, derived not directly through Diodorus, but rather by way of Bossuet's paraphrase (Greenhill 1705, 302–4). He also significantly embellishes Diodorus's remarks about the difference between Egyptian houses and tombs to make them align better with contemporary Christian ideas:

> They despis'd the present Life, and took little care in building their Habitations, looking upon them only as so many Inns or Baiting-Places, where they were to Inhabit but for a Season, whereas the Glory of a future Life, that was to be procur'd by Virtue, they greatly esteem'd. (Greenhill 1705, 305)

Greenhill's practical interest in the embalming techniques of the ancient Egyptians thus leads him to focus on authors and models that can establish ideas of direct relevance to contemporary Christianity, most notably that the soul's immortal life depended on the preservation of the body. Another notable consequence is that he needs to separate out the purely technical procedures from which an eighteenth-century surgeon might in principle draw inspiration from the "magic" and superstitious practices that ancient Egyptian embalming also evidently involved. While he seems to have picked up from other authors the designation of the Egyptian conceptions of the soul as "metempsychosis," Greenhill does not actually understand the soul as moving into other bodies—in line with Christianity, it is solely the survival of the soul after death that is at stake. Despite the rather special aims to which Greenhill puts ancient Egyptian embalming practices, he thus ends up further cementing two highly conventional ideas: that Egyptian mortuary religion aimed centrally at securing the immortality of the soul, and that the means to do so was by preserving the body from decay and corruption.

Conclusion

The shifting interest in universal history in the second half of the seventeenth century (cf. Meyer-Zwiffelhoffer 1995) represents a turning point in the understanding of ancient Egyptian mortuary religion. While earlier approaches were mainly interested in explaining the extant remains of ancient Egyptian culture, the aim of carving out a place for ancient Egypt in universal history encouraged interpretations in cross-cultural terms, which in many cases meant departing from the letter of the classical sources that remained the primary evidence. The main method for this was identifying ideas similar to those of the Egyptians in better attested cultures, which could thus in turn be used to fill gaps in the evidence produced by classical writers—or even override apparent incongruities in their work.

The source of such "corrections" might be a deliberately wide cross-cultural range of ideas and practices, as in the case of Athanasius Kircher. More commonly, however, the models stemmed from Judaism or Christianity, parallels which could be used to bolster a wide range of political, historical, or theological arguments, often implying the sidelining of more objectionable practices, resulting in such very different pictures of the ancient Egyptians as Bossuet's pious moralists and Greenhill's superstitious but capable technicians. The ultimate result of the great majority of such universalist approaches remained the same: the gradual approximation of ancient Egyptian mortuary religion with Christianity, especially in the form of projecting an idea of postmortem judgment on ethical grounds and corresponding rewards or punishments in the beyond. These ideas could in turn be connected to the classical authors with some reinterpretation, for example, by introducing a notion of rewards and punishment into Herodotus's description of metempsychosis or by understanding Diodorus's ritual judgment to be similar, parallel, or even identical to a divine afterlife trial along the lines of the Christian Last Judgment.

FOUR

Death and Initiation: 1700–1750

One of the most striking developments in eighteenth-century engagements with ancient Egypt in general is the increased availability of cultural products from ancient Egypt (prominent among them mummified bodies) paired with growing efforts toward accurate documentation inspired by Enlightenment ideals. While the effort to document ancient Egyptian artifacts and monuments was by no means new (cf. Whitehouse 1992 and the efforts toward "virtual witnessing" discussed in the previous chapter), in the eighteenth century such efforts developed into in what Ebeling terms a "new, more documentary and real object-oriented aesthetic" (Ebeling 2022, 145n2). At the same time, ancient Egypt became deployed in a wider range of ideological and aesthetic projects, from Egypt-themed designs at the court of Louis XVI at Versailles to the reception of Egyptian forms and rituals in Freemasonry (e.g., McGeough 2013).

While partly influenced by such developments, eighteenth-century interpretations of ancient Egyptian mortuary religion also showed significant continuity with the previous centuries (cf. Carré 1932, 1:39) as the basic literary sources remained the same, even as visual and textual representations of monuments and physical specimens of Egyptian objects became more available. With the increasing access to evidence came the ability to confront classical authors with more or less independent sources of knowledge about the topics they discussed. As Suzanne Marchand has shown, this led in particular to a growing skepticism against authors like Herodotus during the long eighteenth century

(Marchand 2021). Although far from universally accepted, such skepticism could be deployed strategically to further particular arguments and agendas. At the same time, Enlightenment thinkers occasionally considered the exotic notion of metempsychosis more seriously as a potential solution to theological problems (McManners 1981, 156–57).

Early in the eighteenth century, the French Benedictine scholar Bernard de Montfaucon published a monumental cross-cultural study of ancient civilizations under the title *Antiquity Explained* (*L'antiquité expliquée*) in a bilingual French/Latin format (Montfaucon 1722–24 [1719–24]; cf., e.g., Poulouin 1995; Aufrère 2021). The fifth volume of the work is devoted to funerary practices first of Greece and Rome and then of "barbarian nations," of which Egypt is the first to be discussed (Montfaucon 1722–24 [1719–24], 5:173–84). The sequence of chapters devoted to this topic begins with descriptions of rites of mourning and embalming based on Herodotus, supplemented by the similar description of mummification techniques by Diodorus (Montfaucon 1722–24 [1719–24], 5:173–76). The next chapter continues with a lengthy, uncommented quotation from Diodorus, now focusing on the judgment ceremony, followed by a brief description of mummified bodies illustrated by plates taken from various earlier publications by other scholars. The chapter ends with another lengthy quotation from Diodorus, this time dealing with the funerals of kings. This topic leads naturally to the topic of the pyramids, which are described first by paraphrasing Diodorus and then with reference to the relatively recently published account by Dutch traveler Cornelis De Bruijn (cf. Aufrère 2021, 289–92). The last chapter devoted to Egyptian funerary practices discusses the sphinx as well as human and animal mummies at Saqqara, and at the other pyramids found there, all based on De Bruijn and other authors including Della Valle and Thévenot (Montfaucon 1722–24 [1719–24], 5:182–84; cf. Aufrère 2021, 289–96 for dependence on other authors). Montfaucon makes no mention in this discussion of any underlying beliefs or other motivating factors beyond the verbatim quotations from Herodotus and especially Diodorus.

By contrast, the second volume of the work is devoted to religion, once again treating Egypt as the first of the ancient cultures after Greece and Rome. However, the discussion in these chapters focuses exclusively on Egyptian idolatry, the various gods and principles as well as their depictions in art, followed by discussions of priests, temples, and festivals (Montfaucon 1722–24 [1719–24],2:269–362). Mortuary religion thus falls between religion thus conceived and funerary practices, and despite his lengthy treatment of Egypt, Montfaucon thus does not enter into the usual discussions of conceptions of souls, the afterlife, and such, except as implied by the uncommented quotations about funerary practices from Herodotus and Diodorus. He apparently sees these practices as a separate cultural domain, as is also indicated by his treating burial practices in a separate volume of his work. Note, however, that this separation is not upheld to the same degree in the discussion of Greece and Rome, where the section on funerary practices includes a lengthy description of concepts of the dead and the underworld (Montfaucon 1722–24 [1719–24], 2:134–70). In this way Montfaucon offers an example that, even if Egyptian funerary practices are difficult to overlook, they did not universally prompt speculation about the underlying motives.

French Expatriates in the Early Eighteenth Century

A closer engagement with Egypt is found in the work of Claude Sicard (1677–1726; cf. Carré 1932, 1:47–55), a Jesuit priest supervising the mission in Egypt from 1712 to his death in 1726, offering him ample opportunity to study the country and its geography (Sicard 1982a, v–xi). Sicard compiled a geographical dictionary, *Parallèle géographique de l'ancienne Égypte et de l'Égypte moderne* (1726), with entries of varying length on numerous localities. It survives only in an incomplete copy, ending midsentence in an entry on catacombs on page 99 (Sicard 1982b, xxiii–xxv). As the dictionary is ordered alphabetically, this indicates a considerable number of lost entries. In the incomplete entry on the catacombs, the discussion deals mainly with the ancient necropolis at Saqqara, which Sicard notes served as a burial place not only for mummified humans but also for "sacred birds" (Sicard 1982b, 162). He notes that Diodorus must have had the real-life landscape of this necropolis in mind when he wrote about the places Greeks later used to imagine the underworld, including the Acheron, the Elysian Fields, the Cocytus, the Lethe, and Charon's barque. The identification of the places corresponding to these mythological localities is not discussed further in the extant *Parallèle* manuscript, but letters about the 1719 visit that gave rise to these observations, both by Sicard himself and especially by fellow Jesuit P. Foynat, who accompanied him, provide additional details on the local waterways that they identified as the models for the rivers of Hades and so forth (Sicard 1982a, 75–76).

In the subsequent discussion, Sicard collects notes on mummification as well as a brief mention of the underlying ancient motivations for their burial practices, noting that these practices are discussed at greater length in the now-lost entry on pyramids. In the brief extant discussion, Sicard (1982b, 163–64) begins by summarizing Herodotus's and Diodorus's descriptions of the procedures of mummification, also relating them to the mention of a forty-day duration for the process in the story of Joseph in Genesis 50:2–3. He goes on to cite Herodotus's passage on a three-thousand-year cycle of metempsychosis as one possible reason for mummification, while giving as an alternative underlying idea George Syncellus's much more rarely cited notion of a general cosmic cycle of 36,525 years. Either way, he notes that "it was imagined that the souls could more easily reenter whole and well-preserved bodies (*corps entiers et bien conservés*)" (Sicard 1982b, 164). He goes on to quote in Latin the first part of Porphyry's description of ancient Egyptian elite funerals relating to the removal of the entrails and their exposure to sun. By leaving out the recitation and the later detail that the entrails are thrown into the river, he is able to align the passage with the general idea of the need for a complete and well-preserved body. After some details on the exact means of desiccating the body as related by Herodotus, the extant text ends just as Sicard turns to discussing how to tell male and female mummified bodies apart based on the iconography of their coffins.

As brief as it is, the section does give us a sense of how Sicard interpreted ancient Egyptian funerary religion not only drawing on the classical authors, but also informed by a significant familiarity with the material remains of the ancient culture. The juxtaposition of Herodotus with George Syncellus indicates that he regarded the cycle between death and the eventual return to the body as a period of cosmic relevance during which the world revolved and returned to its original state—an idea also present in the roughly contemporary letters of Maillet, as seen below. Sicard's wording and his incomplete quotation of Porphyry further indicate that the main aim of mummification as he understood it was simply to preserve the body in its entirety so the soul could more easily return.

While French consul general in Egypt from 1692 to 1708, Benoît de Maillet (1656–1738; cf. Carré 1932, 1:56–62) wrote a series of letters containing notes on his travels in the country, which were edited and published decades later by Jean-Baptiste le Mascrier (Mascrier 1735; cf. Dufrenoy 1975, 41–52). Maillet's text touches in various places on funerary practices in discussions of visits to ancient cemeteries, and the author provides a sense of the framework within which such practices were understood in the early eighteenth century. Thus, in his description of the "plain of Mummies" (*plaine des Momies*; Mascrier 1735, 275) near the village of Saqqara, he understands the tombs there as aiming at safeguarding the bodies of those whose means did not allow them to build a pyramid, and more specifically notes that this was done to "ensure the return of their souls to those same bodies" (*assurer le retour de leurs ames dans ces mêmes corps*; Mascrier 1735, 276). Later on in the book he describes the underlying ideas in more detail based on extrapolations from the notes in Herodotus (see below), and at this point merely expresses surprise that the Greek and Roman authors had so little to say about the "secret mysteries contained in these tombs" (Mascrier 1735, 279). In his description of the discovery and looting of mummies and funerary objects found in the tombs in the area, he refers to a vase filled with "the same balm that was used to preserve the corpses from corruption" (*préserver les corps de la corruption*) (Mascrier 1735, 278). Regarding a particular body Maillet had unwrapped, he notes that under the right hand, which was held across the stomach, were found the strings of a musical instrument, showing that the deceased either played it himself or at least was devoted to music. He theorizes that one should be able to determine something of the nature of every other mummified body by making similar observations on the objects buried with them, thereby indicating that he understood grave goods as being essentially personal objects also used during life.

Having described in relatively indifferent terms the rough treatment the mummies were subjected to, he notes how greatly they must have been venerated in their own time and says vestiges of this profound respect are found among the Egyptians of his own day. He poignantly notes that "only we have been able to imagine the secret of making them objects of trade [*les faire entrer dans le commerce*], which seems highly irreligious to me, as it is certainly useless for conserving the living [*inutile à la conservation des vivans*]" (Mascrier 1735, 279).

In the more detailed discussion of ancient Egyptian religion later in the book, Maillet begins by noting that being the first people to "leave the shadows of ignorance," the Egyptians recognized a supreme being behind the various manifestations they worshipped. He thus draws on the tradition of ancient Egyptian monotheism, but also on the notion that such ideas are largely universal among the peoples of the earth. As another fundamental idea, and one likewise shared across humanity, he goes on to ascertain that the Egyptians yearned for immortality, noting (Mascrier 1735, 45*), "Nothing is more natural to man than this secret yearning for immortality, which, apart from revelation, is one of the strongest proofs of the immortality of our soul; nothing is more gratifying for him than the hope of achieving it."

In other words, in regard both to monotheism and to the immortality of the soul, the Egyptians are understood as instantiating innate human tendencies, whose presence in itself demonstrates the universal truth of these ideas, although they could be only imperfectly realized before the Christian revelation. Correspondingly, he goes on to describe the ways people sought to fulfill the deep yearning for immortality before taking up the more specifically Egyptian ideas about this. He offers a description of transmigration of souls based on Herodotus, though with certain additions. Notably he reinterprets and significantly magnifies the usual three thousand years ("whether it amounts to 30 or 40 thousand years"; Mascrier 1735, 45*), and he interprets the underlying idea as indicating that this period signifies a cosmic cycle "where the universe would return to the same point from which it had begun at their birth" (Mascrier 1735, 45*), implying that it is the entire world that returns to its point of departure, and that this is the rationale for the souls' returning to their original human bodies—all of which indicates that, like Sicard, he also drew on ideas traceable back to George Syncellus. He does not mention the idea of souls' passing through the bodies of animals, which is thus not seen as a central element of the underlying concept, but later on he notes that the rationale for mummifying animals would have been the same one of restoring the life and conditions as found at birth, meaning that the owner could be reunited with cherished pets in their next life (Mascrier 1735, 47*–48*). In fact he notes explicitly how the ancient Egyptian conception differs from the later Greek adoption of a "metempsychosis without end" (Mascrier 1735, 48*), where the nature of each new body depends on the manner of life in the previous one.

Maillet points out that two conditions must be fulfilled for this to happen, and he notes with some cynicism that these conditions would have offered clear advantages to the priests promulgating them (Mascrier 1735, 49*–51*), in a way reminiscent of traditional criticism of the Catholic practice of indulgences, coming not only from Protestants but also from Catholic Jansenists (McManners 1981, 127). The first condition is preserving the body from any corruption once the soul has left it, so that it may be inhabited anew after the very long time span indicated. The second condition is that the deceased must atone for the sins committed during the first life through sacrifices instituted by themselves or offered by their family and friends (Mascrier 1735, 47*). While the former idea is loosely based on Herodotus, the second introduces a model clearly derived from the Catholic notion of purgatory and the efficiency of masses held for the deceased (McManners 1981, 126–29). This presents a notable elaboration of the more basic idea that the transmigration fundamentally depends on a postmortem judgment. Maillet does not elaborate his inspirations further, but it is clear that the application of this model is based on his universalist ideas, where Christianity (and Catholicism in particular) is the culmination and precise articulation of broader innate human intuitions, which thus surface in imperfect form in the religious ideas of pagan cultures. Effectively this means that Christian dogma can be used to understand the rationale behind pagan practices.

In turn, the parallelism with Christianity makes it possible to criticize the ideas of the Egyptians directly. Given that Christianity has perfected the means to satisfy the human yearning for immortality through divine revelation, it follows that pagan reactions to the same yearning can only be imperfect. In the case of the Egyptians, Maillet notes the problem of the soul's returning to inhabit a resurrected corpse robbed of its entrails and with pitch where the brain should be. While he admits that religious ideas do not always make complete rational sense, he notes that ultimately this concession does not redeem the "absurdity" of the ancient Egyptian way of imagining the future resurrection "without the help of revelation" (Mascrier 1735, 48*).

Apart from his writings, Maillet also influenced contemporary understanding of Egypt by acquiring antiquities. He had found a painted and inscribed linen bandage in one of the mummies he unrolled, which he sent to French marine commissary and antiquities collector Jean-Pierre Rigord (1656–1727), prompting an unusually detailed discussion and analysis, including an engraved plate reproducing the imagery, in the learned journal *Mémoires pour l'histoire des sciences et des beaux-arts*, or *Journal de Trévoux* (Rigord 1704; cf. Lüscher 2018, 23–24 and 38–40). Rigord proposes that the linen be understood as an actual book, perhaps meant to be rolled around a stick in the manner of ancient scrolls. Interestingly, and unlike the line of interpretation adopted in the nineteenth century, where such compositions overwhelmingly became understood as guidebooks to the afterlife, as is discussed in chapters 6–8 below, Rigord proposes a more general ritual understanding that in some ways is more in line with recent reinterpretations (cf. Nyord 2020). He refers to various examples of people putting writing on their bodies as a means of protection, including a prince from Borneo and a moribund Ethiopian in Paris. The implication is that the composition in question must have functioned as a sort of ritually efficacious amulet: "This linen might contain the theology of the Egyptians that many carried on them by religious motivation, like some among the Christians today carry the Gospel of St. John" (Rigord 1704, 982).

Accordingly, Rigord interprets the imagery as depicting well-known Egyptian deities and religious principles. Because of his understanding of the composition as a general religious treatise, he makes no mention of more specifically mortuary ideas. Indeed, prompted by the inscription at the bottom of the strip, the article moves on to discuss the different Egyptian writing systems and their possible relation to other ancient scripts, and Rigord does not offer any further thoughts on the purpose or contents of the painted linen.

Moses and the Egyptians

A line of thought roughly similar to Maillet's notion of parallelism between Egyptian religion and Christianity was deployed for more directly polemical purposes by English antiquarian and naturalist John Woodward (1665?–1728), whose lengthy exposition was likely written at about the same time as Maillet's letters, although it was published only posthumously in one of the first issues of *Archaeologia*, the long-lived journal published by the Society of Antiquaries in London (Woodward 1777; cf. Feingold 2019, 120–23; Gascoigne 1991, 180–82). Woodward was explicitly engaged in the debate about the relationship between the ancient Egyptians and Moses, which continued well into the eighteenth century (Assmann 1997b) and occasionally touched on Egyptian mortuary religion. In his treatise he presented a strongly worded argument against what he regarded as a vast overestimation of Egyptian cultural achievements, in particular by writers of "libertine principles, who bear no good-will to Christianity, knowing how much this is built upon Moses, do not care to have it thought his writings came from God, but from Egypt" (Woodward 1777, 225). Not surprisingly given this stance, a large part of the paper is occupied with countering various aspects of Spencer's interpretation of the Egyptian background of the teaching of Moses. As part of the generally dismissive treatment of Egyptian culture, Woodward also presents some brief remarks on ancient Egyptian funerary practices (Woodward 1777, 234–35), which he regarded essentially as the Egyptians' "art in preserving their dead bodies so sound and intire, as we see they are, thorough so many ages" (Woodward 1777, 234), thus tacitly deploying the familiar conflation of result and purpose. He begins his brief discussion by citing Herodotus's passage on metempsychosis, which he presents explicitly as the reason underlying the elaborate funerary practices. In doing so, he paraphrases Herodotus closely, adding only the interpretation that the human body to be inhabited after a three-thousand-year cycle was the same one that was first left, leading to essentially the same understanding as Maillet's. As a consequence, he notes the fallible nature of a practice that would result in the soul's reinhabiting a body from which crucial parts had been removed:

> The soul, at its return, must be forced either to take up a body that was destitute of brains, and the greater part of the bowels; which surely would have afforded it but a very indifferent habitation, or else it must have these reframed to its use and furnished forth anew; and then nobody will be well able to imagine why the rest of the body might not as well have been framed by the same means, without all this trouble of preserving it, and, in truth, but in a very sorry manner after all. (Woodward 1777, 234–35)

To bolster this argument further, Woodward draws on knowledge of actual mummified bodies extant at his time, noting in line with many of his other observations that even the apparent achievement of preserving these bodies was in fact due not so much to the technical skills of the Egyptians as simply to the favorable Egyptian climate. As a final demonstration of this point, he refers to a mummified body brought out of Egypt that he had seen himself, which on exposure to the more humid English climate "began to corrupt and grow mouldy, emitted a foetid and cadaverous scent, and in conclusion putrified and fell to pieces" (Woodward 1777, 235).

As relatively brief and dismissive as it is, Woodward's discussion is interesting for its polemic deployment of the connection between the Herodotus passage on metempsychosis and practices of mummification in a manner clearly paralleling the more detailed treatment of this question by Maillet. In fact, one might have used Woodward's observations as an argument against the direct applicability of Herodotus in the interpretation espoused by Woodward (and a number of previous scholars), since the practice of embalming would not in fact have been suitable for its alleged purpose. However, because of the overall aim of discrediting the Egyptians as a way of arguing against the role of Egyptian wisdom in Moses's teaching (and hence in Christianity), presenting Egyptian ideas and practices as illogical not only is not a problem but is in fact grist for Woodward's mill.

Another noteworthy participant in the same debate was William Warburton, bishop of Gloucester (1698–1779; cf. Assmann 1997b, 96–102; 2014, 61–73), whose book *The Divine Legation of Moses* (Warburton 1738, 1741) became very widely debated during the eighteenth century. Beliefs in the immortality of the soul and postmortem rewards and punishments in different religions were central to Warburton's argument aiming ultimately to demonstrate the divine origin of the laws of Moses: to Warburton, that all other religions of antiquity contain these elements but Mosaic religion does not shows the special, divinely inspired nature of the latter.

Egypt plays a particularly important role in this overall model because of its status as the earliest example of the kind of near-universal beliefs and institutions Warburton is interested in. Thus he notes that "of all Nations, the *Ægyptian* was most celebrated for its Care in cultivating Religion in general, and the Doctrine of a future State in particular" (Warburton 1738, 92; emphasis in the original). Similarly, Warburton cites the Egyptians as the first people to erect statues of the gods, which he sees as a sign that they ascribed human natures to their deities (Warburton 1738, 96). Warburton's general point is that such ideas, along with the connected notion of religious mysteries likewise absent from the teaching of Moses but present everywhere else, were taught out of political expediency by human lawmakers.

Part of the interest in Warburton's argument in the present connection is how little he needs to argue or demonstrate the underlying assumption that the Egyptians *did* in fact believe in a future state of reward and punishment. Unlike other authors collecting evidence from a variety of classical authors and discussing their interpretation, at the time he wrote Warburton could assume that for his readers this idea was so self-evident and commonplace that it could serve as a point of departure for the more specific and idiosyncratic argument that was his main aim. Thus to Warburton it does not particularly matter exactly how one might combine the notion of metempsychosis (explicitly cited, e.g., Warburton 1738, 175, 306) with the notion of rewards and punishment, let alone with mummification, which is of negligible interest to Warburton owing to its cultural specificity. Instead, his concern with the topics connected to Egyptian mortuary religion lies in their capacity to shore up his general model of the development of religious ideas. Thus, for example, concerning the funerary rituals, echoing ideas from Diodorus he notes that

> the *Egyptian* Legislator found afterwards another Use in this Opinion; and, by artfully turning it as a Punishment on insolvent Debtors, grounded on it an Institution of great Advantage to Society. For, instead of that general Custom of modern Barbarians to bury insolvent Debtors *alive*, this polite and humane People had a Law that denied Burial to them when *dead*. (Warburton 1738, 202; emphasis in the original)

Against this background Warburton argues that the Egyptians invented what he calls a "double Doctrine" where the ancient sages taught one thing (notably about a future state of reward and punishment) for the general good of society but did not actually believe it themselves—a method subsequently adopted by the Greeks (Warburton 1738, 303–24). The ultimate aim of this argument is that the Egyptian notion of the immortality of the soul would have logically led to the idea of an eternal, almighty deity (Warburton 1738, 402–3). Since this notion was not taught openly, Warburton concludes that under the method of the "double Doctrine," it was held in secret by the Egyptian sages and taught through the mysteries only to religious initiates, kings, and magistrates. As Assmann notes, these "Greater Mysteries" consisted essentially in "abolishing the illusionary imagery of polytheism" (Assmann 1997b, 98).

This does, however, raise the question of the relation between pagan ideas of a future state and those of Christianity. After all, if this idea was introduced by pagan lawmakers without conviction merely for the good of society following natural reason, as Warburton argues, would this not also cast doubt on Christian notions of eternal life? Warburton (1738, 412) solves this problem by arguing that Christianity is "quite another thing" and that the apparent similarity of pagan and Christian teachings in this regard is deceptive. The view he proposes is one that "shews natural Reason to be *clear* enough to perceive Truth, and the Necessity of its Deductions when proposed and shewn; but not generally *strong* enough to *discover* it, and draw right Deductions from it." (Warburton 1738, 413–14)

The second volume of the work (Warburton 1741) is devoted on the one hand to showing the antiquity of Egyptian civilization and on the other to demonstrating that apparent references to a Mosaic teaching of a future state of the soul have been misunderstood, arguing that Mosaic religion thus does not contain such a teaching. What is at stake in this argument is ultimately the relation between Moses and Christianity, which to Warburton hinges precisely on this point, as when "GOD, by the later Prophets, reveals his Purpose of giving them a NEW *Dispensation,* in which a future State of Reward and Punishment was to be *brought to light*" (Warburton 1741, 455; emphasis in the original).

Assmann has called attention to the lasting effects of Warburton's argument in further entrenching the hypothesis of "dual religion" (i.e., a difference between overt teachings and secret mysteries) in a partly new, eighteenth-century guise (Assmann 2014). As will be seen below, this hypothesis came to play an increasingly important role for consolidating the classical authors' testimonies and would be a key mechanism leading to the eventual rejection of the metempsychosis model in the mid-nineteenth century. But a more specific effect of Warburton's argument was the precise way ancient Egyptian mortuary religion was at the same time paralleled with and subtly contrasted to the eschatological teachings of Christianity. On the one hand, Egyptian beliefs in the immortality of the soul and its reward and punishment were part of a universal pagan phenomenon established for political reasons, and on the other hand this was overtly similar to, yet qualitatively different from, the Christian teaching of eternal life that resulted from divine revelation.

The Egyptian Society

A less rarefied example of the low estimation of Egyptian religion is found in the writings of the later statesman John Montagu, fourth earl of Sandwich (1718–92). As a young man he traveled the Mediterranean, and his memoirs were published posthumously in 1799. In a discussion peppered with quotations from Latin poetry, he notes that the ancient Egyptians were "addicted to all sorts of superstition" and "worshipped many ridiculous objects" (Montagu 1799, 412), although he later notes that, regarding animal worship, "their superstition was not so gross as is commonly imagined," because it was the symbolic qualities of the animals, not the animals themselves, that were worshipped (Montagu 1799, 416). When it comes to funerary religion more specifically, like many others Montagu offers a detailed paraphrase of Herodotus in connection with a visit to the "Field of Mummies" at Saqqara (whence he also brought home several mummified bodies; Montagu 1799, iii), but he does not discuss the underlying beliefs. He does make the following remark on the conducive nature of the Egyptian climate, which indicates he held the aim of mummification to be the preservation of the body (Montagu 1799, 469): "Had the Ægyptians inhabited any other country, they never would have given themselves so much trouble in embalming the bodies of their dead relations, which the nature of their repositories would have rendered ineffectual."

Elsewhere he notes with Herodotus that Pythagoras derived his ideas about the transmigration of souls from the Egyptians, but he does not attempt to relate this idea to the practice of mummification (Montagu 1799, 411). Ultimately, then, while it is not entirely clear what Montagu made of Egyptian burial practices, the remarks he does make are clearly in line with those of other authors, both earlier and contemporary.

Some years after his Egyptian journey, in 1741 John Montagu and a group of other men founded the Egyptian Society in London (Anis 1952; Saumarez Smith 2021, 33–37; Roos 2022). Devoted to the goal of "promoting and preserving Egyptian and other antient learning," the society brought together people of very different backgrounds and is aptly described as "a space in which antiquarians and freemasons, scholarship and amateur dramatics overlapped" (Saumarez Smith 2021, 36). As is explored further below, interpretations of ancient Egypt inspired by Freemasonry would become increasingly influential in the later eighteenth century, making this early and relatively well-documented encounter between scholars, travelers, and aristocrats a moment of considerable interest, even though the society proved short-lived and was disbanded in 1743.

Another cofounder of the Egyptian Society, English clergyman Richard Pococke (1704–65; cf. Finnegan 2019, 181–269; 2021, 42–63) undertook journeys in the eastern Mediterranean, visiting Egypt twice, in 1737–38 and 1738–39, and he offered a detailed account of his travels in the *Description of the East and Some Other Countries,* published in two folio volumes in 1743 and 1745. At the end of the first volume of this work, titled *Observations on Egypt,* Pococke includes a number of chapters on various aspects of ancient Egyptian culture. One of these deals with Egyptian embalming practices, where he paraphrases the descriptions by Herodotus and Diodorus before going on to discuss how they may be interpreted and consolidated. He continues (Pococke 1743, 232) to describe his examination of a mummified body he had brought from Egypt, focusing on the manner of mummification it evidenced (also the topic of a lecture Pococke gave at the Egyptian Society in February 1742; Finnegan 2021, 49; Roos 2022, 277–79), and he afterward discusses topics such as the techniques of painting coffins and the mummification of animals. The latter practice he understands in relation to the myth of Osiris and the idea that each of the twenty-four temples to Osiris consecrated a particular animal to him and on its death buried it in the manner of the god. In relation to the mummification of bulls in particular, he notes that "some say, the soul of Osiris went into a bull, and that this was the reason of the extraordinary worship paid to this animal" (Pococke 1743, 233). Pococke's general understanding of Egyptian religion is that the gods, and especially Osiris, were originally human beings who were honored with deification. Against this background he can understand the practice of mummification simply as an act of imitating Osiris, without attaching to the practice any additional aims of bodily preservation or theological dogma (Pococke 1743, 226).

Danish naval officer and traveler Frederik Ludvig Norden (1708–42; cf. Frandsen 2019) was also among the founders of the Egyptian Society, though at least judging from his published work, his interests seem to have been less oriented toward Egyptian religion. While his own detailed description of the pyramids (cf. Frandsen 2019, 81–83) does not take up the reasons for building them, Norden's travel description (Norden 1755, 1:89–101) contains a letter appended to this section in which he comments in great detail on claims made in Greaves's *Pyramidographia* (chapter 2 above), indicating that even a century after its publication that work still held sway as the most detailed discussion published on the topic. In this discussion, Norden agrees in principle with Greaves that the main motivation behind the pyramids must have been religious, though he adds that ambition must also have played a significant role (Norden 1755, 1:92). Similarly, while he singles out the passage where Greaves speaks of the soul attending the body as long as the latter remains intact, the aspect he criticizes is the question whether the pyramids were derived from the so-called Tumuli Mercuriales (Norden 1755, 1:94). It thus seems he largely accepts Greaves's understanding of ancient Egyptian mortuary religion, since he criticizes many other aspects of his discussion, sometimes in the same passages presenting these interpretations, yet raises no argument against this particular aspect, nor does he bring any of his many detailed observations on Egyptian monuments to bear explicitly on the question. One small indication that Norden may have harbored universalist ideas, although without giving any indication of his stance on the relation between Egyptian and Mosaic religion, is that he interprets a scene in a temple on the west bank of Thebes as alluding to the fall of Adam and Eve (Norden 1755, 2:170–71, pl. 58).

Another member of the Egyptian Society is of considerable interest for his rather different take on Egyptian religion. This was William Stukeley (1687—1765), whose writings on and interpretations of Egyptian rituals were influential in the society (Saumarez Smith 2021). His unpublished manuscript "On the Mysteries of the Antients" appears to have been circulated among the members. In this manuscript Stukeley presents Masonic interpretations of the temple of Solomon, which in turn was understood as the prototype all Egyptian temples imitated, with cosmic symbolism as well as an overall structure reflecting rituals of initiation. Ferdinand Saumarez Smith (2021) has recently presented a reconstruction of the rituals Stukeley described in this manuscript. While it does not relate directly to Egyptian funerary religion, it introduces a set of closely related concepts, since Masonic initiation is understood inter alia in terms of death and rebirth. At the most fundamental level, the temple is described in terms of the cardinal directions, in turn reflecting the solar cycle. Thus the hierophant presiding over the ritual is likened to the rising sun, his role to "admit descending souls into world," and as such he represents the "genius who presides over . . . renascence" (Saumarez Smith 2021, 26). Accordingly, the initiate's garment is said to be "somewhat like Horus's or someway resembling the clothing of an infant" (Saumarez Smith 2021, 26). The goal of this symbolism was to make initiates "look upon themselves as in a state of regeneration, toward a new life, a life of greater perfection" (Saumarez Smith 2021, 27). As Saumarez Smith (2021, 30) notes, however, "the life-cycle theme can equally be conceived of as an afterlife-cycle," an interpretation explicitly drawn on by Stukeley.

Notwithstanding the definitively pagan tenor of much of this description, the overall model remains "the theme of patriarchal Christianity" (Saumarez Smith 2021, 30). Aligning the idea of rebirth with the winter solstice, Stukeley draws on both the ancient Saxons and the cult of Mithras to make the point that pagan ideas of a child's being born at midwinter can be taken to allude to the Christian nativity. In this way Stukeley's Masonic initiation, despite its rather different result, draws on well-established models of aligning pagan religions with Christianity. However, while the salvation and afterlife would remain the standard mode of interpreting Egyptian funerary religion, the notion of a metaphorical rebirth through initiation introduced a viable competitor in some quarters.

Initiation and Egyptian Mysteries

One of the most famous and influential writers in this tradition of initiatory interpretations of ancient Egyptian religion was priest and classical scholar Jean Terrasson (1670–1750; cf. Somos 2014; Geoga 2022), whose novel *Séthos* (Terrasson 1813 [1731]) lays out an elaborate Egyptian system of initiation, which in turn provided inspiration to Freemasonry and most famously to Mozart's opera *The Magic Flute* (e.g., Assmann 2005b). The novel takes the form of a pseudotranslation of an ancient manuscript in Greek to which the author claims to have had access, detailing the life of the Egyptian prince Séthos, his religious initiation, and his travels throughout Africa. While it has sometimes been assumed that this was a hoax that was widely believed by contemporary readers, it seems likely that most readers would have recognized the work for what it was. Not only was pseudotranslation a well-established literary genre at the time (Geoga 2022, 187–88), but attentive readers could also pick up on clear anachronisms, showing that the text could not in fact be ancient (Lefkowitz 2009, 358). Nonetheless, the extensive footnotes "added" to the text lent it an aura of exactitude and scholarship, so that even without necessarily believing in its formal conceit, many contemporary readers came to regard the text as an authoritative presentation of ancient Egyptian culture and society.

In the novel, Terrasson repeatedly makes the point that Egypt's cultural achievements were superior to those of Greece and Rome, which are regarded as mere imitations, a notion also found in classical authors, notably Diodorus. In Terrasson's version this argument entered into a new context as his work intervened in the ongoing "Quarrel of the Ancients and Moderns," an often heated debate in France (and elsewhere) about the relative merits of the achievements of ancient Greece and Rome,—with Egypt occasionally playing a role as well—on the one hand, and those of contemporary Europe on the other (Somos 2014, 289–90; Geoga 2022, 190–95). Nonetheless, the result of staging Egypt as a precursor to Greece and Rome was that ancient Egyptian institutions and achievements naturally came to be understood within the matrix offered by those historical frameworks (Somos 2014).

Terrasson's *Séthos* raises two main questions relevant to the topic at hand. The first is the standard question of how he understands Egyptian mortuary religion and on what basis, while the second is raised by the use of well-known elements of funerary culture—notably the pyramid—in the context of initiation rituals in a manner going far beyond that of roughly contemporary writers like Stukeley. With regard to both of these questions, we are helped along by the copious footnotes that provide a sense of Terrasson's sources, although their use is not always straightforward (Geoga 2022, 195–201).

In the first of the ten books the work comprises, a description of the Egyptian queen's death and burial provides an occasion to present ideas and practices connected to Egyptian mortuary religion (Terrasson 1813 [1731], 1:62–91). Not surprisingly, a main source in this passage is Diodorus's description of funerary practices, though the format of the novel invites a number of additional considerations, especially concerning the reasoning behind the practices, which Diodorus does not have much to say about. Thus Terrasson lets the ancient narrator say that priests "alleged the state of rest and happiness [*repos et bonheur*] into which it could so strongly be hoped the gods would admit her at the following obsequies" (Terrasson 1813 [1731], 1:63), providing the key notions of a blessed afterlife and a judgment by the gods on whether to admit the deceased.

The description continues with a passage drawing on Herodotus for notions of the immortality of the soul and of metempsychosis. However, the narrator notes that the Egyptian doctrine was "not well-defined" (*pas bien démêlée*). Thus, while admitting the doctrine of transmigration of the soul into animal bodies as described by Herodotus, it is noted that "the wisest accepted in the underworld [*les enfers*] a place of punishment for the souls of sinners [*méchans*], and delightful meadows for those of good people [*gens de bien*]" (Terrasson 1813 [1731], 1:64). For the purposes of the narrative, as for the general effort of making sense of the belief by other authors, it thus becomes expedient to add an idea of rewards and punishments, and here this is explicitly relegated to a contrast between an "underworld" or "hell" (*les enfers*) and something like the Elysian Fields (*prairies délicieuses*). The addition of this feature is made the more notable by the fact that, as seen above, Diodorus explicitly disavows this interpretation as a Greek misunderstanding of Egyptian ideas and practices.

After this brief discussion of Egyptian beliefs, the text turns to the process of mummification. Drawing primarily on Diodorus, Terrasson notes that the aim was to restore the body to its "first form [*première forme*], so that the deceased seemed to have retained the air of his face and the port of his person" (Terrasson 1813 [1731], 1:65). Drawing again on Diodorus, he describes the more specific royal rituals of being admitted to the labyrinth at Lake Moeris, including the judgment by a tribunal of priests. The narrative goes on to describe the pomp and circumstance with which the funeral procession is carried out. The body of the queen is adorned in various ways, the significance of which is said to be that "while the death of virtuous persons is sad for those who survive them, it was to them [the deceased] the beginning of their rest, of their happiness, and of their triumph [*de leurs repos, de leur bonheur et de leur triomphe*]" (Terrasson 1813 [1731], 1:74).

Along the same lines as adding places of afterlife rewards and punishments, another way of making sense of the Egyptian ideas and practices by aligning them with Christianity is the approximation of the funerary assessors to gods. This gives the ritual a sense of otherworldly, divine judgment rather than the more straightforward matter of the right to burial as related by Diodorus. Thus it is said that the judges were "regarded as the gods themselves" (Terrasson 1813 [1731], 1:77), and later, the speech the high priest of Memphis makes when presenting the queen to the tribunal is quoted at length, beginning with the address to the tribunal as "Inexorable gods of the underworld" (Terrasson 1813 [1731], 1:79). It is also noted, in a passage clearly reminiscent of Christian notions of divine grace and the difference between human and divine judgment, that the priests are highly anxious about the result of the judgment, "for if the causes which are really good sometimes turn out bad through the injustice of men, it is even more to be feared that causes which appear good really turn out bad before the justice of the gods" (Terrasson 1813 [1731], 1:77–78). The lengthy speech in favor of the queen contains a catalog of her many virtues, and once again what is at stake at the judgment is said to be "her rest and her happiness" (*son repos et son bonheur*; Terrasson 1813 [1731], 1:85). This point is stressed again when, after the favorable judgment of the queen, the assembled masses rejoice, "as suddenly as . . . a man who once again sees alive a beloved person that he thought dead" (Terrasson 1813 [1731], 1:88), the choice of figure implying that there is in fact an underlying notion of resurrection following the successful judgment.

The combination of close paraphrases of classical authors with interjected ideas from contemporary Christianity is instructive. Part of the point of the first book is emphasizing the moral qualities of the queen, as seen most obviously in the lengthy speech by the high priest but implied throughout by everything from the universal sorrow over her death to her successful judgment. Another challenge facing other authors is that, while such a moral dimension is explicitly present in Diodorus, it is understood in terms that are purely social as opposed to religious or eschatological. On the other hand, such a moral dimension is entirely absent from Herodotus. Whereas Bossuet had merely implied a similarity between Diodorus's ritual judgment and the Christian Last Judgment, these two notions are brought much closer here by stressing the divine nature of the judgment, which significantly raises the stakes—as repeatedly noted, it is the queen's "rest and happiness" in the afterlife that is at risk. To bring this point home in relation to Herodotus, his notion of metempsychosis is sidelined in the tradition of the "dual religion" interpretation to allow for a wiser group of the population that believes in postmortem rewards and punishments analogous to those of the Christian heaven and hell, an idea that implicitly informs the understanding of the postmortem judgment as well.

Turning to the topic of initiation, the question immediately presents itself of how Terrasson can arrive at a reconstruction of Egyptian religion that at least superficially differs so markedly from mainstream scholarship of the preceding centuries. A significant part of the answer lies in the model described above, where Greek and Roman culture are regarded as imitations of Egypt and thus can be used to fill in "gaps" in the documentation of Egypt. More specifically, since the Eleusinian Mysteries are regarded as ultimately being based on Egyptian mysteries, Terrasson can draw on Johannes Meursius's 1619 reconstruction of the former alongside other works dealing with secret priestly knowledge in Greece, or even apparently unrelated ideas in Greek and Roman works such as Virgil's *Annaeid* (Geoga 2022, 198–200). A key notion is the secret doctrine of monotheism, an idea that in turn aligns Terrasson not only with ancient authors like Plutarch, but also with more recent ones such as Kircher, Cudworth, and Maillet.

The narrative of Prince Séthos's initiation is the focus of the third and fourth books of the work. It appears immediately puzzling that Terrasson would set the initiation rituals inside and under the Great Pyramid, given that, as has been seen in the preceding discussion, the funerary nature of the Egyptian pyramids had been largely beyond doubt for centuries by his time. The rationale for the connection may be found in the text of Diodorus as elaborated by later scholars, more specifically his idea that the features of the Greek underworld had been derived from ancient Egyptian ritual topography. While, as seen above, travelers like Claude Sicard took this as a point of departure for interpreting actual features of the Egyptian landscape, Terrasson takes the connection in a different direction. After all, Diodorus credits Orpheus, who is famous for his visit to the underworld, with bringing the (reinterpreted) Egyptian ideas to Greece. This can be combined with another concept attested in classical authors (as also seen in Stukeley's text), that of initiation as a symbolic death followed by rebirth (for example, in Apuleius's *The Golden Ass*; e.g., Assmann and Ebeling 2011, 35–36). This brings the ideas of *katabasis*, or descent to the underworld, very close indeed not only to Egyptian funerary practices, but also to putative Egyptian initiation. In *Séthos*, the connection is established by having the Great Pyramid hide a secret initiatory temple underneath, while all the other pyramids are actual tombs (Terrasson 1813 [1731], 2:10–11).

The general structure of the underworld Séthos visits is a parallel society of priests and their families, which Orpheus misinterpreted as a realm of the dead. For example, on entering this underworld he hears children crying. While Orpheus misrepresented this as the children who died at the breast waiting at the entrance to the realm of the dead, the narrator explains that in fact they are the children of the priests placed there to accustom them to the subterranean conditions where they would be spending most of their lives (Terrasson 1813 [1731], 2:133–34).

Similarly, the rewards and punishments of this underworld are meted out to the members of the subterranean society depending on their merits. Thus Séthos sees the "Field of Tears" (Terrasson 1813 [1731], 2:144–47), corresponding to the place of afterlife punishment that was mentioned in the first book as part of the funerary beliefs. Men are punished for minor infractions by having to roll a rock up a hill, while women had to collect water from a well and pour it into a canal (the origin of the Greek myths of Sisyphus and the Danaïdes, as the narrator notes). More severe punishments are meted out for worse transgressions: for violating the secret of initiation, the chest was ripped open and the heart torn out and given to birds of prey to devour—a notion likely inspired by the mythic fate of Prometheus (Assmann and Ebeling 2011, 331n14). Corresponding to the distinction in book 1 between places of punishment and reward, Séthos arrives next at the Elysian Fields, whose wonders are described in some detail (Terrasson 1813 [1731], 2:147–56), before he is shown the secrets of oracles and finally sees the pantheon of Egyptian gods.

As an illustration of the influence of Terrasson's novel, we may look to the travel description of another member of the London Egyptian Society, Thomas Shaw (1694–1757; cf. Finnegan 2019, 61–65, 116–42), who was based in Algiers as chaplain to the English factory of the Levant Company there and visited many parts of the southern and eastern coast of the Mediterranean. While mostly interested in natural history, Shaw includes a chapter on ancient Egypt (Shaw 1738, 389–442), beginning with a detailed discussion of the symbolism of animals, plants, and artifacts, in which he cites the interpretations of a wide range of authorities from classical authors to Athanasius Kircher, then discusses obelisks in Egypt and Rome as "the principal Archives and Repositories, to which this Sacred Writing hath been committed" (Shaw 1738, 410). Shaw then discusses the pyramids, citing the standard interpretation that they were tombs, though he questions the need for their many convoluted corridors and leans toward an understanding of the pyramids as temples for worship of the gods. Showing the influence of the initiatory thinking of the times, he notes that "no Places certainly could have been more ingeniously contrived for the *Adyta*, that had so great a Share in the *Egyptian* Mysteries" (Shaw 1738, 418; emphasis in the original). Correspondingly, he suggests that the sarcophagus inside the Great Pyramid may have been used for the worship of Osiris or else have been a repository of cultic importance for images, vestments, utensils, or holy water (Shaw 1738, 419). Similarly, he suggests that passages may also be found in the other two pyramids (whose entrances were not evident when he visited) and that they "may, all of Them, communicate with the Chambers of the Priests, the artful Contrivers of these *Adyta*, where their initiatory, as well as other mysterious Rites and Ceremonies, were to be carried on with the greater Awe and Solemnity" (Shaw 1738, 422).

If Shaw's understanding thus demonstrates ideas of initiation under the pyramids closely related to those in Terrasson's *Séthos*, he does make a few comments on funerary themes as well. One of his first observations in the chapter is that among the many things posterity learned from the Egyptians is Pythagoras's doctrine of the transmigration of the soul (Shaw 1738, 390). More concretely, he describes mummified animals and grave goods he saw at Saqqara. However, beyond suggesting that "Instruments and Utensils, in Miniature" found in a box at the feet of each mummified body "may be supposed to have belonged to the Trade and Occupation of the embalmed Person, when he was alive" (Shaw 1738,423), he does not make clear how he understands the motivations behind the observed burial practices.

The further reception of Terrasson's *Séthos* well into the nineteenth century has been studied in detail by previous scholars (Macpherson 2004; Assmann and Ebeling 2011, 55–57; Ebeling 2018, with an abbreviated English version in Ebeling 2022; Geoga 2022, 201–7). While the main audience for whom its description of Egyptian initiation rituals was of interest was no doubt Freemasons and similar groups, ideas such as the interpretation of descriptions in ancient texts of descents to the underworld as masked initiation rituals would also make their way into more mainstream scholarship like that of William Warburton (Geoga 2022, 203–4). Even more important for present purposes, a seed had been planted where ancient texts and images could be expected to provide detailed descriptions of journeys through the realm of the dead. As is discussed further in chapters 6–8 below, this idea would turn out to be highly influential as imagery from ancient Egyptian tombs began to come to the attention of European scholars.

Interpreting Egyptian Imagery

An early example of this connection between prevalent understandings of Egyptian mortuary religion and concrete ancient imagery may be found in Scottish antiquarian Alexander Gordon's interpretation of the decoration of a coffin in the collection of William Lethieullier (1701–56). Lethieullier had joined the Society of Antiquaries in London in 1724, two years after returning from Egypt with the coffin, and antiquarian and engraver George Vertue (1684–1756) was commissioned to make an engraving of the decoration on the coffin's lid (fig. 5). In his

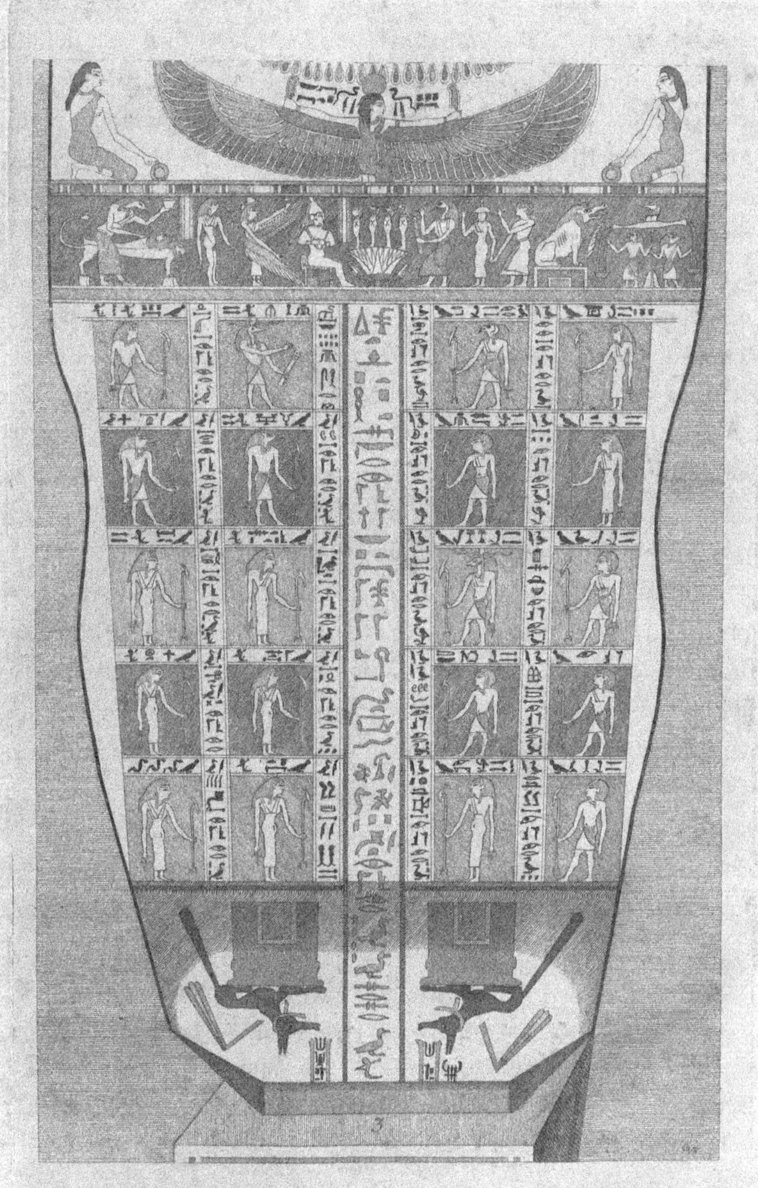

Fig. 5: Detail from the front of an Egyptian mummy case, engraved by George Vertue (1724). © Royal Academy of Arts, London; photographer: Prudence Cuming Associates Limited.

essay interpreting the decoration on the coffin (Gordon 1737), Gordon passes quickly over the embalmed body inside to turn to a detailed discussion of the individual iconographic elements on the lid. In his detailed description, Gordon is apt to identify prominent female figures as the goddess Isis, drawing on authors such as Plutarch and Apuleius to establish her central importance for the Egyptians. Of particular interest for present purposes is his interpretation of the "entire symbolical Picture" found on the horizontal band extending across the torso of the anthropoid coffin lid, which he understands as containing "a twofold Representation of DEATH and JUDGMENT" (Gordon 1737, 5; emphasis in the original). The theme of death is identified relatively straightforwardly through the image of a mummified body on a bier on the left being treated by what he identifies as an ibis-headed figure, which occasions quotations on the procedure of mummification from Diodorus and Clement of Alexandria (Gordon 1737, 5–6).

In the central part of the decorated band, Gordon identifies the enthroned Osiris in his role as Pluto, ruler of the realm of the dead, through a detailed discussion of the figure's iconography. As seen above, there is nothing surprising by this time in ascribing postmortem judgment a central role in Egyptian religious beliefs, but the identification of this theme in an actual ancient Egyptian source is new, making the way this identification is made particularly important. The pivotal element for his interpretation of the scene as pertaining to postmortem judgment lies in a scale depicted on the right. On this, Gordon writes,

> [the two figures by the balance] perhaps may symbolize the opposite GOOD and BAD *Principles*. . . . These seem each, by pulling the Scales down towards their own Side, to claim, as it were, the *Soul* of the *Deceased* for its own. The Balance symbolizing, that after the Actions of the Deceased are as it were weighed, the *ἱερογραμματεύς* [*hierogrammateus*] or sacred Scribe already mentioned, enumerates them before *Pluto* the supreme Judge of the Shades, that he may pass Sentence on the Deceased, who seems as it were led in by the *Agatho Dæmon* before his Tribunal already described. (Gordon 1737, 9; emphasis in the original)

The balance as a symbol of judgment, and particularly postmortem judgment, would have been well known to an eighteenth-century observer through the conventional European motif of *psychostasis*, or weighing of souls, in religious art, especially connected to Saint Michael's separating the virtuous and sinful souls in depictions of the Last Judgment (e.g., Dobrzeniecki 2015; Bates 2021, 82–83; cf. Podemann Sørensen 2013, 41–42). What shows this source of inspiration especially clearly, though it is not stated explicitly, is the more specific interpretation of the two figures attending the balance as trying to tip the scales in their favor to claim the soul. This idea is evidently derived from the more specific tradition in late medieval depictions of the Last Judgment with "devilish figures pulling at the scale-pan of sin in an attempt to secure a conviction, while saints mediated in a spiritual tug-of-war" (Bates 2021, 83).

However fortuitous its inspirations, Gordon can conclude his detailed analysis of the scene by suggesting "that the foresaid Representation alludes to the Belief which the *Egyptians* had at the time of embalming this Mummy, of the IMMORTALITY OF THE SOUL, of a FUTURE EXISTENCE after Death, and an INTELLECTUAL JUDGE, who was to pronounce the Deceased worthy or unworthy of *Eternal Bliss*" (Gordon 1737, 12; emphasis in the original). The similarity to Christianity is made all the more striking by Gordon's omission of the notion of metempsychosis that was still prevalent in many contemporary treatments of the topic. As seen above, all of the tenets Gordon listed had already come to be strongly associated with ancient Egypt in preceding scholarship. What is new, and would eventually prove highly influential, is the way these ideas could now seemingly be derived directly from interpretations of ancient Egyptian imagery (even if in practice the interpretation derives purely from conventional ideas combined with a specious similarity to Christian iconography). Gordon, however, takes this new evidence in a different direction to intervene briefly in the discussions about the interrelation between Egyptian religion, Judaism, and Christianity. Noting that the Egyptians clearly believed in the immortality of the soul at the time when this coffin was made, and that no such beliefs can be found in the Pentateuch, he concludes that these beliefs must have arisen after the Israelites' sojourn in Egypt because "that Doctrine of living happily after Death, is of so alluring a Nature to Mankind, as could not possibly have been concealed from either, but become a mutual Belief" (Gordon 1737, 13).

With its combination of entrenched ideas about postmortem judgment with ancient imagery that was seemingly immediately understandable based on well-known European iconography, this interpretation would have been as intuitively satisfying in the 1730s as it has remained to this day. The reason it did not immediately catch on was that neither the interpretation in Gordon's privately printed pamphlet nor reproductions of the imagery it was based on was widely available at this point. Rather, it would take the vast machinery behind the production and distribution of the *Description de l'Égypte* in the early nineteenth century to make the idea rise to its full prominence.

Shortly after the publication of Gordon's analysis, British physician Charles Perry (1698–1780)—another member of the Egyptian Society—undertook a journey through the eastern Mediterranean from 1739 to 1742 (Baigent 2004; Finnegan 2019, 143–80; Roos 2022, 281). During his visit to Egypt, he took a keen interest in Egyptian antiquities and acquired among other things a mummified body that, like Lethieullier, he brought back to England (Perry 1743, 470–75). In his published travelogue Perry writes at length about Egyptian antiquities and his interpretations of their imagery, and he engages among other things in a lengthy polemic against a recently published study by Noël-Antoine Pluche (1688–1761) on connections between ancient astronomical concepts and Egyptian mythology (most focused in Perry 1743, 421–33, but also in various other places throughout the work).

Noting that "the Customs and Manners of the antient *Egyptians* are as well touch'd by Herodotus, as by any other Person we know of, whether antient or modern" (Perry 1743, 242; emphasis in the original), Perry follows this authority very closely, including a detailed paraphrase of his presentation of Egyptian beliefs on metempsychosis (Perry 1743, 241–42). He also relates Herodotus's description of burial and mummification (Perry 1743, 246–47) but does not initially connect the two ideas. Later in the book, however, he returns somewhat reluctantly to the topic of Egyptian religion, "lest we should incur the Reproaches of our Readers, by being perfectly tacit as to that Article" (Perry 1743, 389). In the discussion that follows, Perry takes a very positive view of the ancient Egyptians and notes that they must have concluded the existence of a supreme being that created the world, and that it was this "Divine Author" (Perry 1743, 390) that they worshipped through different parts of his creation, such as celestial bodies, animals, and plants. Additionally, Perry establishes the two key concepts of the immortality of the soul and its transmigration. On the societal usefulness of these two ideas, he makes the following observations:

> The First was extremely well adapted to the most prevailing Wishes and Desires of the People of all Ages and Nations: And the latter (which perhaps was rather the Result of Policy, than the real Opinion of the Priests and Sages) was highly conducive to the Ends of Submission and good Discipline in the People. (Perry 1743, 390)

In this way the two ideas that are intrinsically connected in Herodotus become distinguished, with immortality being a universal idea (because it is also a Christian one), while transmigration has mainly political utility and thus is in fact suspected not to have been an earnest belief of the religious experts. Perry further clarifies his understanding of the ambiguity in Herodotus by noting the comfort believers could take in the notion that "after a certain Revolution of Years (no matter how many) their Souls and Bodies (after the Separation that's made by Death) shall be reunited, and preserve their Reunion for ever" (Perry 1743, 390). As is also evident from the quotation above, he regards the successful outcome of this as depending on one's conduct during one's first life, though he does not elaborate on this idea or the consequences of not achieving this aim. Instead, he goes on to explicate how, given that the ultimate goal is for the soul to return to its own body, this in effect implies a resurrection of the body along Christian lines:

> with this Difference only, that the Resurrection of all Bodies, as insinuated by Holy Writ (and as typify'd, or rather specify'd, by our Blessed Saviour) is to happen and be completed on one certain Day; whereas, according to the antient notion (and the modern one too,

> for that matter) of Transmigration, the Reunion of the Souls and Bodies of each Individual is to happen after a certain determinate Revolution of Time from the Death or Separation of each respectively. (Perry 1743, 390)

This effectively adds a third option to Christian theology's two alternatives of judgment immediately upon the death of the individual and a collective one at the Day of Judgment, namely the staggered judgment of each individual after a set period when the soul returns to its body. Perry finally notes briefly that this belief was likely also the reason for the invention of embalming, implying that—unlike writers such as Woodward—he understands a mummified, and hence preserved, body to be a more fitting home for the returned soul. The practice of mortuary sacrifices, interpreted as "Expiations" along broadly Catholic lines, can likewise be understood as motivated by the same belief, if one assumes that they could help secure the successful transmigration (Perry 1743, 391).

From his detailed discussion and considerations, it becomes clear that Perry builds his generally highly positive view of ancient Egyptian religion on an understanding that parallels key Christian tenets, notably the belief in a supreme being, the immortality of the soul, and the resurrection of the body. Egyptian religion, then, can be understood within this broadly Christian framework with the addition of a few exceptions that may not even have been earnestly believed in, namely the transmigration of souls into animals (the main point of which was to introduce an element of postmortem rewards and punishments) and the slight difference in the timing of the resurrection of the body to a specific period after death rather than the collective Last Judgment.

Meanwhile, back in France, another grand cross-cultural work on antiquities in the tradition of Bernard de Montfaucon bookended the half-century discussed in this chapter. Appearing in 1755, the work of Anne-Claude-Philippe de Tubières, Comte de Caylus, was titled *Recueil d'antiquités égyptiennes, étrusques, grecques et romaines* (Caylus 1752–67; cf. Browne 2023, 381–83). Caylus remarks about the Egyptians that "no nation has carried respect for the dead further; but in the religious care that these people took for the body, they only seem to have been occupied by securing rest and peace that nothing might disturb them, and, if you will, a near-eternal duration" (*une durée presqu'éternelle*) (Caylus 1752–67, 1:8). In commenting on a golden leaf found between mummy bandages, he proposes that it is an Egyptian coin, and that the rationale behind it could be similar to the Greek practice of giving the dead a coin for the ferryman Charon. After all, he notes, the name Charon is derived from Egyptian, so perhaps this is true of the entire concept (Caylus 1752–67, 2:21), a proposal with clear consequences for Egyptian mortuary religion, although he does not pursue it further. As these examples show, Caylus is not particularly interested in elucidating underlying beliefs in souls, afterlife, and such. On the other hand, he presents numerous discussions of mythology and iconography more widely as part of object-centered discussions of his plates. As with Montfaucon's earlier work, lengthy interpretations of a relatively wide range of ancient Egyptian antiquities were still entirely possible without invoking any specific beliefs in the afterlife.

Conclusion

By the mid-eighteenth century, the range of prevalent ideas relating to ancient Egyptian mortuary religion is well illustrated in writings of the members of the London Egyptian Society. From the dismissive and mostly practical considerations of Montagu and the architectural discussion by Norden to Pococke's understanding of mummification as primarily an imitation of Osiris, to Stukeley's and Ward's interests in initiation rituals, these show a remarkable overt variety of approaches. At the same time, however, it is clear that a number of shared ideas delineated what could meaningfully be said and understood about ancient Egyptian mortuary religion. The deliberate paralleling with Christianity looms large here. As most explicitly presented by an author like Perry, there tended to be widespread agreement that Egyptian religion could be effectively described using the familiar categories of immortality, postmortem rewards and punishments, and sometimes more detailed notions such as expiatory sacrifices to help the soul of the deceased.

FIVE

Describing Egypt: 1750–1798

The 1750s saw a grand synthesis of ancient history: the three-volume work *Origin of Laws, Arts, and Sciences* by Antoine-Yves Goguet (1716–58), who served as counselor to the Parliament of Paris (Goguet 1758; cf. Rohbeck 2002; Wolloch 2007). Within a biblical framework beginning with the flood and closing with the end of the Israelites' Babylonian exile, Goguet surveys the evolution of cultural history in the major ancient cultures, of which Egypt is one. As a late echo of the quarrel of ancients and moderns, Goguet frequently criticizes the achievements of the ancient societies he discusses as falling short by the cultural standards of eighteenth-century France (Wolloch 2007, 432–33). While this harsh judgment is certainly also extended to Egypt, whose architecture he characterizes, for example, by words such as "no grace [*grace*], no elegance [*élégance*], no attractiveness [*agrément*]" (Goguet 1758, 3:69), Goguet still credits Egypt as the general origin of Greek culture (cf. Rohbeck 2002, 258–59).

In line with his overall focus on material culture as the underlying condition of intellectual and spiritual development, it is in relation to tomb architecture that Goguet (1758, 65) discusses ancient Egyptian mortuary religion. His understanding of the motivation underlying the building of pyramids rests fundamentally on Servius, and he correspondingly notes that the Egyptians believed the soul would not be separated from the body as long as the body remained whole (*demeurer en son entier*). Accordingly, mummification as well as tomb construction aimed at preserving and protecting bodies to allow souls to survive. This idea is further connected to Diodorus's description of Egyptian tombs as eternal dwellings. Goguet (1758, 65) suggests that these ideas were sufficient to motivate the construction of pyramids, as the kings sought to "shelter [*mettre à l'abri*] their corpses against all events and assure them some manner of eternal duration [*durée éternelle*]." The specific shape of the pyramid, in turn, was chosen simply as "more suited than any other, due to its structure, for braving the injuries of time" (Goguet 1758, 66).

In this way Goguet offers a very simple explanation, focused on the concept of preservation, consistent with his main aim of explaining the construction of pyramids. With no specific interest in reconstructing religious ideas or theology, Servius proves perfectly adequate for Goguet's needs and allows him to be explicitly dismissive of the speculations by previous scholars on the motivations behind the pyramids as "commonplace and trivial morality" and "vain declamations repeated from mouth to mouth" (Goguet 1758, 64).

Several decades after Norden visited Egypt, another royal Danish expedition (1761–67) explored a number of countries of the Middle East, starting in Egypt. The sole survivor of the ill-fated expedition was cartographer Carsten Niebuhr (1733–1815; cf. Lage 2022, 211–34), who published a detailed account of his travels in his *Beschreibung von Arabien* (1772) and *Reisebeschreibung nach Arabien und andern umliegenden Ländern* (2 vols., 1774–78). He includes a chapter on Egyptian antiquities where he describes the aspects that particularly captured his interest, namely the task of examining and measuring the pyramids and his efforts to copy a large number of hieroglyphic inscriptions (Niebuhr 1774–78, 1:190–209). In the course of doing so, he explicitly relates his own findings to those of previous travelers like Maillet, Pococke, Norden, and Perry, though he also cites the occasional classical author, giving a sense of the sources of authoritative knowledge of Egyptian antiquities at this time. He does not, however, discuss Egyptian funerary practices more generally and thus does not provide evidence of what he thought about this aspect of the ancient culture.

Skeptic Voices

A direct result of Niebuhr's travels was the Danish King Christian VII's giving one of the mummified bodies Niebuhr had acquired to the Sozietät der Wissenschaften in Göttingen (Graepler 2007, 52–55). A commission of four professors from different disciplines was formed to study the body, including classical scholar Christian Gottlob Heyne (1729–1812), who had published a detailed discussion of mummification methods the year before the body's arrival (Heyne 1780). In his earlier study, Heyne was primarily interested in elucidating the technical procedures of mummification, notably compared with the narratives of Herodotus and Diodorus. As such, and in common with many other such "mummy studies," his discussion of the underlying religious motivations is brief. He notes that it is certain that the practice had "some religious motivation" (*religionis momentum aliquod*), but he expresses some doubt whether the Greek writers' ascription of beliefs about the immortality of souls and their return to the bodies was really accurate—entirely in line with his critical approach to the more technical descriptions of embalming techniques, which he checked against the empirical evidence of actual mummified bodies. Either way, he proposes that the practice of "desiccation" predated any such religious motivation (Heyne 1780, 76). It is thus characteristic that the skepticism toward the technical descriptions of Herodotus and Diodorus is carried over to their cultural observations as well. The result is a relatively new critical stance on the general reliability of Greek interpretations of Egyptian religion, but it is also worth noting that Heyne's lack of commitment to studying these religious aspects makes it much easier for him to adopt this stance than for contemporaries who are primarily interested in elucidating religious questions for which the classical authors were still about the only available source. Another of the four collaborators on the committee, professor of medicine Johann Friedrich Blumenbach (1759–1840; cf. Di Biase-Dyson and Grosskopf 2019) developed a more lasting interest in ancient Egyptian mummified bodies, although his attention tended more toward identifying the place of the ancient Egyptians in craniometric definitions of human races than in elucidating underlying religious motivations for the practice (e.g., Blumenbach 1865).

The skepticism toward the veracity and accuracy of the classical authors was not inspired solely by empirical studies of mummified bodies but was an important part of the *Zeitgeist* more generally (e.g., Marchand 2021), which did occasionally involve studies of Egyptian mortuary religion—even if, as noted, the lack of alternative sources of knowledge remained a challenge. In his comparative work *Recherches philosophiques sur les égyptiens et les chinois*, Dutch diplomat Cornelius de Pauw (1739–99; cf., e.g., Lage 2022, 89–149) sought to dispel several myths as he saw them, notably the long-standing idea—argued for example by Athanasius Kircher, and in de Pauw's own time by the prominent French Orientalist Joseph de Guignes (1721–1800)—that China had started as an Egyptian colony. To make this overall point, he set out to demonstrate the many differences between the two cultures. The notion of transmigration of souls came to play a role in this connection, since de Pauw regarded it as certain that the Chinese held this belief, which they had derived from the Tibetans and Hindus (Pauw 1773, 1:11). For this reason alone, but also in line with a general tendency toward pronounced skepticism in relation to established authorities, de Pauw did not accept that the Egyptians could have believed in metempsychosis. He rejects the explanatory model mobilized by a number of scholars that the Egyptians might have had two sets of beliefs held by different parts of the population, noting that the apparent contradiction between ideas found in classical authors never existed among the Egyptians (Pauw 1773, 2:154–55). He argues this point by noting that all subsequent authors commenting on Egyptian metempsychosis had the idea from Herodotus, who in turn was certainly wrong—a notion he substantiates by pointing to the many misunderstandings by Greek and Roman authors of the religion of the Jews as a parallel case.

De Pauw further notes the apparent contradiction that others before him had wrestled with concerning the role of the preservation of the body in a system of metempsychosis, arguing that prime examples of such a belief (again bringing forward Tibetans and Hindus) never had such customs (Pauw 1773, 2:155–56). Instead he invokes the funerary prayer from Porphyry, where the intestines are discarded as the seat of transgression to make the deceased acceptable to the gods. De Pauw argues that this idea is incompatible with either a "fatal or physical" version of metempsychosis (like the mechanical system of Herodotus) or a "moral or real" version that can encompass an idea of rewards or punishments (such as that described in Plato and the Hermetic writings), and notes that Plutarch similarly denies the notion that souls would enter into animals (Pauw 1773, 2:156–57). Consequently De Pauw asserts the beliefs of the Egyptians as follows:

> The Egyptians completely rejected the eternity of punishments [*l'éternité des peines*], and believed only in purgatory, called in their language *Amenthes*; but from this place no path led directly to heaven, and all those who entered the *Amenthes* would one day be resurrected [*ressusciter*], and revive [*ranimer*] the same body or the same matter that they had animated the first time. (Pauw 1773, 2:158)

The use of Christian dogma as a default model is notable here. Having rejected the more exotic belief in metempsychosis, it becomes a matter of asserting which parts of the Christian framework were applicable. As seen in the quotation this leads to a rejection of hell and eternal punishment, the acceptance of purgatory, and a somewhat reworked notion of resurrection in the flesh, which could in turn be connected to the practice of mummification. Corresponding to the idea of *Amenthes* as purgatory, De Pauw adds that philosophers and others of the highest moral standard would be able to go straight on to live among the gods—bypassing both purgatory and the bodily resurrection—and that only in this regard does Egyptian religion approximate Hinduism. The result, then, apart from the theological addition of the *Amenthes* as a purgatory, comes quite close to minimalist interpretations like those of Gryphius and others who merely assume on intuitive grounds that the soul was meant to return to the body, given all the efforts apparently invested in preserving it.

Another skeptic was Scottish explorer James Bruce (1730—94), who published a five-volume work describing his travels to discover the source of the Blue Nile (see Smith 2006 for the transmission of this work). The first part of his travels naturally took him through Egypt, and his book includes descriptions of his visits to the necropolises of Giza and Luxor. Given his much broader aims, it is not surprising that describing and interpreting ancient Egyptian antiquities and monuments is not his foremost concern, and he shows no particular commitment to interpreting the ancient mortuary religion. Nonetheless, he visited seven tombs in the Valley of the Kings on an outing that would end in a violent clash with the locals (Bruce 1790, 1:135–38). In describing the wall paintings he saw when descending into one such tomb, he adds some interpretive notes on their significance, preferring to see them as geographic or cosmic symbols rather than, as others had suggested, as emblems of resurrection:

> My own conjecture is, that the apis was the emblem of the arable land of Egypt; the crocodile, the typhon, or cacodæmon, the type of an over-abundant Nile; that the scarabæus was the land which had been overflowed, and from which the water had soon retired, and has nothing to do with the resurrection or immortality, neither of which at that time were in contemplation. (Bruce 1790, 1:127)

Bruce unfortunately does not develop this idea any further, but it seems reasonable to suppose from his remarks that he regards resurrection and immortality as specifically Christian ideas, or at least believes they are characteristic of later cultural developments. If this conjecture is correct, Bruce offers a rare and hence notable example of an eighteenth-century thinker who understands such ideas as being specific to Christianity rather than having universal relevance. The result of such a stance would be a clear rejection as anachronism of the ideas of many of his contemporaries (and indeed both earlier and later scholars), who apply such frameworks without question.

Despite such skeptical voices, the traditional interpretation drawing on interpretive reading of Herodotus continued among other travelers. Thus Constantin-François Volney (1757–1820; cf. Carré 1932, 90–103), in a travel description dealing mostly with modern affairs, includes a chapter on ruins and pyramids. Arguing against ideas that were hardly widespread among his contemporaries, that the pyramids might have been observatories or temples, he reasserts the notion that they were in fact tombs, noting as an explanation that "since before the time of Moses, it was the belief in Memphis that the souls would return after 6,000 [*sic*] years to inhabit the bodies they had left: It is for this reason one took such care to preserve these same bodies from dissolution" (Volney 1787, 1:250).

Although Volney thus does not offer much new material for the main question occupying us here, it is worth noting the more general influence of his volume. David Prochaska (1994, 74) understands the volume as the culmination of "at least a century of French Orientalist studies" and emphasizes that Napoleon Bonaparte not only had read Volney's book, but in fact brought a copy with him on his invasion of Egypt during the last years of the century (see chapter 6 below).

While he may not have traveled widely throughout Egypt during his two-year stay from 1777 to 1779, orientalist and later translator of the Quran Claude-Étienne Savary (1750–88; cf. Carré 1932, 80–90; Hamilton 2019) nonetheless published a three-volume work on numerous aspects of the country titled *Lettres sur l'Égypte*. Among the many letters discussing Egyptian religion in the third volume of his work is one devoted to more general concerns of the Egyptian cult. Savary begins by noting that Egyptian religion held only two dogmas, "that of the infinite spirit [*esprit infini*] responsible for creation, and that of the immortality of the soul" (Savary 1786, 3:274), with the rest of the apparent beliefs being purely allegorical. In accordance with the first idea, he understands the different gods of the Egyptians as so many qualities of the Supreme Being, thus following the idea that the apparent polytheism of the Egyptians is just a surface obscuring an original monotheism. Unlike other authors who regarded this original wisdom as having been lost in the course of history, Savary regards this as impossible owing to the general thrust of history, "for men who have once elevated themselves by the sublime effort of reason to the knowledge of a single God, or who have received it by tradition, as they form an enlightened body, would not be able to descend back into idolatry which always presupposes profound ignorance" (Savary 1786, 3:275).

A more specific discussion of the belief in the immortality of the soul is found earlier in the book, prompted, as with numerous other travelers, by a description of the "plain of Mummies" at Saqqara—though Savary relies on others' descriptions of this place and in fact may never have traveled farther south than Giza (Hamilton 2019, 283). He notes that, unlike other authors who attributed the construction of pyramids like those still visible in the Memphis necropolises to the sheer vanity of the kings constructing them, he preferred the explanation of a concern with "what was going to happen after this short life" (Savary 1786, 2:13), a notion for which he refers to Herodotus's book on Egypt. He goes on to relate that the soul would not leave as long as the body was preserved from decay, and that after three thousand years the soul would once again animate the body thus preserved.

This brief exposition thus draws primarily on Herodotus, though without fitting in his idea that the soul must go through a series of animal bodies. Instead, the idea of the soul's lasting as long as the body is preserved is seemingly taken from Servius (possibly by way of some other author, obscuring this genealogy), though with the change that it is a matter of the soul not "leaving" (*quitter*) the body. Even though the soul would thus remain in or near the body, in Savary's understanding it is only after the three thousand years that it would "reanimate" (*reanimer*) the body. While this contradicts details of both Herodotus and Servius, it nonetheless provides an internally consistent explanation of why bodies were preserved, pivoting on the central dogma of the immortality of the soul.

One of Savary's contemporary readers was the poet Jean-Antoine Roucher (1745–94). A pronounced anti-Jacobin, Roucher was arrested in 1793 and incarcerated in the Sainte-Pélagie prison in Paris, a fate he shared with the painter Hubert Robert (1733–1808). In a letter to his daughter, Roucher asks her to get him the copy of Savary's *Lettres sur l'Égypte* to divert the painter, who is unable to practice his art during his imprisonment (Roucher 1797, 20–22). Beyond Savary's more detailed notions of Egyptian immortality, his description of Egypt seems to have evoked in the two prisoners thoughts pertinent to their predicament, notably the question of how human beings facing imminent death can nonetheless live on in the memory of others (Breguet 2007, 60–62).

Gathering the Threads

The accomplishments of Danish antiquarian Georg Zoëga (1755–1809) were highly regarded at his time; yet, as noted by the editors of a recent volume devoted to this scholar, they "fell almost entirely into oblivion with the end of the Enlightenment" (Ascani, Buzi, and Picchi 2015, 1). A convert to Catholicism, Zoëga was charged by Pope Pius VI with studying ancient Egyptian obelisks in Rome. Published only in 1800 (despite the title page carrying the date 1797), but occupying Zoëga at least as early as 1786 (Ciampini 2015, 185n3), the resulting massive book in Latin, *De origine et usu obeliscorum* (The origin and use of obelisks) covered a wide variety of subjects regarding ancient Egyptian culture, well beyond the description and analysis of the type of monuments indicated by its title. However, the book was not only delayed but apparently also difficult for contemporary international readers to get. Thus a detailed anonymous discussion in the Edinburgh periodical *Critical Review* laments not only the delay in the book's publication, but also its very limited availability, noting that "the copies at Rome [where the book was published] were all bought up, before even one found its way hither [to Britain], and that the book is not likely to undergo a re-impression" (Anonymous 1802, 494).

Important for the understanding of Egyptian mortuary religion at the end of the eighteenth century, the book contains a series of chapters relating to this topic (Zoega 1797, 245–312), including notably one chapter on "the doctrine of the Egyptians on the status of the soul after death" (Zoega 1797, 294–312). It is fitting that Zoëga's detailed and erudite discussion brings together most of the main strands of previous scholarship on the eve of the eighteenth century, in a book dated to the year before Napoleon's invasion of Egypt (though as noted, actually appearing only during the occupation) would usher in a new era of more direct, colonial European engagement with Egypt.

Zoëga begins by discussing the variety of human treatments of the dead through the ages, from the complete destruction of bodies to various other practices, based on a wide range of classical and ethnographic sources (Zoega 1797, 245–50), before turning to the practices of the ancient Egyptians. He notes that the Egyptians had perfected an art also practiced by many others of "keeping the bodies of the deceased as incorrupt [*incorrupta*] as possible and passing down the memory of their parents and friends to future times" (Zoega 1797, 250). His point of departure for the specificities of Egyptian embalming practices is, not surprisingly, Herodotus and Diodorus, both of whom are quoted verbatim at length in the original Greek and then in Latin translation (Zoega 1797, 250–57), followed by discussions of the information given in those passages in light of other ancient authors and especially more recent studies of actual specimens brought to Europe, which also allow him to summarize patterns of decoration, use of materials and amulets, and so forth (Zoega 1797, 262). Moving on to discuss the uncertain dates of the beginning and end of the practice of mummification (Zoega 1797, 265), he rejects several previous suggestions regarding the original incentive for the practice, contending that "piety for parents and affection for friends urged them to protect [*servare*] the corpses, particularly since it is the persuasion of most peoples that also after death the soul adheres [*adhaerere*] to the body."

As a point of departure, then, Zoëga posits a widespread cross-cultural belief that souls continue to adhere to bodies as the reason for wanting to embalm, and thus preserve, them. Helped along by the country's arid climate, the Egyptians eventually took this inclination to the extreme, rendering the bodies "eternal" (*aeterna*) and extending the practice to the populace at large (Zoega 1797, 265). In accordance with this understanding of Egyptian mummification as a perfection of a natural inclination, Zoëga goes on to list a number of other cultures, in the Old World as well as the New, that have made some effort to preserve their dead at least for a time, returning also to the topic of various other approaches to dealing with dead bodies (Zoega 1797, 266–74).

The next chapter begins by elaborating the point made more briefly earlier on, according to which the innate human desire for a life after death (*vitae post obitum desiderium*), along with the experience of seeing deceased persons in memories and dreams leads to the notion that the "shadow of the soul" (*umbra animae*) continues to be attached to the body as long as the latter is not destroyed (Zoega 1797, 275–76). For this reason a "chamber" (*cubiculum*) is prepared for the deceased equipped with all manner of necessities of life such as food and clothes, but also sometimes servants or wives. Even among people who believed the soul went to Hades, its fate was understood as being bound up with that of the bodily remains. After these general remarks, including some considerations about the supposed origins of burial practices by placing the deceased in caves, Zoëga returns to the topic of ancient Egyptian burials more specifically (Zoega 1797, 279). From the idea of primitive cave burials, Zoëga suggests that the rock tombs of Thebes exemplify early artificial developments of this practice, citing descriptions by both classical authors and recent travelers, and he goes on to discuss burials at other sites, noting differences in burial practices (Zoega 1797, 280–90). The footnotes to this section contain numerous etymologies of various names and designations citing both Greek and Coptic evidence.

The next, short chapter is devoted to the topic of the judgment of the dead, taking as its point of departure a lengthy quotation of Diodorus's ninety-second chapter describing the judgment episode of the funerary ritual (Zoega 1797, 290–92). Unlike the theological explanations by earlier authors, in some instances even relocating the judgment to the afterlife as seen above, Zoëga's explanation is remarkably practical. He notes that the original practice of keeping the dead in one's house would have gradually become unworkable, both because of the increasing numbers and because of the imperfect conditions for preserving the body from air and moisture. He connects this with the idea from Diodorus that the bodies of deceased relatives were used as security for loans, and that the body could not be buried until the debt had been repaid. This, Zoëga suggests, is the origin of the judgment rite described by Diodorus, since the town prefect would need to make sure all arrears had been settled before allowing a body to be buried in the necropolis. It then became natural to inquire about additional affairs of the deceased's life beyond the strictly financial, and at the major cemeteries, counsels were appointed to take care of these proceedings as their scope expanded (Zoega 1797, 292–93). Despite this highly secular explanation, Zoëga does shift to more religious language at the end of this passage when he describes the consequence of a negative judgment and the resulting prohibition against burial as entailing being "exiled from the domain of Osiris and the quiet republic of the ancestors [*avorum quieta republica*], to be likened to the Elysium of the Greeks, and compelled to stay (*de-*

gere) among the living, although dead" (Zoega 1797, 293). This wording seems to imply that despite its secular origin, Zoëga understands the consequence of being barred from burial as also entailing banishment from the realm of the dead. The chapter ends with a brief note citing the passage from Herodotus according to which persons who had been eaten by a crocodile or who had drowned in the Nile were regarded as being particularly sacred (Zoega 1797, 293–94).

The last of Zoëga's chapters on Egyptian mortuary religion is devoted to the underlying concepts of the soul and its fate in the afterlife. He begins by noting the belief in the underworld (*inferi*) "where Osiris was thought to rule the shadows [*umbris imperare*]," but he also notes that on the one hand the soul was supposed to remain with the corpse, and on the other it was expected to move into new bodies in a process of transmigration (Zoega 1797, 294). By contrast, he explicitly dismisses the idea in recent authors that the Egyptians believed in the resurrection of the body, "of which I find nothing in the ancient authors" (Zoega 1797, 294), and he also warns that ancient writers confused the Egyptian belief in metempsychosis with details taught by Greek philosophers. With this caveat, he turns to Herodotus's passage on metempsychosis, once again quoted in full in the original Greek and translated into Latin (Zoega 1797, 295).

Zoëga reconciles the different ideas about the fate of the soul by combining them into a sequential scenario, in which the soul first descends to the underworld presided over by Osiris and Isis, where its happiness is in accordance with its conduct during life, and once the body decays, the soul returns from the underworld to inhabit a new body (Zoega 1797, 295). Adding further specificity to the Herodotus passage, Zoëga asserts that the soul must travel through the different species in order "from the lowest species of animals to the nobler" (*ab infimis animalium generibus ad nobiliora*) before returning to a human form. It follows from the logic of this scenario that the second human body is a new one, since in Zoëga's model the transmigration starts only once the original human body is destroyed. This raises the question whether the number of such migrations (from human through all species of animals and back to human) is finite or whether it would continue forever—a question to which Zoëga notes we have no answer, though he cites fifth-century BCE Greek poet Pindar for the idea that souls would be allowed to stay in the underworld after completing three perfect cycles of migration (Zoega 1797, 295–98). The following pages discuss how these ideas were in turn transmitted to the Greeks through teachers like Pythagoras and Plato (Zoega 1797, 298–302).

The last part of this chapter concludes Zoëga's discussion of Egyptian mortuary religion by focusing on conceptions of the underworld (Zoega 1797, 302–12). He clarifies that the Egyptians thought the "entire human" (*totum hominem*) descended to the underworld (*inferi*), presided over by Isis and Osiris (Zoega 1797, 302). The former of these Zoëga identifies as the painted figure seen on mummies spreading her wings as mother and protectress. Osiris is likewise identified in ancient imagery, first in the scenes of Ozymandias (Ramesses II) described by Diodorus (1:49), where the king is depicted "as though he were submitting proof before Osiris and his assessors in the underworld that to the end of his days he had lived a life of piety and justice towards both men and gods," and then in depictions on the coffin first studied by Gordon in 1737 (see chapter 4 above), which William Lethieullier had bequeathed to the British Museum in the meantime (EA 6695), and another coffin drawn in Cairo by Carsten Niebuhr (fig. 6; Niebuhr 1774–78, vol. 1, pl. 39), which Zoëga describes in detail. On the first of these coffins, Osiris is shown "holding the office of a judge and promising to reward [*remunerare*] the souls" (Zoega 1797, 304). Referring to Gordon's study, Zoëga understands the weighing scene in front of Osiris as a balancing of "merits and faults" (*merita et delicta*) carried out by two opposing forces, the falcon-headed figure being "the symbol of immortal mind and virtue," while the "dog-head" (*cynoprosopus*) denotes "the inferior soul and sensuous desire (*appetitus*)" (Zoega 1797, 303), combining concepts drawn from the Platonic tradition with ideas from Christian iconography of the Last Judgment, although his exact sources beyond Gordon are not made clear.

Zoëga's interpretation of the pictorial scenes thus remains entirely mythological, with the weighing scene referring to events in the underworld. Unlike later authors (see chapters 6–8 below), he does not make any direct connection to the judgment described by Diodorus and discussed by Zoëga earlier in his book, since this takes place on

Fig. 6: Hieroglyphs and symbols on a mummy coffin. Carsten Niebuhr, *Reisebeschreibung nach Arabien und andern umliegenden Ländern*, vol. I (1774), pl. 39. Universitätsbibliothek Heidelberg.

earth before burial and determines whether the deceased is allowed to go to the underworld in the first place. By contrast, to Zoëga the scene found on coffins shows the judgment the soul undergoes once it arrives there in order to determine the quality of its sojourn in the underworld.

Throughout the discussion, Zoëga refers to the idea that Osiris was a human being who was deified and became ruler of the underworld after his own death. He also notes the alternative appellation of Osiris as Serapis, whose name in Egyptian he interprets to mean "father of shadows" (*pater tenebrarum*) (Zoega 1797, 306). In connection with the cult of the Apis bull, Zoëga discusses the ritual descent to the underworld that celebrates the legendary feat of King Rhampsinthus (Herodotus, *Histories*, 2:122). In this ritual the blindfolded priest is led by two "wolves," and Zoëga points out the frequency with which this animal is depicted on mummies and coffins, being associated with the underworld because of its nocturnal nature (Zoega 1797, 307–8).

At the end of the chapter, Zoëga explicates his understanding of the apparently diverging ideas about the fate of the dead, notably the stay in the underworld with rewards and punishment, against the notion of metempsychosis. As I noted above, his overall solution consists in making these ideas different stages in a sequence, but he also points out that this was a priestly compromise to reconcile the learned idea of metempsychosis with the popular opinion that the soul would depart to a new body only once the old one became corrupted (Zoega 1797, 310–11). He cites Servius for the latter notion and Herodotus for the idea of metempsychosis and briefly compares the idea described by Herodotus to the metempsychosis taught by Greek philosophers. Notably, while later thinkers understand the nature of the body into which the soul transmigrates as being a reward or punishment, to the Egyptians transgressions were punished by barring the deceased from the grave and from the kingdom of Osiris (*arceretur a sepultura et a regno Osiridis*), or in less serious cases by acts of cleansing before embalming or in the underworld. But for the most part, the underworld existence was a happy one that the Egyptians wanted to prolong by preserving and protecting the corpses "so that no event would disturb those who rested with Osiris [*qui cum Osiride quiescerent*]" (Zoega 1797, 312).

Conclusion

Zoëga's discussion explicates important assumptions and underlying considerations that are absent or implicit in much of the earlier scholarship. His vision of Egyptian religion is explicitly universalist: ancient

Egyptian funerary practices are simply one reaction, albeit in some ways extreme, to universal human ideas and experiences concerning death. While universalist, his understanding differs markedly from the "universal history" approaches of the previous century or the more contemporary interpretations of traditions of hidden wisdom and initiation. His emphasis is not on how particular ideas were diffused to or from the ancient Egyptians; rather, what is of interest is the common human background that led the Egyptians in one direction and other cultures in more or less markedly different ones. As such, Zoëga's approach is also secular, at least overtly so. Unlike other authors, some very close to his own time, he does not aim to determine in what theological respects the ancient Egyptians were right or wrong; he seeks to understand what they did against the background of universal human experiences. Explicit comparisons with, or deployment of, specific Christian concepts like resurrection of the body or the Last Judgment are largely absent.

Nonetheless, from the perspective of this book it is clear that many of the "universal" concepts are in fact couched in remarkably Christian terms of "body and soul," "eternity," and such. Similarly, the ideas taken over from previous scholarship, such as the emphasis on judgment, rewards, and punishments, carry with them the Christian models that first inspired them. Engaging more closely with the source material than most previous discussions, Zoëga's book takes an important step toward mapping such ideas onto the ancient source material, notably depictions of mythological scenes. The method of attaching specific traditional ideas to concrete Egyptian imagery, then quite new, would become a dominant approach in the following century. Although specific details of his understanding of the scene of weighing the heart would be questioned in the nineteenth century, his idea that Osiris acts as a "judge" and that the Egyptian imagery of weighing represents a judgment between dueling principles of virtue and vice signifies an important step toward an entrenchment where ideas of postmortem judgment are no longer purely abstract, textual ideas derived interpretively from classical authors. Now they are projected onto concrete ancient Egyptian images, which can in turn be used didactically to illustrate Egyptian beliefs.

SIX

Invasion and Aftermath: 1798–1822

While Zoëga's volume on obelisks was still in publication, a French expeditionary force led by General Napoleon Bonaparte invaded Egypt in July 1798, completely changing the circumstances of European engagement with Egypt, both ancient and modern (e.g., Cole 2007). It is no exaggeration, then, when Donald Malcolm Reid notes that "Egyptology was born amid violence, imperialism, and Anglo-French rivalry" (Reid 1997, 31). The immediate geopolitical motivation behind the invasion was to disrupt British colonial interests in India and the Mediterranean, though intellectually it was shored up as an Enlightenment project of "exploration" by tasking a commission of 151 scholars from various fields with describing the natural and cultural history of the country (Prochaska 1994; Godlewska 1995; Bret 2019; Sarfatti 2022). While the scope and access afforded by a large-scale military invasion were unprecedented, intellectually the project had deep roots in French orientalism of the preceding century (Laurens 1987).

Among the first publications resulting from Napoleon's invasion was an account by artist and antiquarian Dominique-Vivant Denon (1747–1825; cf. Carré 1932, 1:117–41), who had taken part in the invasion with the task of documenting and collecting Egyptian artifacts (cf. Moore 2002). In his travelogue *Voyage de la Basse et la Haute Égypte* (Denon 1802), he does not address ancient Egyptian mortuary religion as an overarching concern, and though he cites classical authors on occasion (e.g., Herodotus on the construction of Khufu's pyramid; Denon 1802, 1:63), he does not draw on their discussions of such topics as embalming and mortuary beliefs. He does, however, touch on the topic a few times in his commentary on the numerous plates of Egyptian antiquities in the work's second volume.

One of Denon's plates depicts an illustrated funerary papyrus written in hieratic script (Denon 1802, vol. 2, pl. 136), which he identifies as a "manuscript found in the wrappings of a mummy" (Denon 1802, 1:309), although his analysis of the offering scenes reproduced in the plate does not connect the imagery to this funerary context. Another plate reproduces the twelfth hour of the Amduat on a funerary papyrus (Denon 1802, vol. 2, pl. 137). In his description and interpretation of the imagery, Denon notes that the subject seems to be a mortuary ceremony (*cérémonie mortuaire*), and that the mummy in a boat in the lower register is traversing a river, "perhaps the Styx" (Denon 1802, 1;311). Other than this association that would imply an Egyptian origin for the Greek notion of crossing the Styx roughly along the lines of ideas expressed by Diodorus and others, Denon does not provide many details about how he understands the relevance of the scene.

The final plate of the volume reproduces a weighing of the heart scene from a much longer Book of the Dead manuscript found at Thebes. Denon notes that for him this vignette holds considerable interest and emphasizes that he himself engraved it very carefully for the volume, using a system of striation at different angles to convey the painted colors (Denon 1802, 1:313). He proposes that the human figures with animal heads depicted on the papyrus represent people wearing masks, "outward signs indicating dignity associated with degrees of initiation and worn by the initiated during ceremonies." Accordingly, the persons without such marks of distinction are suggested to be "an aspirant" or "young ones" (Denon 1802, 1:314). The scene of the balance is understood as referring to the "equilibrium of waters," and the subsidiary figures are understood in the same vein, with the rationale that "it is always to obtain water that one prays in Egypt, because it is always water which produces everything there" (Denon 1802, 1:314). In other words, unlike Zoëga he interprets this scene not in a funerary vein, but rather in an initiatory, more generally religious one.

The same is true in another publication resulting, albeit less directly, from Napoleon's invasion: the discussion and engraved copy of a Book of the Dead manuscript (now Bibliothèque nationale de France, égyptien 1–19) bought by the engineer Simmonel, who in turn sent it to mine inspector Jean-Marcel Cadet (1751–1835). Cadet presented the results of his study of the papyrus at a public session of the Society for Agriculture, Sciences, and Arts in 1805 and published his paper along with notes by other scholars and an engraved copy of the images in the manuscript (Cadet 1805). The most prominent vignette on the papyrus is a large version of the weighing of the heart (fig. 7), and Cadet's interpretation of this image sets the tone for his understanding of the composition as a whole. There is no indication that Cadet had read Zoëga's interpretation of the weighing scene, and indeed, as noted above, his volume may not have been widely available outside Rome, its place of publication. Although taking the same point of departure as Zoëga in regarding the scene as one of judgment, rather than understanding it as relating to a postmortem assessment, Cadet suggests that "based on passages from Critias, from Timaeus reported by Plato, and by those of Herodotus, Plutarch, Diodorus of Sicily, Horapollon, Marcellinus, etc.," one can conjecture that the scene of the weighing of the heart shows "an assembly of judges without hands, a judgement, or rather an initiation into the mysteries of Isis, and the trial by blood undergone by the initiand" (Cadet 1805). Images in the later part of the papyrus are interpreted as representing various astronomical phenomena. Unfortunately, the vague references to multiple ancient authors do not make it clear precisely how Cadet understands the imagery or how the classical authors inform the interpretation. None of the authors mentioned seem to lead directly to an understanding relating to the "mysteries of Isis" and initiation, though other writers like Apuleius and, much closer in time, Terrasson might have exerted an unstated influence in this direction. Be that as it may, Cadet provides another example of an understanding of the weighing of the heart scene along nonmortuary lines that would soon fall outside mainstream interpretations.

On the eve of the eighteenth century, Arnold Hermann Ludwig Heeren (1760–1842; cf. Blanke 1983), a student of Heyne's who would be appointed professor of history in Göttingen a few years later in 1799, published a work titled *Politics, Trade, and Commerce in the Ancient World* that became highly influential well into the following century.

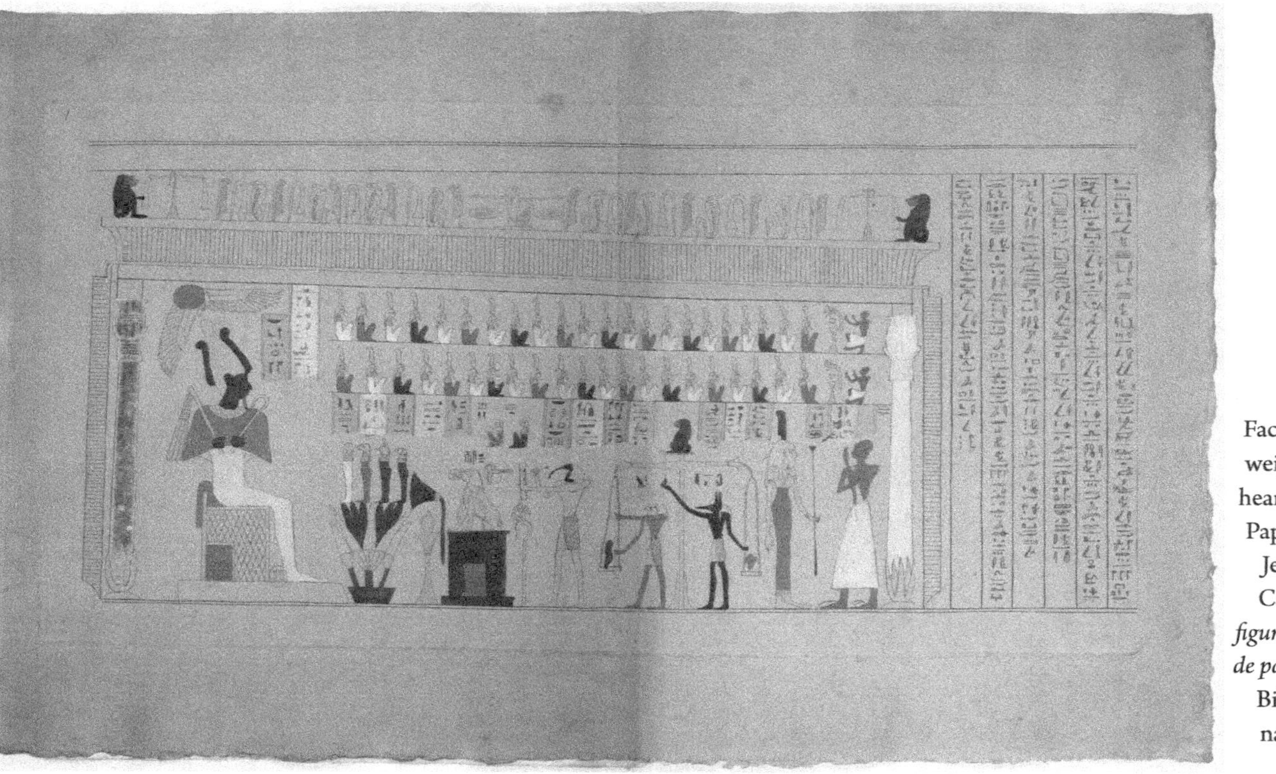

Fig. 7: Facsimile of the weighing of the heart scene from Papyrus Cadet. Jean-Marcel Cadet, *Copie figurée d'un roleau de papyrus* (1805). Bibliothèque nationale de France.

The work, which was published in new editions during the first decades of the nineteenth century and eventually in an English translation appearing in the 1830s (cf. Gange 2013, 80), was innovative in its focus, as indicated by the title, on the intersection of economic and political history. As such, mortuary religion is not a major emphasis, but this topic is discussed briefly as holding some interest in relation to social groups, not least the "priestly caste [*Priestercaste*]," playing an important role in Heeren's social model of ancient Egypt. As is discussed in more detail below, the second and subsequent editions of the book engage directly with Denon's plates and interpretations, which makes it expedient to discuss Heeren's interpretations at this point. The references given are to the second German edition (Heeren 1804).

Heeren begins his discussion by pointing out the immense importance for private citizens, as well as for public administrators, of the Egyptian conceptions of "continued existence after death" (*Fortdauer nach dem Tode*) (Heeren 1804, 670), which warrants discussing the topic in the context of the book. He immediately goes on to note that while all writers agree that the Egyptians held such beliefs, it is less straightforward to determine more specifically what those beliefs were. Heeren begins his discussion of this topic by quoting Herodotus on the transmigration of souls, and he points out that the passage clearly implies that the human body inhabited after the cycle of transmigration is not the original, but rather a new one (Heeren 1804, 671). Immediately, however, this idea seems to be at odds both with the practices of the "preservation" (*Erhaltung*) of the body through mummification and entombment, on the one hand, and with the concepts of an underworld or Hades on the other. Unlike additive approaches such as Zoëga's, Heeren argues that the approaches are so contradictory as to be impossible to reconcile. In the second and subsequent editions of the work, he refers to Zoëga's attempt to reconcile these ideas by assuming a sequential model, but he questions the logic of transmigration's taking place only once the body has decomposed, since, as he notes, "the body was embalmed in such a manner as to never decay" (Heeren 1804, 672).

To solve this problem, Heeren suggests a scenario in line with his sociopolitical interests: that the different teachings and practices stem from different social groups, with the doctrine of metempsychosis as a "priestly religion" (*Priesterreligion*), as opposed to a "popular religion" (*Volksreligion*) (Heeren 1804, 672). As seen above, this idea is also present in earlier authors such as De Pauw. By contrast, Heeren sees the popular beliefs as underlying Diodorus's passage about tombs as eternal abodes, which he proceeds to quote, noting that this passage holds the "key to one of the most important parts of Egyptian antiquity" (Heeren 1804, 673).

What Heeren has in mind is the importance of the continuance of the body and the influence of this notion on "practical life." He sees this as a "coarse popular concept" (*roher Volksbegriff*) (Heeren 1804, 675) of the identity of body and person—an idea that may then in turn be elaborated philosophically in one way or another. Correspondingly, it becomes possible to explain the practice of mummification: "Who can help seeing that everything must depend on this preparation [*Bereitung*], which secured the body's permanence [*Fortdauer*] not merely for some time, but—insofar as it was not subjected to violent destruction—forever?" (Heeren 1804, 675).

Tombs were created for the related purpose of securing places of habitation (*Wohnungen*) for the dead, and the Egyptians were aided in this by the presence of cliffs bordering the Nile Valley where such constructions could conveniently be made. Another element of this "natural" conception was that the future life was seen as a continuation of the present, so people were mostly buried in family tombs whose decoration included scenes of both "religion and domestic life" (Heeren 1804, 677–78).

Heeren sees another idea following naturally from the practice of building tombs on the edge of the desert—the notion of a "realm of the dead [*Todtenreich*]" (Heeren 1804, 679), onto which the expectations of the continuance of the present life were projected to people it with gods, inhabitants, and animals. Though not originally part of this basic conception, it became possible to add onto it the notion of postmortem punishments and rewards (*Strafen und Belohnungen*) administered by the judges in the underworld (Heeren 1804, 681), simply by expanding the idea of a parallel society in the realm of the dead. Because of this hypothesized secular origin of the idea, Heeren stresses that the notion of postmortem judgment is thus fundamentally different from "what it is among us [*wie bey uns*]" (Heeren 1804, 682). To bring out this difference, Heeren emphasizes the practical aspects of Diodorus's description—unlike many other authors who either focus on the ethical aspects or leave it deliberately vague whether the judgment takes place among the living or in the beyond. To Heeren, projecting the judgment to the realm of the dead is thus a later, secondary interpretation of the social institution determining the right to burial (683). It is the latter that is depicted in scenes like the one analyzed by Zoëga, and the one published by Denon—Heeren notes explicitly that Denon's interpretation of the weighing of the heart as an initiation ritual is thus "completely wrong" (*ganz falsch*) (Heeren 1804, 684). In other words, the origin of the notion of postmortem judgment is entirely different and relates from the outset to the right to remain in the realm of the dead, but Heeren nonetheless admits the possibility that in time new associations were formed that "more closely approximated our concepts of postmortem rewards and punishments" (Heeren 1804, 685).

Heeren's discussion, not surprisingly given its cross-cultural context, thus proceeds in quite a different manner than most other contemporary discussions of Egyptian mortuary religion (with Zoëga as a notable exception). Rather than describing exotic beliefs or approximating Egyptian religion to Christianity, he takes as his point of departure universal human experiences, especially the identity between body and person. He proceeds to show how the main elements of Egyptian mortuary religion can be produced deductively from this basic idea, as long as Herodotus's notion of metempsychosis is removed from the equation by understanding it as the result of learned priestly speculation. This leads to the interesting, if somewhat ironic, result that the Egyptian postmortem judgment (first constructed, as has been seen above, by a combination of Christian eschatology with a particular interpretation of Diodorus's account) is explicitly contrasted to the corresponding idea in Christianity. To Heeren, the former simply results from projecting the affairs of this life into the afterlife, and thus any similarity to the Christian ethical judgment resulting in rewards and punishments is a secondary development.

This deductive approach sets Heeren apart from most scholars interested more specifically in ancient Egypt, who instead tend to approach

Egyptian mortuary religion through a combination of classical sources, Egyptian monuments, and received convention. Nonetheless, because Heeren was so widely read and discussed, his ideas became influential in this area as well. In particular, the idea that one could obtain a much tidier model of Egyptian mortuary religion by sidelining Herodotus's description of metempsychosis as priestly speculation would become pivotal during the nineteenth century.

The first volume of the *Description de l'Égypte* was published in Paris in 1809, containing detailed descriptions and illustrations of a number of Upper Egyptian sites (cf. Carré 1932, 1:156–60). Of particular interest for our purposes is the lengthy discussion by the work's eventual editor and prolific contributor, Edme-François Jomard (1777–1862; cf. Carré 1932, 1:161; Grinevald 2014; Sarfatti 2022, 117–23, 191–202) of the Theban necropolis (Jomard 1809). As an "engineer-geographer" (i.e., surveyor) educated at the technical college École des ponts et chausées in Paris, Jomard's work in Egypt was focused on surveying and topography, but tasked with editing the *Description* as a whole after the demise of two predecessors in the role, he ended up contributing to a wide range of topics.

Jomard begins his discussion of the Theban necropolis by outlining the general architecture and decoration of the Theban rock tombs, using the wall paintings to address habits, dress, tools, and the like, often with comparisons to those of modern Egypt. Next he describes the various objects found in the tomb, not least mummified human and animal bodies, using the former not only in elucidating the embalming techniques employed, but also to contribute to the ongoing debate about the racial characteristics of the ancient Egyptians that would become more prominent later in the century (e.g., Challis 2013; Riggs 2014, esp. 70–76). In his discussion of the interpretation of other grave goods found in the tombs, Jomard warns against "the common fault of antiquaries who have often made bold decisions in these obscure questions" (355), preferring to proceed by more descriptive means.

Jomard particularly emphasizes the importance of "papyrus manuscripts that were found intact in the mummies of Thebes" (357). On one of these he identifies a particular scene discussed by previous scholars: the weighing of the heart. Unlike Denon and Cadet, but continuing in the tradition of Zoëga (though without referring to the interpretations of any of these scholars), Jomard suggests that in all probability the scene depicts the judgment of the soul (*jugement de l'ame*) of the person at the right of the scene, although he also indicates by his wording (Isis "presented by a woman dressed like the goddess" and "masked priests") that he understands the scene as a representation of some ritual rather than mythological depictions of the deities themselves (363). In an influential inference, he deduces that if the weighing scene thus depicts an Egyptian equivalent to the Last Judgment, it stands to reason that the many other images in the papyrus "might indicate the trials which the soul of the dead is meant to undergo before the judgment which would determine his fate [*fixoit son sort*]" (364). Apart from pointing out a few details of particular interest, Jomard does not speculate further on how the vignettes might conform more specifically to this interpretation. It is worth noting that similar interpretations were presented elsewhere in the *Description* as well, for example, by the engineers Jollois and Devilliers (1809, 165–68), who use Zoëga's model directly to interpret the weighing of the heart scene in the "Temple of Isis" at Dayr al-Madīnah (later studied also by Champollion, as discussed in the following chapter) as a judgment of the soul of the deceased, weighing the good deeds against the wicked deeds.

This approach to funerary papyri is novel and would have significant influence (whether directly through Jomard or by scholars arriving independently at the same chain of inference), so it is worth outlining its suppositions and its relation to previous ideas. As indicated by the discussions of Zoëga, Denon, and Cadet, around the turn of the century the scene of weighing the heart had taken on increasing importance for understanding Egyptian mortuary religion. Zoëga combined the idea with a number of other sources to create a complex model of mortuary religion, while Denon and Cadet went in the direction of understanding it as an initiation ritual, which would accord it a less central role for the understanding and illustration of Egyptian mortuary religion. By contrast, Jomard does not overtly cite any classical discussions and simply takes over Zoëga's idea that the scene provides pictorial evidence of the postmortem judgment that had become more and more firmly established in the literature of the previous centuries. This move would become increasingly popular through the nineteenth century, whereby the scaffolding of the classical authors is removed, leaving the conclusions originally drawn from combining these sources with expectations from Christian eschatology. By applying this framework to concrete motifs and sources, one gets the impression that the interpretations emerge naturally from the sources themselves. Only detailed examination of how these interpretations came about during the preceding centuries allows us to see the inner workings and suppositions of this interpretive move.

Moving beyond the weighing scene itself, Jomard suggests that if the weighing of the heart thus depicts the final judgment of the soul, the rest of the imagery in the Book of the Dead should depict the trials leading there. In its specificity this is a new idea, since the classical authors do not give any particular reason to suppose there would be such postmortem trials and tribulations in the first place. However, eighteenth-century thinking about ancient Egyptian initiation was certainly influential here, and as seen above, the distinction between death and initiation was frequently blurred. Against this background there is only a small interpretive step from Cadet's "initiation into the mysteries of Isis" to Jomard's suggestion that a deceased Egyptian needed to go through a series of trials similar to those Terrasson's Séthos faced under the pyramid. Indeed, the hypothesis seems to fit the Book of the Dead imagery fairly well: not only could one imagine a broad range of things happening in the beyond in the Egyptian mind, but the prevalence in the imagery of religious activities such as worship and sacrifice appears to fit such an underworld journey with initiatory inspirations reasonably well. Thus, for example, the imagery of what is now known as the vignette to chapter 110 (fig. 9) of the Book of the Dead is understood as one of a series of tasks or "stations" beginning with the depicted agricultural work and followed by ritual acts of sacrifice and arrival at a series of temple gates to finally reach the judgment shown by the weighing of the heart (Jomard 1809, 367).

Jomard's interpretation thus distinguishes itself from most earlier scholarship by how much it draws on Egyptian images, but also, consequently, by the increasingly concrete conception of the details of the Egyptian afterlife. Until this point there had been a certain reluctance to make detailed description of what the afterlife the Egyptians desired actually looked like, certainly due in part simply to the paucity of evidence suitable for such a reconstruction, but also paralleling a general theological resistance in Christianity to detailed descriptions of heaven (e.g., McDannell and Lang 1988, 145–80; McManners 1981, 130–33; Marshall 2002, 188–231; Sawicki 2002, 41–55). In popular Christian conceptions of the eighteenth and early nineteenth centuries, this lack of concreteness and specificity in conceiving the afterlife had begun to change with Swedish visionary Emanuel Swedenborg's (1688–1772) visions of heaven, resulting, as Colleen McDannell and Bernhard Lang argue, in "a radical realignment of the Christian concept of heaven" (McDannell and Lang 1988, 181). This "modern" conception of heaven presented a sharp contrast to conventional imagination and in turn it held a number of features that would come to characterize popular nineteenth-century Christian notions, and hence the model of the ancient Egyptian afterlife developed during the same time. A notable feature of this new conception is a focus on individuals and their experience and spiritual development in the afterlife (cf., e.g., Rowell 1974; Wheeler 1994; Sawicki 2002). Jomard's influential suggestion of an afterlife journey in the beyond that he understood to be depicted in the Book of the Dead forms part of the new, anthropocentric conception of the hereafter that would increasingly be applied to traditional interpretations of the ancient Egyptian afterlife. At this point it is worth noting this backdrop to the increasingly concrete and specific conceptions of the Egyptian afterlife based on ancient imagery and the way it interacted with eighteenth-century notions of initiatory journeys to shape the interpretation of the newly available funerary papyri. I will return to the more specific effect of nineteenth-century concepts of heaven when I discuss Lepsius's seminal interpretation of the Book of the Dead in the next chapter.

While the implications of this line of thought becomes crucial in later interpretations, as Jomard shows in dealing with "some remarkable symbols" in the tomb paintings, the idea of metempsychosis, although not strictly necessary for his interpretation of funerary papyri, is still very much part of his framework. In discussing the difficulties involved in interpreting the meaning of ancient Egyptian symbols, Jomard explicitly uses the notion of metempsychosis as an example of "a conjecture

Fig. 8: Weighing scene from the tomb of Ramesses VI as drawn by Jomard. Edme-François Jomard, *Description de l'Egypte*, Antiquités, Planches, vol. 2 (1812), pl. 83. Universitätsbibliothek Heidelberg.

that is isolated, yet founded on the testimony of serious authors, on the nature of an authentic and well-studied monument, and finally on ideas generally attributed to the Egyptian nation" (Jomard 1809, 377), and thus gains great cogency. What has hitherto been missing in the case of Egyptian metempsychosis, Jomard argues, is the connection to concrete ancient monuments. He proposes to find this connection generally in the symbolism of the scarab:

> Regeneration of beings, animated nature not perishing through the dissolution of its parts, or dying only to take on new life in another form, this was the fundamental idea at the basis of the doctrine of the transmigration of souls, and the scarab portrayed this generative faculty, always acting, always surviving death. (Jomard 1809, 377–78)

Jomard returns to the funerary papyrus to examine a number of scenes (again referred to as "stations" in accordance with his interpretation of the images as giving a sequential account of a postmortem journey) that feature scarab imagery. In these concrete cases, he understands the scarab once again as a "symbol of regeneration, of the new life the figure seeks in some way to *grasp*" (Jomard 1809, 379; emphasis in the original).

Jomard ultimately emphasizes one scene in particular that would come to be regarded as the locus classicus for demonstrating Egyptian metempsychosis based on monuments through the next several decades. The scene comes from what is now known as the thirty-third scene of the Book of Gates (cf. Manassa 2006) in the version from the tomb of Ramesses VI (KV 9), illustrated in a drawing by Jomard himself in the plates of the *Description* (fig. 8). Given the presence of the seated god on the left and the balance in front of him, Jomard quickly concludes that it is another version of the same motif as that found on funerary papyri—"the judgment of souls" (*jugement des ames*; Jomard 1809, 379). Of particular interest is the imagery in the upper right of the scene, which sets this version apart. Here one sees a boat containing a pig (or possibly a hippopotamus, as Jomard notes) chased by one baboon and led by another, both carrying sticks. Jomard was particularly struck by this image as providing the direct proof of Egyptian metempsychosis that had long been missing:

> When I first saw this painting on site, it seemed to me that this was the striking image of the transmigration of souls into the bodies of animals; and whatever study of it I have made afterwards, I confess that nothing has presented itself to my mind that appears more probable. I think it can be interpreted in the following manner: The god has just judged a soul, he found it guilty, and he condemned it to *return* to earth to inhabit the body of a swine or a hippopotamus. (Jomard 1809, 380; emphasis in the original)

He notes further that the Egyptian version of the Greek Hermes Psychopompos who guides the souls of the dead to the underworld, that is to say the Egyptian god Thoth, could appear in the form of a baboon. Jomard also refers to a hieroglyph of a man with blood spurting from his head under the enthroned god, asking "was this not one of these guilty ones [*coupables*] the judgment of whom was represented in our scene, since the souls of the wicked were to pass into the bodies of foul or fierce animals?" (Jomard 1809, 381). The implication of this connection is that the decapitated figure shows the fate of the body of the transgressor, while the imagery above represents the fate of the corresponding soul.

Similarly, Jomard interprets the "hawk with a human face" (*épervier à face humaine*) hovering above Osiris as having a role relating to "regeneration and the transformation of the body." More specifically, he proposes that this figure is to represent "the journey [*trajet*] of a human soul traversing heavenly spaces in order to go and animate a new body," referring to Plato's *Phaedro* for the idea that souls undergoing metempsychosis had wings, allowing them to fly through space (Jomard 1809, 381). Note that the human-headed birds in the upper left of the scene are from the modern point of view a misinterpretation of four upside-down hartebeest heads (cf. Manassa 2006, 117–20), reinterpreted in the plate of the *Description*. However, since for a long time this plate would be scholars' main access to the scene, this version would be depended on as the authoritative interpretation, so that the row of human-headed birds was accepted as a well-established fact.

This empirical anchoring of already established interpretive concepts in ancient monuments is of utmost importance for the dominant modes of thinking about Egyptian mortuary religion in the nineteenth century (and beyond). It is worth noting the two main sources for interpreting Egyptian imagery. As seen especially in the transmigration scene, classical authors continue to play an important role in inspiring interpretations. At the same time, as shown by Jomard's interpretation of Book of the Dead vignettes, the idea of the judgment of the dead in the underworld might at one time have been anchored in a specific reinterpretation of Diodorus's description of the funerary ritual, but by the nineteenth century it had become partly a conventional understanding of Egyptian religion and partly an intuitive idea that simply seemed reasonable to expect from a people so invested in burial practices (inspired ultimately by the Christian notion of postmortem judgment). A case of source amnesia was gradually presenting itself, and scholars increasingly assumed that the interpretations arose naturally from the newly discovered Egyptian imagery.

The topic of metempsychosis and its connection to the observable monuments returns in the following chapter of the same volume of the *Description*, Louis Costaz's (1767–1842) description of the royal tombs at Thebes (Costaz 1809). A mathematician originally tasked with leading one of the two commissions setting out in 1799 to document the antiquities of Upper Egypt, Costaz headed the initial exploration of the Theban necropolis. In this capacity he gave descriptive designations to some of the major tombs the commission explored, which appeared in his published contribution discussing the royal tombs at the site.

Costaz thus explicitly names what is now known as the tomb of Ramesses VI (KV 9), in which the scene Jomard discussed occurs, as the "Catacomb of metempsychosis" (*catacombe de la métempsycose*) (Costaz 1809, 407). His discussion of the scene largely follows Jomard, who, judging from the wording in his own chapter, seems to have originated it. Costaz adds a few more details, including that the figures standing at the stairs before the enthroned god have "passed the Styx" and are now approaching the "formidable tribunal" (*redoutable tribunal*) (Costaz 1809, 408). He adds a further spatial observation in that the barque carrying the pig is facing the opposite direction from the humans to be judged below, corroborating that it is returning to earth.

Another, more complex wall scene from the Book of the Earth (part

A) in the same tomb is interpreted in the same vein, expressing "the necessity of dying, the grief that accompanies a recent death, the descent to the realm of shadows (*séjour ténébreux*) where the souls are to stay after death, and the return to the upper regions" (Costaz 1809, 409). Based on these two scenes, Costaz notes that the importance of the "dogma of the transmigration of souls" is clear and that the name given to the tomb is thus well deserved.

Recent scholarship has tended in general to downplay the importance of the *Description* as a watershed moment in the history of Egyptology (e.g., Reid 1997, 31; Bednarski 2005, 95–96), especially in relation to older heroic narratives that tended to take Napoleon's (at least in part retrospective) scholarly justifications of the invasion at face value. As we saw above in this chapter and the previous one, it is certainly true that the new, empirical mode of approaching Egypt can be seen earlier in the eighteenth century as well, rather than being engendered ex nihilo by the publications resulting from the French invasion. Nonetheless, as far as European understanding of ancient Egyptian mortuary religion is concerned, the *Description* held significant importance in bridging the gap between this relatively recent interest in, and availability of, empirical data from ancient Egypt on the one hand and the authority of the classical authors on the other. More specifically, the notion that funerary papyri contained literal descriptions of a journey through the Egyptian afterlife would prove highly successful and remarkably long-lived, and the judgment scene from the Book of Gates came to provide what had hitherto been a conspicuously missing link between Herodotus's description of ancient Egyptian beliefs in the transmigration of the soul and Egyptian monuments. The effect of the *Description* was not, however, either universal or immediate.

As an example of this, in 1816 French autodidact archaeologist Marie Alexandre Lenoir (1761–1839) returned to the Book of the Dead manuscript made available by Cadet, publishing a lengthy speculative interpretation (Lenoir 1816) that shows the influence of Denon's understanding of the weighing of the heart and naturally drew on Cadet's publication as well, but does not show influence from the new ideas expressed in the *Description*. Lenoir's interpretation of the papyrus builds on controversial ideas he had previously laid out in a sixteen-page pamphlet published in 1812 (Lenoir 1812). The pamphlet poses two critical questions in reaction to Diodorus and his later reception: whether the Egyptians had a tribunal judging kings after their death, and whether the pyramids were intended as tombs for kings. Both are answered no.

Regarding the first, Lenoir is skeptical in the first instance about who would have instituted the practice of passing judgment over kings (he does not address the idea in Diodorus that ordinary people were also meant to undergo such a judgment), and he goes on to cite various cases, from the Egyptian king Amasis, who was so unjust that he was assassinated by his successor yet was still buried, to the infamy Louis XIV gained from revoking the Edict of Nantes (cf. Thibaut-Payen 1977, 178–95, and chapter 2 above for the implementation of the edict), ending an era of official tolerance of Protestants. On the second question, Lenoir does not find it credible that the pyramids were royal tombs, among other reasons because no kings had in fact been found to be buried in them. Instead, he suggests that the Great Pyramid must be the tomb of Osiris, whom he understands as the sun god. The pyramid is thus a monument of the solar cult intended to receive the sun when it sets.

In the larger book on Cadet's papyrus, Lenoir begins by stating his fundamental understanding of Egyptian mortuary religion based on the concept of metempsychosis, to which he also adds a conception of "purgation of the souls [*purgation des âmes*] after death" (Lenoir 1816, 7). However, unlike the authors of the *Description*, he does not see this idea as being prevalent in the funerary papyrus. Instead, he understands the imagery in largely astronomical and mythological terms, and the weighing scene at the manuscript's beginning is interpreted along the broad lines Denon suggests as representing "the opening of the year under the sign of the Balance [Libra]," with imagery expressing the inundation of the Nile (Lenoir 1816, 16). While this mode of interpretation means that mortuary religion does not become a significant concern in the book, Lenoir nonetheless includes a lengthy footnote running across several pages presenting a stand-alone treatise titled "Observations on the Egyptian Mummies and Tombs" (Lenoir 1816, 34–41). Here he sharpens the argument in the previous work considerably: "I have said: *The pyramids of Egypt were not meant to serve as tombs for the kings*; I may add: *There are no Egyptian tombs*" (Lenoir 1816, 39; emphasis in the original).

The point of his denial of Egyptian funerary practices and alternative interpretations in an astronomical vein has to do with Lenoir's larger, universalist project (Schwartz 2016) drawing inspirations not only from Masonic ideas, but especially from French scholar Charles Dupuis's (1742–1809) controversial thoughts about the commonalities of all human cultures originating in natural phenomena (cf. Buchwald and Josefowicz 2010, 47–69). Thus in other works he was interested in drawing wide-ranging parallels both between ancient cultures, and with the Christian faith. Of interest for present purposes is thus not only his selective use of contemporary sources, but especially the idea that for Lenoir, the funerary aspects of ancient Egyptian culture were so specific that they needed to be fundamentally denied for such a universalist project to include Egypt.

Leaving Lenoir's idiosyncrasies, a more telling example of the generally accepted understanding of Egyptian mortuary religion on the eve of the decipherment of hieroglyphs is offered by two papers published in 1819 by English polymath Thomas Young. Young is known best in histories of Egyptology as having played a crucial role as a precursor to, and rival of, Champollion in the process of deciphering the hieroglyphic script (Buchwald and Josefowicz 2020). Of particular interest for our topic, Young offers an example of the way ancient monuments were increasingly understood in the light of classical authors (and vice versa). As seen above, an increasing number of copies of Book of the Dead manuscripts, and especially the scene of the weighing of the heart, had come to the knowledge of Europeans in the wake of the French invasion, and in the *Description*, Jomard had cemented the significance of such scenes as a depiction of the Egyptian equivalent of the Last Judgment. It was also noted above that during this process, the fact had largely been forgotten that the conventional concept of Egyptian postmortem judgment based on which the ancient scene had first been interpreted had originally been developed from a somewhat loose reading of Diodorus's description of funerary rituals as events in the afterlife. This meant that the weighing of the heart scene could now be compared *against* Diodorus's description to determine the accuracy of the latter. This is precisely what Young did, albeit in a slightly unlikely place.

In January 1819, Young presented a paper at the Royal Society of London on probability calculations, titled "Remarks on the Probabilities of Error in Physical Observations, and on the Density of the Earth, Considered Especially with Regard to the Reduction of Experiments on the Pendulum" (Young 1819). As one might expect from the title, much of the paper deals with technical mathematical calculations, but Young's other area of expertise, ancient Egypt, surfaces as part of one of his arguments. Young notes that, in principle, if a number of persons between 2 and 100 were gathered on some business, and if a person correctly reports the number of participants in the meeting, "the chances must be about 100 to 1 that a person reporting it truly must have some good information" (Young 1819, 83). Young goes on to point out that one manuscript of Diodorus's text gives the number of judges at the ritual tribunal as forty-two, and that this is also the number of figures presented "as judges assisting Osiris" in a number of ancient manuscripts that depict the judgment of the deceased. From this, Young (1819, 83) argues, several conclusions can be drawn that mutually strengthen the two sources of evidence:

> It is therefore perfectly fair to conclude from this undeniable coincidence, that we might venture to bet 100 to 1, that the manuscript in question is in general more accurate than the others which have been collated; that Diodorus Siculus was a well informed and faithful historian; that the graphical representations and inscriptions in question do relate to some kind of judgment; and lastly, that the hieroglyphical numbers, found in the rolls of papyrus, have been truly interpreted.

Young's point is precisely that sometimes probabilities in historical research can be quantified with some precision, and that to make this argument it is naturally necessary to focus on the similarities between the two sources for which an authentic connection is argued. As such, Young does not address the issue that Diodorus explicitly describes a funerary ritual, while as seen above, the interpretation of the weighing of the heart was increasingly that of events taking place in the afterlife. This tension is carried over into Young's lengthy *Encyclopaedia Britannica* entry on Egypt published the same year (cited here in the 1824 version; Young 1824 [1819]).

Among the many topics the entry covers, Egyptian mortuary religion does not play a major role. The relative reliability of classical authors, on the other hand, is a topic of some interest. As in his Royal Society paper, Young again uses the example of Diodorus's funerary ceremony as an illustration of the veracity of the author. Young contrasts Diodorus partially to Herodotus, whom Young points out is "by no means free from a frequent mixture of fable" and in some areas is "almost universally mistaken," although other parts of his descriptions have "many marks of authenticity" (Young 1824 [1819], 52). Diodorus, on the other hand, is vindicated through the "coincidence" of the number of judges he gives with "a variety of Egyptian monuments still existing" (Young 1824 [1819], 52). He goes on to quote Diodorus's description and, as in the Royal Society paper, points out the correlation with ancient Egyptian evidence. In conclusion to this discussion, Young can thus aver a little more explicitly than in the Royal Society paper that the correlation "demonstrates also the truth of the received opinion, that the Egyptians believed in a future state of rewards and punishments" (Young 1824 [1819], 52).

In the first instance, the importance of this discussion lies simply in the confirmation that this idea was established as a "received opinion" at least partly separate from whatever concrete evidence one might cite to support it, or rather to illustrate it. The second point of interest is the clear and circumscribed way Young exemplifies the efforts to correlate classical authors and the newly available ancient Egyptian evidence, while in reality having "received opinion" strongly framing the scope of the possible interpretations of both.

A much more detailed example of a similar approach, which also serves to illustrate the international influence of the *Description de l'Égypte*, is provided by a lecture given by Danish professor of Latin Børge Thorlacius (1775–1829) at the Scandinavian Society of Literature in August 1822, just a month before Champollion's announcement that he had deciphered the hieroglyphic script (Thorlacius 1823;

cf. Podemann Sørensen 2022). Thorlacius begins by emphasizing the importance of the evidence made available through the *Description de l'Égypte*, noting in a manner similar to Thomas Young that until the end of the eighteenth century, while classical authors had established that "the Egyptians thought of death as a transition to another spiritual state [*aandelig Tilstand*] dependent on the behavior [*Opförsel*] of the deceased," yet the evidence connecting these testimonies to Egyptian monuments had hitherto been lacking until the results of the French campaign had "cast an unexpected light over several branches of human knowledge" (Thorlacius 1823, 166).

To Thorlacius the main interest of ancient Egyptian burial practices lies in the evidence they provide for religious ideas and in that "underneath the careful attention to the preservation of the physical body [*Bevarelsen af det physiske Legeme*], one had in addition an eye to something higher, something more important, something eternal" (Thorlacius 1823, 167). Thorlacius thus saw mummification as aiming to preserve the body, and he clarifies that he sees this as motivated by the idea that the soul would remain with the body as long as its putrefaction could be prevented (Thorlacius 1823, 168). As seen above, this idea ultimately stems from Servius, but Thorlacius does not cite him or anyone else on this, so he may have received it more indirectly, most likely from his compatriot Zoëga, whom he cites in highly approving terms later in his paper.

After a lengthy quotation of Herodotus's description of embalming practices, Thorlacius turns to Diodorus's description of the judgment determining the deceased's right to burial, which he connects with Porphyry's purification ritual of removing the intestines and the accompanying recitation (Thorlacius 1823, 171–73). He finally links these passages to depictions on mummies, citing one in the royal museum in Copenhagen on which "a balance is depicted, which is meant incontrovertibly to determine the worth of the deceased [*den Dödes Værd*] who presents himself to Osiris in a reverential posture in the same painting" (Thorlacius 1823, 173). Although he thus regards mummification as primarily a means of preserving the body, he also understands the outward shape of mummies as a "visible image of Osiris" (Thorlacius 1823, 174).

To Thorlacius the myth of Osiris fundamentally reflects the cycle of the Nile, but it is in turn "transferred to the human soul, its strife [*Kamp*] and consequential victory [*Sejr*]" (Thorlacius 1823, 174). A lengthy description of the techniques and iconography of a number of embalmed bodies mostly from European collections follows, characterizing the range of different approaches attested. Along the way, Thorlacius notes that he understands the images on an inner coffin of a mummified body in Darmstadt as depicting "the solemn incorporation of the deceased in the world of the dead [*Dödeverdenen*])" (Thorlacius 1823, 179). Such interpretations as scenes of judgment coexist with a more initiatory understanding, which is how Thorlacius explains a scene of a mummified body lying on a lion bier tended by a priest wearing the head of a jackal, with four canopic jars under the bier. Without further explanation, he simply notes that "the aim of the depiction is to show the initiation of the deceased [*den Dödes Indvielse*]" (Thorlacius 1823, 180).

At the end of the discussion of burial practices, Thorlacius (1823, 184) divides grave goods associated with mummified bodies into main groups depending on their function: "on the one hand a number of amulets or things intended to avert the effect of evil genii on the deceased, and on the other items that were pleasant to the deceased or served to preserve his memory." Of these, funerary papyri are described as showing depictions of "the activities of the dead, his mortuary judgment, and his presentation before Osiris" (Thorlacius 1823, 185), evidencing the acceptance of Jomard's interpretation of the imagery as depictions of the postmortem journey of the soul.

Whereas earlier authors would have resorted to the descriptions of mourning and burial in the classical authors, Thorlacius can turn instead to a detailed description of a scene showing funerary rituals from a tomb at al-Kāb published in the *Description de l'Égypte* (Thorlacius 1823, 188–91). After a lengthy description of the architecture and decoration of tombs at different sites, Thorlacius returns to the main matter of his lecture, "the state of the soul after death" (Thorlacius 1823, 204). He notes that the rulers of the underworld were once human, and in particular he describes Osiris in explicitly Christological terms before turning to more exotic details of the Egyptian conception:

> Osiris, who had sealed his acts of charity [*Velgjerninger*] to humanity by his suffering, his blood, and his death [*sine Lidelser, sit Blod og sin Död*], and thereupon appears victorious as a phallic deity, is enthroned as chief judge [*throner som Overdommer*]. . . . The ordering of the realm of the dead was the capstone as it were of the Egyptian formation of myths. By the doctrine that there is a life after this one, and by the judgement of the souls, the entire teaching was hallowed. (Thorlacius 1823, 205)

So far, the overall framework of Thorlacius's interpretations of Egyptian mortuary religion has thus been largely along the lines of a personal afterlife with rewards and punishments in the Christian vein. However, at this point he turns to Herodotus's description of metempsychosis as well as Diodorus's contrasting of dwellings and tombs (Thorlacius 1823, 205–6). He points to earlier authors who have attempted to resolve this apparent contradiction by assuming metempsychosis as a priestly faith (notably De Pauw and Heeren), though he adds a number of nuances to this overall model, arriving at three basic tenets that he argues can be deduced from classical authors, imagery on monuments, and observed practices:

> 1. After death there is a reckoning, determining whether one is allowed to join one's forefathers in the Underworld or not. 2. Those who gain access rejoice there over their deeds in this life and await the time when they shall migrate to a more exalted state. 3. Those who have behaved badly in this world are relegated to inhabit lowly creatures, for example, the bodies of repulsive animals. The good on the other hand rise after a certain period to the form of higher beings. (Thorlacius 1823, 208–9)

As can be seen from this, the model Thorlacius arrives at is basically the same additive one that Zoëga presented, with the stay in the underworld as an intermediary state, though he is more explicit about the nature of transmigration to animal bodies as a distinctive punishment. And notably, he can go on to illustrate each of these ideas with reference to concrete monuments.

Not surprisingly, the main source for the idea of "reckoning" is scenes of the weighing of the heart, of which he describes one in detail before pointing out some notable variants. The importance of the idea of reckoning is further emphasized by other scenes in Books of the Dead showing "a multitude of tableaux depicting intercessions to various gods for the soul of the deceased, invocations of Isis, Horus, and others, offerings of lotus flowers, kneeling before uraeus-serpents, etc." (Thorlacius 1823, 211). Similar to Jomard's interpretation, such images are understood to "express the preparations of the soul for the important act where Osiris passed judgment over its behavior in life" (Thorlacius 1823, 212).

Scenes of "daily life" in tombs are understood as mementos of life on earth. On the other hand, Thorlacius's second stage, the joyful time spent in the underworld while the soul remains, does not appear to be depicted anywhere in the monuments. By contrast, according to Thorlacius the third and last stage, the transition to other forms of existence, either lower or higher, does occur in representations. The transition to lower forms follows Jomard's understanding of the hippopotamus (as interpreted by Thorlacius) in the judgment scene in the Book of Gates, with Thorlacius adding that the four flying birds in Jomard's rendering of the scene represent "acquitted [*frifundne*]" souls (Thorlacius 1823, 214–15). Desirable transformations are much more frequent, and Thorlacius proposes that much of the animal imagery in the funerary papyri can be understood along these lines, on the model of the soul of Osiris transmigrating to the Apis bull (Thorlacius 1823, 215–16), and he proceeds to summarize Jomard's interpretations of soul imagery such as birds and scarabs in a similar vein (Thorlacius 1823, 216–19).

Thorlacius's detailed discussion is instructive in several respects. First, it exemplifies once again the new commitment to bridging the gap between classical sources understood through the lens of their traditional interpretation on the one hand and the monumental evidence on the other. It also shows that while the "additive" approach adopted by Zoëga is in principle quite compatible with the wish to connect theological ideas to monuments, in practice the idea of metempsychosis was being increasingly sidelined, even when it was not explicitly dismissed as elite priestly speculation. The notion of judgment and afterlife simply proved much more generative, amenable as it was to a description in purely Christian terms as seen in various places in Thorlacius's discussion. Nonetheless, to Thorlacius, transmigration of souls still offers a key to interpreting the prevalent animal imagery in funerary papyri.

One feature shared by the more empirical works of this period and continuing through to the twenty-first century is the production and maintenance of circumscribed "facts" about ancient Egyptian religion, consisting of particular motifs or objects along with the conventional interpretation of these in terms of underlying beliefs. More concretely, this is seen with the idea of the judgment of the dead, which was no longer understood as emerging primarily from Diodorus's description, but rather as being at the same time illustrated and demonstrated by the weighing of the heart scene (still de rigueur in this capacity in any introduction to the topic today). The same was true of the scene of the pig/hippopotamus being chased away from the judgment hall of Osiris in the Book of Gates as an illustration cum demonstration of the belief in metempsychosis, though this latter "fact" would prove less long-lived for reasons that have been hinted at and are explored further below.

This new, empirical method was far from the only option for scholars during this period, however. A much more traditional approach, if only in the sense of being based almost exclusively on extrapolations from classical sources, but not in terms of the resulting interpretation, was taken by physician James Cowles Prichard (1786–1848; cf. Augstein 1996) in support of a larger project of aligning ancient Egyptian religion with Hinduism. While the aim was thus fundamentally similar to that of much earlier scholars like Athanasius Kircher, the intellectual framework was very different. Prichard's larger aim was to procure arguments in favor of the idea of monogenism being hotly debated at the time. Monogenism was a hypothesis that all of humanity stemmed from a single shared origin (laid out more clearly in other works such as Prichard 1813 and later editions; cf. Augstein 1996, 135–52), as opposed to polygenism, which held that human races had different origins. Ultimately, Prichard's aim through his studies of comparative religion was to reconstruct "the elements of the primitive faith, or the first system of religion that prevailed," which turns out to contain central precursors to Christianity, notably a creator god rewarding and punishing humans through a system of "purgatorial chastisement" (Prichard 1819, 294).

Prichard's monograph *An Analysis of the Egyptian Mythology* demonstrates an approach to comparative mythology strongly inspired by the thinking of German Indologist Friedrich Schlegel (1772–1829; cf. Augstein 1996, 467–84). As part of his argument, Prichard devotes a chapter to Egyptian mortuary religion that is worth examining in some detail (Prichard 1819, 195–217). The chapter begins by noting the slim nature of the available evidence—to which, as shown by his subsequent discussion, he counts mainly the classical authors, not ancient monuments—providing "little more than a foundation for conjectures" (Prichard 1819, 195). The point of departure of his own discussion is the 1775 English translation of Goguet's somewhat minimalist interpretation, which as seen in the previous chapter was in turn based mainly on Servius's idea that the soul remained attached to the body as long as its decay was prevented. Prichard criticizes the quality of Servius's testimony, noting that "from the manner in which Servius states it, it may well be doubted whether he had any better ground for his assertion than a specious conjecture" (Prichard 1819, 196), and Prichard rejects the idea on this basis. He similarly rejects the notion of the resurrection of the body, "since not the slightest hint respecting it has reached our times" (Prichard 1819, 198).

Instead, Prichard turns to Herodotus's description of transmigration of souls, which he regards as the likely foundation of Egyptian mortuary religion. The rejection of the idea of preservation of the body for the sake of the soul, as well as that of bodily resurrection, leaves the purpose of mummification unaccounted for, and Prichard suggests a more generic explanation along the lines of other ancient burial practices, namely that "these solemnities expedited the journey of the soul to the appointed region, where it was to receive judgment for its former deeds, and to have its future doom fixed accordingly" (Prichard 1819, 200), a notion he sees corroborated by Porphyry's account.

The idea of an ethically based postmortem judgment that determines the fate of the soul is thus introduced here without direct support from the classical authors, and as has been seen, the idea was widely accepted at this time, more or less independent of the classical testimony that had first given rise to it centuries earlier. No doubt this "received opinion" and its compatibility with Christian eschatology played a role, though in the context of his wider argument Prichard also has a clear interest in making Egyptian religion similar to the notion of *saṃsāra* (the cycle of death and rebirth) in Hinduism, which thus probably also helped inspire this particular case. This is also the one question on which Prichard turns to Egyptian evidence—the weighing of the heart scene from Papyrus Cadet—which he even reproduces as the book's frontispiece. The following explicit description, however, is relegated to a footnote:

> [In the scene] the infernal judgment of Sarapis seems to be represented. The presiding god sits in the office of judge; and Thoth, distinguished by the head of the Ibis, holds the tablet, which seems to contain a testimony respecting the actions of the dead; while Anoubis, or Mercury the conductor, holds the scales, and seems prepared to execute the sentence. (Prichard 1819, 204–5)

He does not cite the "new" example of transmigration from the Book of Gates presented in the *Description*, and in general there is no clear evidence that he was familiar with the contents of that work, making it uncertain whether he arrived at the understanding of the weighing of the heart as postmortem judgment independently or from a different source.

To Prichard, the realm of the dead thus served as a "temporary receptacle" where the soul remained for a time after death until it was sent back to earth to enter a new body as described by Herodotus (Prichard 1819, 202). He thus understands the model as being very similar to that described by Anchises in book 6 of the *Aeneid* (724ff.), which he quotes at length first in the original Latin and then in English translation (Prichard 1819, 202–4). Although his ostensible inspirations for this interpretation are thus pagan, Prichard nonetheless reverts to clearly Christian language to develop its significance. Thus transmigration is regarded as "a sort of purgatorial chastisement inflicted on the soul, as the consequence of previous delinquencies" (Prichard 1819, 205), and he concludes on this basis that transmigration must have been thought to continue only for a limited period until any transgressions had been expiated. Like Zoëga (but probably independently), Prichard cites Pindar for the notion that the transmigratory cycle needs to be completed at least three times (Prichard 1819, 206).

Prichard establishes similar ideas of cyclical emanation and return of souls in gnosticism, Jewish mysticism, and most significantly the Hermetic writings, so that he can use them to elucidate details of the number and nature of the heavenly spheres through which the soul descends (Prichard 1819, 208–10). While Prichard admits it is questionable how many of these details can be projected back to ancient Egypt, he can, "with greater confidence, ascribe to the Egyptians the doctrine of emanation, and refusion, and purgatorial transmigration" (Prichard 1819, 210–11).

By rejecting the ideas relating mummification to Egyptian mortuary religion, Prichard thus can arrive at a model that is quite different from those of contemporary authors, instead aligning Egyptian religion much more with ideas attested elsewhere in the Mediterranean, and notably (as demonstrated later in his book) India. He does so exclusively through classical authors and other traditional texts, while his use of the scene of weighing the heart—the only ancient Egyptian evidence he cites—is solely as an illustration of ideas known from the texts. Despite his unusual understanding of several details, he ends up cementing notions like the postmortem judgment of ethical merits (and its illustration in the Book of the Dead) and the notion of a purgatorial system for transgressors. In fact, as seen above, divine judgment was precisely one of the key points that the primordial religion preserved in the systems of the Egyptians and the Indians had in common with Christianity (Prichard 1819, 294–95; Augstein 1996, 473–74), bringing the genealogy of the ideas full circle. As Franziska Augstein concisely characterizes the overall structure of Prichard's argument,

> [Prichard] chose his own criteria of comparison, that is, the main Christian doctrines; then he projected them back on ancient pagan mythologies. Where Egyptian mythology defied this operation, Indian traditions came into play. At the end, he concluded triumphantly that the existence of the main Christian doctrines in the

> earliest stages of all ancient mythologies proved that they all had sprung from one common source. (Augstein 1996, 475–76)

Lest it seem that such erudite attempts at reconciling the major parts of the evidence were the only approach taken during this period, it is worth citing a couple of examples of more generic interpretations. The British traveler William Richard Hamilton (1777–1859) includes in his travel description a passage on ancient embalming practices, prefacing it with the following broad and noncommittal characterizing of the underlying motifs:

> the priests appear to have had in view a regard to the preservation of the general health, and to the doctrine of their religion, touching the immortality of the soul, the future connection of the soul with the body it had once animated, and its supposed disposition to migrate from that body, either after a certain period of years, or in case it should have become putrid. (Hamilton 1809, 318)

These ideas can all be recognized (and from his following discussion, Hamilton seems to have put particular stock in hygienic considerations), but rather than attempting to reconcile them as other scholars had done, he simply lists them side by side as possible explanations or differing ancient opinions.

Noted Italian explorer, collector, and former circus strongman Giovanni Belzoni (1778–1823) offers an even more laconic account. Interested in the pyramids primarily for the challenge of accessing their internal chambers, Belzoni gave the following brief remark in the 1820 description of his adventures in Egypt:

> As to their [the pyramids'] architecture, I can only say it is in conformity with their ideas. It is to be recollected, that they had a notion of returning to life again, body and soul, after a period of three thousand years: whence we may presume, that they intended to make their edifices last so long, that they might see them again in good preservation. (Belzoni 1820, 176)

While clearly based ultimately on Herodotus, as shown by the detail of the three thousand years, this idea departs from his description in several respects, showing that Belzoni probably received it indirectly, with possibly more than one layer of interpretation. Thus transmigration is not mentioned, and the resurrection is supposed to involve both "body and soul." Unlike many other scholars, however, for Belzoni the key function of the monument is not to protect the body during this period, as he makes no mention of that, but is simply to make sure the tombs are still extant when their builders come back to life. This is a straightforward exoticizing model that has no need for journeys of the soul, rewards and punishments, and such, partly because the only piece of evidence it is intended to explain is the building of monumental tombs.

Conclusion

As these varied examples show, there was no single established consensus about the specific tenets of ancient Egyptian mortuary religion on the eve of the deciphering of hieroglyphs. Nonetheless, the more scholarly treatments, and many of the less scholarly ones, did have a number of ideas and assumptions in common, and authors could refer to "the received opinion" confident that their readers would understand roughly what they had in mind. The main commonality was the Egyptians' belief in a life after death in which persons would each be rewarded or punished according to their merits. As in earlier periods, this basic idea could be related to different pieces of evidence in various ways depending on the role a given scholar accorded to traditional ideas such as the need to preserve the body, the doctrine of metempsychosis, and the existence of a separate realm of the dead.

At the same time, a consequential innovation was taking place in the more scholarly works that would have the greatest influence on ideas in the following decades, namely the increasing effort to anchor such traditional ideas in concrete ancient Egyptian imagery, which was becoming much more widely known during the first decades of the nineteenth century. Jomard provides a prominent example of this approach of connecting specific Egyptian images to existing expectations about Egyptian beliefs. The most successful effort in this direction was no doubt the interpretation of the weighing of the heart scene from the Book of the Dead as an ancient illustration of the belief in postmortem judgment that European scholars had come to associate with Egyptian religion. A similar example—which, however, as we shall see in the following chapter, was destined to be rejected—was the judgment scene from the Book of Gates, which was understood to similarly illustrate the coupling of Herodotus's metempsychosis with the notion of rewards and punishments.

In both cases the ancient images quickly shifted their status. Once they had been interpreted in light of ideas conventionally attributed to the ancient Egyptians, they could in turn be used to illustrate and demonstrate those same ideas, seemingly decreasing the need to rely on the classical authors who had originally enabled this understanding. Weighing imagery thus became transmissible as icons consisting of the visual images along with their conventional interpretations—a way the Book of the Dead vignettes of the weighing of the heart are still used today to illustrate the Egyptian concept of postmortem judgment.

In turn, this approach to specific images strongly implied that the rest of the visual context of the papyri on which they were found would be similar in nature. Jomard himself draws this conclusion in the most general sense of suggesting that the rest of the Book of the Dead depicts the trials and tribulations of the next world, though he does not explore the implications of this interpretation in detail. Other scholars began this work during the first decades of the nineteenth century, but it is only after the decipherment of hieroglyphs that we can appreciate the full consequences of this intuitive mode of understanding funerary papyri as literal descriptions of the soul's postmortem journey.

SEVEN

The Decline of Metempsychosis: 1822–1860

Traditional histories of Egyptology tend to emphasize the seismic shift in knowledge about, and approaches to, ancient Egypt resulting from Jean-François Champollion's (1790–1832) successful decipherment of the hieroglyphic script. The details have been frequently narrated, especially during the two hundredth anniversary in 2022 (a nuanced recent exploration is found in Buchwald and Josefowicz 2020). Drawing on the trilingual inscription on the Rosetta Stone, aided by his knowledge of Coptic, and building on earlier work by scholars such as Johan David Åkerblad and Thomas Young, Champollion was able to lay out the main principles of the script, the different sign types, and a number of sign readings, taking a decisive step toward making ancient Egyptian writings available to modern scholars.

In an age of electronic mass communication, it is easy to imagine the effects as being akin to flipping a switch by which all Egyptian texts became available overnight, and the disciplinary trope of 1822 as the "birth of Egyptology" does little to add nuance to this impression. It is true that when it came to identifying royal and divine names on monuments and making sense of simple captions, the change was almost immediate, and the effects can be seen in the writings of Champollion himself as well as of others during the decades after the decipherment. However, not many scholars rivaled Champollion's familiarity with the hieroglyphic writing system, and with his untimely death in 1832, the exploration of Egyptian language suffered an enormous setback. Additionally, the kind of brief inscriptions that could be read at first were not the most forthcoming when it came to the questions of religion and theology occupying us here. The disappointment this seeming lack of progress caused can be glimpsed in the preface to the updated 1838 edition of James C. Prichard's *Analysis of Egyptian Mythology*, discussed in the previous chapter:

> It was at one time generally expected that the clue afforded by the Rosetta inscription towards the decyphering of Egyptian hieroglyphics and enchorial [i.e., demotic] writings would have led to very important discoveries with respect to the religious notions and practices and the philosophical dogmas of the Egyptian priests. Hitherto little or nothing has been obtained to verify this sanguine hope. It may indeed be questioned whether from this source it could have been discovered that the remarkable doctrine of the metempsychosis was held by the Egyptians. (Prichard 1838, xii–xiii)

While Prichard had his own reasons to belittle the relevance of Champollion's decipherment, not least that Champollion had been vocally opposed to the kind of cross-cultural diffusion Prichard held as fundamental, nonetheless the quotation expresses a more widespread sentiment regarding the promise of Egyptian texts for elucidating such abstract ideas. The full translation of lengthier texts was still far away, with the first relatively full, annotated translations of an autobiographical inscription (that of Ahmose son of Ibana; Rougé 1853) and a literary narrative (*The Tale of Two Brothers*; Rougé 1852) being published in the early 1850s, while larger compilations of inscriptions, making them accessible to readers beyond a small group of experts, would start appearing only in the 1870s, half a century after the announcement of Champollion's decipherment. To historian David Gange (2013, 164), it is only the last two decades of the nineteenth century that can be characterized as "the moment when hieroglyphic, hieratic and archaeological sources finally began to define the shape of histories of Egypt." As we will see below, by then a clear consensus about the nature of the ancient Egyptian afterlife was firmly entrenched, and the newly available textual evidence did little to change that.

Nonetheless, Champollion's decipherment did significantly affect understandings of Egyptian mortuary religion in other ways. While Champollion is known indirectly to have worked intensively on the manuscripts of the Book of the Dead available to him (e.g., Lüscher 2018, 25–26), his publications address that source, and Champollion's understanding of Egyptian mortuary religion more generally, only piecemeal. A relatively detailed description by Champollion of a Book of the Dead manuscript found on a trip to Egypt shortly after the publication of his decipherment was included as part of Frédéric de Cailliaud's multivolume travel description (Champollion 1827). In his introduction, Champollion lays out his basic understanding of the work as notably encompassing, apart from formulas regarding embalming and procession to the tomb, "a host of prayers addressed to all of the divinities who might decide over the fate of the soul, whether in Amenti where it was judged or in the mystic regions which it was supposed to inhabit before resuming the cycle of its transmigrations" (Champollion 1827, 22–23). Despite the brevity of this characterization, the continuity with earlier ideas is thus clear, with an implicit sequence of judgment, then a stay in the "mystic regions" where perhaps the soul was punished or rewarded in accordance with its merits before finally transmigrating to a new body, again presumably corresponding to the result of the judgment. Elsewhere he refers to "the sacred myths pertaining to the separation of the soul and the body and to the various purifications it would successively undergo in the interval between its transmigrations" (Champollion 1827, 43), confirming both the dualistic split between body and soul and that the Book of the Dead was thought to deal specifically with the stage between incarnations. Another idea implicit in Champollion's description is that the divinities the soul encounters in the beyond might be swayed by the prayers contained in the Book of the Dead.

Champollion concludes his contribution with a discussion of the painted decoration on a coffin (reproduced in Cailliaud 1823, pl. 67), which adds a few details to his understanding and shows further developments in the connections between traditional concepts and ancient Egyptian imagery. The lid of the coffin shows a scene of worship where the coffin's owner is depicted with hands raised in adoration facing an offering table with the deities Osiris and Isis behind it. Champollion understands the scene as "the examination of the material faults [*fautes matérielles*] of the deceased, since his body itself appears before the supreme judge of the Amenti." As a counterpart to this, a scene on the other side of the lid depicts the judgment of the soul understood as "the examination of its thoughts and its voluntary determinations" (Champollion 1827, 46–47). This interpretation is prompted by the representation of the deceased as a human-headed bird rather than a human as in the first scene. The chief interest in this interpretation for present purposes is that it expands the earlier understanding of the weighing of the heart as depicting the last judgment of the soul by also applying this understanding to less specific scenes of worship. Consequently the intuitive split between body and soul can also be deployed as an interpretive measure, leading to the idea of a dual judgment of body and soul, perhaps implicitly inspired by earlier ideas of an earthly judgment in the vein of Diodorus and a divine judgment in the beyond.

As this shows, and as we saw in the previous chapter, during the first decades of the nineteenth century the idea that the weighing of the heart motif in ancient Egyptian imagery depicted a judgment of the souls of deceased humans in the beyond had crystallized. During Champollion's travels in Egypt in 1828 and 1829, he studied a monumental version of this scene in the temple of Hathor at Dayr al-Madīnah (Bourget and Gabolde 2008, 56–57), and he offers a detailed description and interpretation with translation of the accompanying captions in a letter to his brother, which was published posthumously (Champollion 1833, 313–21).

Champollion begins his description of the leftmost of the three shrines of the temple where the scene occurs by noting that it is dedicated to the goddess Thmeï (Maat), and that the scenes of the shrine depict the roles that goddess plays in "Amenti, the western regions or underworld [*enfer*] of the Egyptians," and he goes on to characterize the latter as "this terrible place where the souls were judged (*les ames étaient jugées*)" (Champollion 1833, 318). Although this basic understanding was well established by Champollion's time, he seems to be the first to explicitly use the term *psychostasia* for the motif of weighing the heart, a term used in Christian art for Saint Michael's weighing of souls at the Last Judgment that had long formed an important inspiration for European interpretations of the weighing imagery, as noted in previous chapters. In describing the scene in the temple, Champollion identifies the "42 assessor judges of Osiris," as well as the "monster . . . opening its large maw threatening the guilty souls," whose name is read as "the devourer [*dévoratrice*] of the west or the underworld." He reads the caption to the goddess Maat in the following way: "Thmeï who dwells in the Amenti, where she weighs the hearts on the balance: No villain [*méchant*] escapes from it" (Champollion 1833, 319). Next to the person undergoing the trial, Champollion reads "Arrival of a soul in the Amenti." With his knowledge of hieroglyphs, he is also able to identify the iconography of the "infernal balance," noting that one pan holds the heart of the accused and the other the feather as emblem of justice (Champollion 1833, 320). He ends by noting that even though the scene is more frequently known from funerary objects and tombs, there are no grounds for supposing that the temple belonged in this category.

Champollion thus uses the new insights into Egyptian inscriptions to flesh out an interpretation very much in line with the results of scholars of the preceding decades. While he notes the special emphasis on the goddess Maat in this particular version, the overall understanding is largely identical to those of Jomard and Zoëga: the scene shows a soul newly arrived in the afterlife who needs to undergo a judgment of his ethical merits to determine his afterlife fate. In principle, the decipherment now offers an opportunity for interpreting the imagery in terms of indigenous concepts and categories. However, because the understanding of the scene was thus already established, Champollion's indubitable linguistic mastery leads instead to an incipient approximation of the ancient Egyptian terms to modern ones. The *Amenti* is the Egyptian "underworld/hell [*enfer*]," the figure approaching the balance is a "soul," and in particular the wider framework that is not described explicitly is characterized in terms like "infernal," "judgment," "*psychostasia*," and such. This co-optation of indigenous terminology is another reason the transition to the postdecipherment era turned out to be so surprisingly seamless in interpretations of mortuary religion.

Another of Champollion's letters, this one from the Valley of the Kings, offers further insight into his understanding of Egyptian mortuary religion. As part of his general description of the royal tombs found there, based—like the *Description* discussed in the previous chapter—on the tomb of Ramesses VI (KV 9; Piankoff 1954), he offers some thoughts on the underlying religious beliefs. Noting the general assimilation between the king and the sun in the decoration, he describes how the deceased king, like the sun, "was also going to be reborn, whether to continue his transmigrations, or to inhabit the heavenly world and be absorbed in the bosom of Ammon [*sein d'Ammon*], the universal Father [*le Père universel*]" (Champollion 1833, 226). While thus not committing to either of the rival theories of the Egyptian afterlife (transmigration versus going to "heaven"), the wording of the second one in particular makes its inspirations clear with its close paraphrase of the notion of the Judeo-Christian notion of the "bosom of Abraham" as an afterlife destination, variously understood as a place where souls await the Resurrection or as the final destination of the blessed dead after judgment (e.g., Baschet 1996; O'Kane 2007, 489–96). Later on, in his interpretation of the scenes from the Book of Gates and Book of Caverns in the outer sections of the tomb, it becomes clear that it is only the specific fate of the king that is uncertain, not the validity of transmigration of souls in general, as Champollion draws on the notion of metempsychosis, with the type of body the soul is incarnated in depending on the result of the judgment in the underworld (Champollion 1833, 230). The basis for this idea is once again the scene of judgment from the Book of Gates, and Champollion supports the interpretation of the pig (described here as an "enormous sow," *énorme truie*) as the body appointed to a condemned soul, reading the sign underneath as meaning "greed" or "gluttony," and hence indicating the "capital sin of the offender" (Champollion 1833, 230–31).

Another scene in the underworld books depicts the "Elysian Fields" where dwell "the blessed souls [*ames bienheureuses*] resting after the troubles of their transmigrations on earth" (Champollion 1833, 231). The counterpart to this is found in images in the lower register inhabited by the "guilty souls" (*ames coupables*), which is explicitly compared to Dante's *Inferno* as a place of "torment" (*tourments*) and punishment (Champollion 1833, 233). After a detailed description of the punishments taking place there, Champollion offers a summary of the underlying ideas:

> This double series of scenes thus present to us the *Egyptian psychological system* in its two most important and most moral points, *rewards and punishments*. Thus everything the ancients tell us about the Egyptian doctrine *of the immortality of the soul* and the positive objective [*but positif*] of human life is found completely demonstrated. It is decidedly grand and successful, this idea of symbolizing the *double destiny* of the souls through the most striking of celestial phenomena, the course of the sun through the two hemispheres, and of linking the painting to that of this imposing and magnificent spectacle. (Champollion 1833, 235; emphasis in the original)

Ultimately, Champollion's overall understanding of Egyptian mortuary religion thus does not differ significantly from that found in the *Description*, and in the quoted passage he explicitly emphasizes how this view is in accordance with the testimony of classical sources. In the outline of the plans for Champollion's stay in Egypt reproduced in the beginning of the volume it is pointed out that the funerary nature of much of the evidence for Egyptian religion means they provide "only detailed information on the mystical figures [*personnage mystiques*] protecting the dead and presiding over the various states of the soul [*divers états de l'âme*] after its separation from the body" (Champollion 1833, 3). This religion "of the tombs" is contrasted with that of the higher classes expressed in temples and chapels, which seems to be regarded as relating more to mythology and theology than to mortuary religion. It appears, then, that Champollion's overall model is a fairly simple one where the soul is separated from the body at death and subsequently goes through a series of "states," with the underworld judgment of the soul as depicted in the weighing of the heart scenes possibly being situated before or (as in Jomard's interpretation) after these. Where he adds significant new detail, however, is in translating the accompanying inscriptions, and not least in his detailed analysis of the underworld books in the royal tombs, with the notable separation of their imagery into one area corresponding to the Elysian Fields (in turn understood as a sort of heaven or paradise) and another to torments along the lines of Dante's *Inferno*. The result of this is that, while he repeatedly mentions the idea of transmigration of souls, in practice, Christian-style rewards and punishments are much easier to identify in the imagery.

Like the discussion in the *Description de l'Égypte*, Champollion's letters are strongly tied to the specific monuments discussed, which they analyze in a systematic fashion. However, as the interpretations became increasingly narrowly tied to the evidence, the crystallizing of the ancient Egyptian afterlife was able to enter a new phase. Rather than using the concept of postmortem judgment to explain scenes of weighing the heart as it occurred on specific objects and monuments, one could now take the scene out of those contexts and use it instead to *illustrate* the ancient Egyptian concept of postmortem judgment—extending a step already taken by James Prichard, as we saw above. Thus, some years after the publication of Champollion's letters, a full translation of his discussion of the weighing of the heart scene in the Dayr al-Madīnah temple is reproduced in an 1838 guidebook to the British Museum, ostensibly to contextualize the roles of the four Sons of Horus represented on canopic jars in the museum's collection (Anonymous 1838, 298–300). Apart from demonstrating Champollion's influence, this also illustrates the changing status of museum collections, with the British Museum through new acquisitions and exhibition installations gradually becoming positioned as an important source of knowledge about ancient Egypt for the museumgoing public in its own right, in ways that could be connected directly to the published results of expeditions to the country (Moser 2006, esp. 125–70).

Rosellini's Empirical Methods

While Champollion's studies during his trip to Egypt were thus documented directly in the form of his letters, his stay formed part of the Franco-Tuscan expedition led by Champollion assisted by his Italian mentee and collaborator, Ippolito Rosellini (1800–1843; cf. Betrò 2010; Betrò and Miniaci 2013). The massive publication resulting from this trip was written by Rosellini under the title *I monumenti dell'Egitto e della Nubia*, appearing during the course of the 1830s, with the last volume published posthumously in 1844. Of particular interest for present purposes is the lengthy chapter on funerary rites in part 2, volume 3

(Rosellini 1836, 285–502). Not surprisingly given the close connection between the two scholars, Rosellini's interpretations generally correspond to the framework laid out by Champollion, though by assigning more than two hundred pages to the topic Rosellini is able to go into much greater detail and also to provide a more comprehensive treatment of aspects left out of Champollion's discussion, such as the problem of the relation between afterlife beliefs and practices of mummification.

Rosellini starts out by noting the importance of grounding interpretations in firm evidence, avoiding "vain errors" (*vani errori*) of previous scholars as well as "preconceived systems" (Rosellini 1836, 286). In particular he notes the tendency in past scholarship to take as one's point of departure the "works of Pythagoras and of Plato" and to use the ancient monuments, if at all, only to confirm the ideas found in the Greek texts (Rosellini 1836, 287–88). According the Rosellini, not only does this lead to a wide variety of interpretations in previous scholarship, but it puts undue trust in the classical authors, who did not transmit Egyptian beliefs accurately but shaped them to serve their own purposes. Correspondingly, Rosellini argues in favor of swapping the priorities, emphasizing the necessity of grounding interpretations in the monuments and only secondarily—if at all—comparing these against what is found in the classical sources (Rosellini 1836, 289–90).

More specifically, he points to the Book of the Dead (which, following Champollion's usage, he refers to as the "funerary ritual") as the main source for understanding Egyptian afterlife beliefs, since that composition contains texts and accompanying images "symbolizing the transformations and passages [*le trasformazioni e i passaggi*] of the soul after the death of the body" (Rosellini 1836, 290; cf. also the similar characterization in Rosellini 1838, 3), making a future detailed study of the texts and imagery of the Book of the Dead an important desideratum.

Given his strong emphasis on the primacy of the monuments, it is slightly ironic that Rosellini in practice notes that because the monuments are full of confirmations of this idea, Plato's model (in *Phaedon*) of immortal souls spending three thousand years wandering on earth before returning to their divine origin can be regarded as authentically Egyptian, with the exception that wicked souls are condemned instead to repeat the migratory cycle. In this way the traditional idea that the

Egyptians held this belief and transmitted it to the Greeks can be vindicated (Rosellini 1836, 291–94). On this basis Rosellini proceeds to discuss the differences between the models described in Plato and in Herodotus, notably whether the cycle of transmigration is automatic and unavoidable, as Herodotus implied, or is the result of the nature of individual souls as understood by Plato. Dismissing scholars drawing on other authors or hypothesizing a split between priestly and popular beliefs, Rosellini argues in favor of taking Herodotus's description at face value without connecting it to the practice of mummification (Rosellini 1836, 294–303). After what thus turns out to be a highly traditional discussion concerning the possibility of reconciling the different classical sources, Rosellini ends his discussion of conceptions of the soul after death by turning briefly to the monuments, more specifically the judgment scene from the Book of Gates where a wicked soul is returned to earth "in the foul body of a sow [*nell'immondo corpo di una porca*]" (Rosellini 1836, 303).

Rosellini's rejection of a connection between beliefs about the soul and mummification raises the question of the purpose of the practice, and he takes up this discussion in the following section. Certain that such a laborious and long-lasting practice must have had a significant religious rationale, Rosellini supposes that it must have been connected to Egyptian ideas about the afterlife, even if it cannot be explained solely either by the soul's adhering to the body as long as it does not decay or by the notion of transmigration as described by Herodotus (Rosellini 1836, 304–8). Instead, he suggests that the precondition for the cycle of transmigration to take place at all was "the condition of the incorrupt body [*la condizione del corpo incorrotto*] after the soul had departed," a notion that he sees confirmed in the text and images of the Book of the Dead (Rosellini 1836, 308–9).

Since the precondition of proper burial rites does not seem to have any obvious connection with the long-term preservation of bodies, Rosellini suggests that this specific quality of the practices of embalming was introduced instead owing to their public benefits as a "local sanitary measure" (*sanitario provvedimento locale*) (Rosellini 1836, 311). He goes on to argue the likelihood of this scenario at some length, pointing to the potential dangers of infection in a landscape like that of Egypt as well as to the excellent health the ancient Egyptians were reported to enjoy (Rosellini 1836, 311–14). Realizing these benefits to public health, Egyptian sages deliberately connected the practice of mummification to the religious ideas of metempsychosis to encourage its continuance. From their original role as simple places of storage for dead bodies, practices of decorating tombs developed, Rosellini suggests, not only to beautify them in general, but more specifically to "foreshadow the doctrine of the soul's survival after the death of the body [*sopravviver dell'anima alla morte del corpo*] and of the continuance of its journey as an inhabitant of this world" (Rosellini 1836, 319).

The next section discusses the soul's ultimate fate after it completes the cycle of migration. Rosellini understands the necessity of transmigration in explicitly Christian theological terms such as "expiation of guilt" (*espiazione della colpa*) or "purgation" (*purgamento*) of a stain (Rosellini 1836, 320). As noted above, Rosellini understands the judgment of the behavior of the soul as taking place after the completion of a full transmigratory cycle to determine whether the soul can return to the gods whence it came or needs another purgatory stay on earth, an idea for which he cites the Hermetic writings. He notes that wicked souls are shown in the royal tombs being subjected to "torments of fire and iron" (*tormenti di ferro e di fuoco*), though he avoids a more detailed discussion of these scenes (Rosellini 1836, 323). It further follows from Rosellini's understanding of mummification as being a precondition of transmigration that this practice essentially served as a backup that was necessary only if the soul had to undergo additional purification rather than returning to the gods. He sees this as underlying Porphyry's description of the funerary ritual, which was performed for human beings rather than animals and thus related to a soul at the end of its cycle and undergoing judgment to determine whether it should return to the gods.

Rosellini goes on to support each of the elements in Porphyry's description with regard to the monuments. The differentiation between good and wicked souls, with only the former allowed to approach the sun god, is shown through translations of inscriptions copied from the underworld books in the tomb of Ramesses VI, where enemies are kept away from the sun god while the "just souls" (*anime giuste*) are allowed to enjoy his proximity (Rosellini 1836, 326–29). Rosellini briefly notes that the negative statements in Porphyry's prayer correspond to statements made in the "confession" (*confessione*) of the deceased. Finally, as confirmation of the idea of transgressions being blamed on individual parts of the body, he refers to another inscription from the royal tombs that he translates as "Justice to his spirit, his wickedness to the matter" (*La giustizia allo spirito suo, la malvagità sua alla materia*), noting that the latter word refers to the corpse as "the material part of man" (Rosellini 1836, 330). The correlation between Porphyry and the monuments allows him to conclude that the author "truly expresses a doctrine and a rite of the ancient Egyptians" (Rosellini 1836, 331).

Having laid out his understanding of ancient Egyptian doctrines of the afterlife, Rosellini's lengthy chapter continues with sections on a tomb painting that he understands as representing the ages of man; the practicalities of mummification, comparing the relations by the classical authors with Rosellini's own observations; the practices of embalming priests; and representations of funerary processions, none of which adds substantial new ideas to the outline presented here. After these sections there follows one dealing with the topic of judgment regarding the right to burial (Rosellini 1836, 430–42) that is worth discussing in more detail.

Not surprisingly, Rosellini (1836, 430–34) begins this part of his account by quoting Diodorus's passage on the ritual judgment of the dead, continuing to note the additional practices that author relates on the pawning of mummified ancestors and the extension of the judgment ritual to kings as well as private citizens. Rosellini understands the ritual judgment as "an image, an imitation" (*una immagine, una imitazione*) of the judgment taking place in the beyond (Rosellini 1836, 435)—in the same vein as Sponde's much earlier Catholic notion of the funeral as a reflection of the Resurrection (chapter 2 above). He goes on to point to two private tomb scenes depicting rites before the tomb that he sees as illustrating the ritual judgment described by Diodorus, interpreting a priest holding an adz before the face of the mummified body as expressing the "approval" (*approvazione*) resulting from a positive judgment (Rosellini 1836, 436–37). In accordance with the idea of the earthly judgment as a reflection of that in the next world, Rosellini notes that "the ideas of mountain, of tomb, of underworld [*inferno*] and of Amenti were assimilated and almost identified" (Rosellini 1836, 439). In a female figure emerging from the western mountain to embrace the tomb owner, Rosellini sees the goddess Tme (Maat) receiving the deceased to lead him to the "infernal judgment" in the presence of Osiris, thereby establishing the sequential nature of the two judgment procedures (Rosellini 1836, 441).

The remaining three sections of the chapter concern various individual themes and motifs that are interpreted in significant detail with attention to both text and image. While they do provide additional depth and nuance to Rosellini's understanding of Egyptian mortuary religion, especially concerning the burgeoning realization of the importance of commemorative rituals taking place after the funeral, for present purposes there is no need to go into the details, though it is worth mentioning a few of his notes on the realm of the dead, Amenti, which is the topic of the last section of the chapter. Referring to Plutarch's interpretation of the name as meaning "receiver and giver," Rosellini connects this to the idea that souls are arriving in Amenti only to be relayed somewhere else after judgment, whether it is back to the gods or back to earth (Rosellini 1836, 479). After a discussion of another scene showing funerary rituals, Rosellini turns to the weighing of the heart scene as an appropriate way to end the long chapter, based once more on the vignette from the Cadet Papyrus that, like the *Description*, Rosellini reproduces as part of his plates (Rosellini 1836, 490–502). His detailed description follows earlier interpretations quite closely and differs mainly by being able to draw on the hieroglyphic captions identifying the various beings depicted. One notable difference is that in Rosellini's interpretation, rather than an agent of punishment as with Champollion, Ammut is a "vigilant guardian of the terrible abode of Amenti, similar to the Greek Cerberus" (Rosellini 1836, 495). Like Young before him, Rosellini points to the variant manuscript of Diodorus, which has forty-two judges, which he notes as the number regularly depicted in scenes of the weighing of the heart, although the Cadet vignette happens to have forty-three instead (Rosellini 1836, 499). He also briefly points to variants of the scene that have the "negative confession" (*confessione negativa*) as part of the accompanying text.

As conclusion to the discussion of the weighing of the heart vignette, Rosellini returns to the question of its relation to the ritual described by Diodorus, suggesting that, given their close connection, it would have been regarded as certain, or at least highly probable, that the result of the infernal judgment would be the same as that of the earthly ritual. Essentially, this offered a double punishment for evildoers, an "observable punishment of infamy [*sensibile punizione d'infamia*] after the death of the body" in addition to "the threat of the condemnation of the soul [*minaccia di condanna dell'anima*]" (Rosellini 1836, 501). In other words, the split between the two judgments, one ritual and one transcendent, corresponds to the two parts of the dualistic conception of the human being, determining respectively the fates of the body and the soul.

Another idea present here in a germinal form is the notion that the deceased might have work to carry out in the beyond. In discussing the funerary figurines from the tomb of Seti I now known as *shabtis*, Rosellini makes brief reference to the idea that the agricultural tools these figurines hold were needed "so that they could cultivate the celestial fields of Tme, as depicted in one of the sections of the *Ritual*" (Rosellini 1836, 472). The reference here is no doubt to the agricultural tasks depicted in Book of the Dead chapter 110, which Lepsius would shortly afterward interpret authoritatively as the "Elysian Fields" that formed the paradisial destination in the afterlife (see below). To Rosellini (1836, 472), the several interlocking parts of his model of the ancient Egyptian afterlife make things a little more complicated, but the imagery of tilling celestial fields is seen in similar terms as expressing the hope that the deceased will begin the "journey back to the superior worlds" (*ritorno ai mondi superiori*) rather than being incarnated in a new "earthly body" (*corpo terreno*).

A few notable general features in Rosellini's discussion are worth emphasizing. The first has to do with his method. As noted, he is keen to stress the primary importance of the monuments, and indeed his discussion is unprecedented in the amount of detail it draws on from texts and images. On the other hand, when it comes to establishing the overall framework in practice, Rosellini simply notes that the monuments confirm the classical authors, which in turn allows him to use them as his point of departure. This ostensible empirical grounding is worth noting because it would continue not only through the nineteenth century, but in many respects to the present. Rather than deriving a framework from the sources, the framework preexists, and the sources are fitted into it, which in turn makes the framework seem not only grounded in the empirical data, but actually derived from them.

The second main feature is the slight reshuffling of the elements of Egyptian mortuary religion in Rosellini's model. Metempsychosis plays an important role, but since most decorated tombs were those of human beings, an identity that places the soul in question at the end of the transmigratory cycle, their texts and images are actually found to be occupied exclusively with the cycle's very end, and especially with the aspirational result of escaping the cycle. This gives transmigration a background status where one would not necessarily expect to find it expressed in monuments constructed for human beings, and the main role it plays in the larger model is as a temporary purgatorial system.

A final notable feature of Rosellini's system is its sidelining also of mummification, which is regarded as originally a purely practical institution for reasons of hygiene which became artificially connected to afterlife beliefs as a precondition for the transmigration of the soul (presaging concerns of Paduan professor Ferdinando Colletti, who in the 1850s espoused cremation as a contemporary more hygienic alternative to burial; cf. Conti 2023, 454–57). In the basically Platonic model Rosellini espoused, one would not expect to find the positive outcome of the soul's return to the divine world described in much detail, so what is left in particular is the central theme of judgment, which now happens in two interconnected stages, one determining the right to burial as a practical ritual on earth, and the other, infernal judgment determining whether the soul is condemned to undertake another transmigratory cycle.

Several other scholars traveled to Egypt in the wake of the deciphering of hieroglyphs, which, along with the new political situation after the Napoleonic Wars, had generated a new wave of interest in ancient Egyptian culture. Some of the resulting publications were deliberately modeled on the *Description de l'Égypte* as systematic efforts of documentation of monuments for an audience back in Europe, while other projects were more specific in their aims, such as John Gardner Wilkinson's effort to write an ethnographic account of life in ancient Egypt based primarily on Theban tomb paintings. While strongly empirical and heavy with illustrations of monuments and their inscriptions and decoration, in terms of mortuary religion they tended not surprisingly to fit such newly documented material into the dominant narrative established by the *Description* and further cemented by the writings of Champollion and others.

British Orientalist Edward William Lane (1801–76; cf. Thompson 1997) traveled to Egypt in 1825 to 1828 in the immediate wake of Champollion's decipherment. He would go on to become most famous for his ethnographic description of the "manners and customs" of the modern Egyptians (Lane 1836), but in the years after his return, he also completed several drafts of a travelogue containing significant passages on the ancient culture. This work, though accepted for publication in 1831 (meaning that at least parts of the latest extant manuscript were written without knowledge of Champollion's posthumously published letters), remained unpublished during Lane's own lifetime, but the third and final draft of the manuscript was recently edited and published by Jason Thompson (2020).

Of greatest interest in the present connection is the "Supplement" appended at the end of the travelogue itself, dedicated to ancient Egyptian history and culture. As part of a chapter on religion and laws, Lane devotes a couple of pages to "the state after death" (Thompson 2020, 523–24). He takes as his point of departure Herodotus's description of transmigration, with the minor addition that the soul's journey begins not at death, but rather "on the dissolution of the body," no doubt inspired by combination with Servius's ideas in the existing literature. However, Lane immediately goes on to cast this idea into doubt in line with a generally mounting skepticism toward Herodotus, by noting that "the information which this historian obtained from the Egyptian priests must always be received with much distrust" and that therefore "the testimony of the monuments must of course be preferred" (Thompson 2020, 523).

Surveying such evidence, he mentions depicting souls as birds with human heads as Jomard had established, but also as "a simple human figure, sometimes painted *black* to denote a *depraved* soul" (Thompson 2020, 523; emphasis in the original). Having already discussed scenes of weighing the heart, understood as judgment of souls in the manner of Jomard (Thompson 2020, 518, with addition that the figure of Ammut is understood as "the Egyptian Cerberus"), he goes on to note that the royal tombs at Thebes have "representations of a state of rewards and punishments; the latter perhaps purgatorial, and both preparatory to perfect fruition to be enjoyed by the soul when reunited to the human body which it had formerly occupied on earth" (Thompson 2020, 523–24).

Although the idea that the souls were to return to the same human body after transmigration could in principle be connected to the practice of mummification (as other scholars had previously done), Lane rejects the idea from Servius that the continuance of the soul depends on that of the body, and instead prefers the explanation that mummification was meant to make the corpse into an "emblem" of Osiris (Thompson 2020, 524). He concludes his discussion by referring to Diodorus's description of the tribunal determining the deceased's right to be buried, demonstrating that this passage had by now become entirely divorced from the interpretation of the weighing of the heart as postmortem judgment, which the Diodorus passage had originally helped establish.

The increased access to Egypt during this period was also reflected in a veritable boom in interest in ancient embalmed bodies and the more or less public revelation of what was hidden under the bandages (e.g., Pearce 2002; Moshenska 2014b; Riggs 2014, 37–76; Baber 2016; Stienne 2017, 2022), in line with more general developments toward the "medicalization of death" in the late eighteenth and early nineteenth centuries (Carol 2023). Looming large in the public examinations of Egyptian mummified bodies is English physician and antiquarian Thomas Pettigrew (1791–1865; cf. Moshenska 2014a; Stienne 2017, 193–204), famous (and in some quarters infamous) for his public unwrapping of mummified bodies. His *History of Egyptian Mummies* from 1834 aggregates the results of his early unwrappings, aiming primarily at amassing details of embalming and burial practices. It deals not only with Egyptian human remains based on Pettigrew's own examinations as well as the existing literature, but also with a number of other cultures whose funerary practices are in one way or another regarded as comparable to those of the

Egyptians. One chapter in the book, however, is devoted to the ancient Egyptians' religious motivations for mummification.

In light of Pettigrew's primary interest in embalmed bodies, it is no surprise that he comes to a somewhat different conclusion than the marginalization of embalming practices argued by contemporary scholars like Rosellini. Proceeding from the idea that the Egyptians thought the soul was eternal, he presents two possible motivations for preserving the body from decay: either the aim of "retaining the soul within the body as long as the form of the body could be preserved entire" or else "facilitating the reunion of it with the body at the day of resurrection" (Pettigrew 1834, 13). Pettigrew begins his discussion with references to Herodotus and Servius and adds a number of further classical authors making remarks on Egyptian embalming practices, but he does not discuss them or attempt to resolve the differences between them.

In the end, Pettigrew's understanding is thus a fairly simple extrapolation of the notion of preservation: Just as the bodies were evidently preserved, so also was the soul, and the soul needed the preserved body either for its own survival or to have a body to return to at the resurrection. This framework makes his approach quite similar to that taken in earlier centuries, especially by predecessors in the discipline of "mummy studies," in that it is the mere fact of mummification that needs to be explained with reference to classical authors, unlike the increasing reliance on ancient Egyptian monuments by his contemporaries.

Wilkinson on Egyptian Life and Death

Pioneering Egyptologist John Gardner Wilkinson (1797–1875; cf. Thompson 1992) was first encountered in the introduction above, and his work—and hence also his understanding of Egyptian mortuary religion—was widely read in the mid-nineteenth century, even if its initial success would prove relatively short-lived (Thompson 1992, 158; Gange 2013, 55–88). Wilkinson's voluminous *Manners and Customs of the Ancient Egyptians* aimed to treat ancient Egyptian culture within a genre popular at the time that combined elements of a travelogue with descriptions of a more ethnographic character (Thompson 1992, 141–59; Gange 2013, 79–89). The data for Wilkinson's descriptions of various aspects of the Egyptians' way of life were drawn primarily from his extensive studies of the wall paintings from Theban tombs, though more traditional sources like the classical authors also fed into his reconstructions. The work appeared in two multivolume "series," the first published in 1837 and the second in 1841.

Although, as Gange argued, a "major novelty" in the work "was to limit discussion of religion—ancient Egyptian, Muslim and Christian—to the barest minimum" (Gange 2013, 88), nonetheless ancient Egyptian religion plays a visible role in the second series of volumes of the *Manners and Customs*. As part of these discussions, ideas relating more specifically to mortuary religion come up in a few places, notably in connection with conceptions of the divine, sacred animals, and especially in a lengthy discussion devoted to funeral rites more specifically.

To Wilkinson, a fundamental idea in Egyptian religion is the doctrine of "emanation" borrowed by Pythagoras from the Egyptians, which in turn means it can be elucidated through Greek authors building on that intellectual tradition, whether or not they explicitly connect their ideas to Egypt. This doctrine entails a "universal soul" that dwells in all parts of the world, analogous to the way the human soul dwells in the human body (Wilkinson 1841, 1:316–18), a notion that authors like Plutarch and Porphyry ascribed to the Egyptians. The implication is that individual souls are emanations of the world soul, and that they return to this divine origin upon death, after having been purified of the "evil propensities" and "sinful actions" incurred during life in the human body (Wilkinson 1841, 2:112). The means of this purgation was the soul's passing through animal bodies, and Wilkinson follows Plato in understanding some animals as being more suitable for wicked souls, with the nature of the animal corresponding to the sins of the soul. This idea can explain both why some "higher" animals were considered sacred and thus embalmed, and also why "intermediary agents and Dæmons" inhabited the bodies of animals and hence were depicted with the heads of such animals (Wilkinson 1841, 2:112–13).

Turning to more specifically funerary questions at the end of the work, Wilkinson draws on his familiarity with the decoration of Theban tombs by taking as his point of departure representations of the ancestor cult there, although he is also quick to connect these ritual actions to the broader beliefs he understands as underlying them. Thus, in accordance with the overall notion of emanation, Wilkinson suggests that the recipient of mortuary offerings was "that particular portion of the divine essence which constituted the soul of each individual, and returned to the Deity after death" (Wilkinson 1841, 2:381). He adds further notions that are not necessarily straightforward to reconcile, namely that returning to the deity also implies an "admission into the regions of the blessed," but equally that bodies are mummified in the likeness of the god Osiris "in token of his having assumed the character of that deity" (Wilkinson 1841, 2:382).

After this brief outline of the motivations behind Egyptian burial practices, Wilkinson goes on to describe in detail the kind of rituals depicted on tomb walls, in accordance with the ethnographic aims of the "manners and customs" genre of writing. Wilkinson suggests that the reason for decorating the tombs and equipping them with grave goods may be that the soul "took pleasure in contemplating the scenes it delighted in during its sojourn upon earth" (Wilkinson 1841, 2:393), though he suggests that the reason for depositing grave goods in the tomb might also be that they would be of use when the soul was supposed to return to the body, foreshadowing his discussion of the transmigration of the soul (2:395). After describing the architecture and uses of the tombs themselves, Wilkinson returns to the question of ancient rituals in discussing mourning practices. His point of departure is Herodotus, but he compares the description with contemporary practices of mourning described by Lane's ethnography of early nineteenth-century Egypt before turning to the depictions of the funeral procession in tomb imagery (Wilkinson 1841, 2:402–24).

The description of the tomb scenes is detailed, and it is occasionally supplemented with quotations from Diodorus inserted in new contexts. For example, Wilkinson uses a quotation applying the description in Diodorus of the king's sacrifices in the library of the temple of Ozymandias to elucidate the contents of a priestly recitation at a funeral:

> Before him stood an altar laden with offerings; and a priest, opening a long roll of papyrus, read aloud the funeral ritual, and an account

> of his good deeds, "in order to show to Osiris and the Assessors the extent of his piety and justice during his life." (Wilkinson 1841, 2:414, citing Diodorus 1, 49.3 without reference)

After the lengthy description of depictions of the burial procession, Wilkinson turns to the "remarkable ceremony" where the right to burial was determined (Wilkinson 1841, 424). Quoting Diodorus's description of this ritual at length (Wilkinson 1841, 2:426–28), Wilkinson remarks on the connection between the ritual and the ultimate fate of the soul, stating about the negative judgment depriving the unworthy deceased of burial that "the awful sentence foretold the misery which had befallen the soul of the deceased in a future state" because "a belief in transmigration suggested to them the possibility of his soul being condemned to inhabit the body of some unclean animal" (Wilkinson 1841, 2:428). In other words, Wilkinson makes the by now familiar connection (e.g., from Rosellini) between the ritual judgment described by Diodorus and the divine judgment in the beyond determining the nature of the transmigration of the soul. This is corroborated when he says that the judges in the ritual were "equal in number to the assessors who were destined to examine the deceased at his final judgment" (Wilkinson 1841, 2:430).

In line with his understanding of incarnation in animals as a form of purgatorial preparation of the soul for returning to the universal soul, the punishment is only temporary. Additionally, inspired by Catholic practices of expiation, Wilkinson supposes that sacrifices were meant to shorten this period: "when the devotion of friends, aided by liberal donations in the service of religion, and the influential prayers of the priests, had sufficiently softened the otherwise inexorable nature of the Gods, the period of this state of purgatory was doubtless shortened" (Wilkinson 1841, 2:429).

The wording here is somewhat acerbic, echoing Protestant critique of Catholic indulgencies, as Wilkinson is apt to see the potential weaknesses of this system. He does, however, note that there must have been limits to the potential for priestly corruption, since blatant cases would have damaged the "credit of the priesthood," so that the priests can be assumed to have been motivated by virtue, at least "until society had undergone those changes, to which all nations are subject at their fall" (Wilkinson 1841, 2:429).

Wilkinson goes on to cite with approval, and offer examples of, Diodorus's idea that Greek conceptions of the underworld were derived from Egyptian funerary rituals, concluding that it cannot be doubted that "the fable of Charon and Styx owed its origin to these Egyptian ceremonies" (Wilkinson 1841, 2:433). Although the main tenor of the discussion is thus the widespread parallelism between the ritual judgment regarding the right to burial and the underworld judgment determining the soul's fate, the latter was ultimately more encompassing. The deceased might have succeeded in concealing their sins from everyone present at the human judgment, but Wilkinson supposes the divine judgment to be based on omniscience: "But the all-scrutinising eye of the Deity was known to penetrate into the innermost thoughts of the heart; and they believed that whatever conscience told them they had done amiss was recorded against them in the book of Thoth, out of which they would be judged according to their works" (Wilkinson 1841, 2:439).

After the discussion of the judgment ritual, Wilkinson returns to the topic of metempsychosis in more detail, based on passages from Herodotus, Plutarch, and Plato (Wilkinson 1841, 2:440–42). As we saw above, Wilkinson understands the series of transmigrations as ending with a return to the same human body that the soul originally inhabited, noting that "there is reason to believe" this is why the Egyptians sought to preserve the bodies of the dead for long periods and to have them equipped with useful or precious objects. He goes on to note, however, that the practice of mummifying animals could not be explained in a similar way, so that perhaps the practice originates in sanitary concerns or simply the wish to preserve the outward form out of "a feeling of respect for the dead" (Wilkinson 1841, 2:444–45). As we saw in the introduction above, ultimately Wilkinson leans toward the Egyptians' believing in bodily resurrection (Wilkinson 1841, 2:445). Accordingly, Wilkinson suggests that the well-attested practice of reuse of tombs must thus have happened only after the three thousand years had elapsed, with the tombs' having outlived their purpose once the original occupants had been resurrected.

As noted above, Wilkinson understands the ritual judgment before burial and the afterlife judgment in front of Osiris as separate events but closely connected. He thus moves on to the topic of the "future judgment," which he studies based on scenes in tombs and papyri, since the classical authors have little to offer on this. He uses the by now well established scene from the Book of Gates to illustrate the result of a negative judgment of a dead man, as Osiris "condemns his soul to return to earth under the form of a pig, or some other unclean animal." On the other hand, a successful judgment of the deceased will "entitle him to admission to the mansions of the blessed," as shown in Book of the Dead scenes of admitting him into the presence of Osiris (Wilkinson 1841, 2:446–47). He goes on to discuss differences in the details of various versions of the scene, including the temple scene from Dayr al-Madīnah studied by Champollion.

One challenge that underlay this discussion, as it had for many previous ones on this topic, is that while the monuments were able to add a number of details to the suppositions based on conventional readings of the classical authors, they still remained unclear about the nature of the afterlife for the blessed dead, which one might have expected to be a main theme. In principle, Wilkinson's point of departure in the Platonic doctrine of emanation might have led to the idea that a dissolution in the universal soul was the goal after sufficient purification. However, he remains beholden to the more intuitive Christian idea of the individual experience of rewards and punishments as central to eschatology, and the admission to the god's presence is understood within this framework. Thus he notes that "the deceased on admission to that pure state must be born again, and commence a new life, cleansed from all the impurities of his earthly career" (Wilkinson 1841, 2:449). Later on he gives a further clue to his understanding of the nature of this existence in noting that "the Egyptians who, from their virtues, were admitted to the mansions of the blessed, were permitted to assume the form and name" of Osiris (Wilkinson 1841, 2:455).

The final lengthy section of the chapter explores practices of embalming in detail, beginning as usual with the descriptions by Herodotus and Diodorus before moving on to a series of observations on details in the two descriptions, dealing mostly with the practical execution rather than the religious motivations. A few exceptions to this pattern are worth emphasizing, however. In discussing in greater detail the previous interpretations of the reasons for the practices of embalming, Wilkinson rejects Servius's idea that the soul remained attached to the body as long as the body did not decay, noting that this is in opposition to "the known opinion of the Egyptians, which, as we see even from the sculptures, was that the soul left the body at the moment of death" (Wilkinson 1841, 2:462). Another erroneous idea in the classical authors that Wilkinson sets out to correct is Porphyry's and Plutarch's account of discarding the intestines to purify the rest of the body. This is also contradicted by evidence from the tombs as well as the general religious ideas of the Egyptians, and Wilkinson dismisses the notion outright, noting that "no one . . . could for an instant suppose that they would on any consideration be induced to pollute the stream, or insult the dead by a similar custom" (Wilkinson 1841, 2:464–65). This leads Wilkinson to a lengthy warning concerning the general unreliability of the classical authors when compared with the evidence of the tombs. Nonetheless, he accepts that the "confession" related by Porphyry "partakes of the character of truth" and "indeed is an imperfect portion of that recorded in the sculptures" (Wilkinson 1841, 2:467).

Wilkinson's discussion has a number of points in common with those of the previous decades, and its chief innovation is new evidence, especially that resulting from his extensive study of the private rock tombs at Thebes. Although he draws on them for most of his general framework, Wilkinson is highly skeptical of the classical authors when it comes to matters of detail that can be directly checked against the monuments. Probably for a similar reason, he is often cautious in ascribing specific religious motivations to observable practices, and as exemplified above, he sometimes lists several possibilities advanced by classical authors or later scholars without making a definitive choice between them.

Strictly speaking there are a number of contradictions in Wilkinson's model, owing partly to his tendency to juxtapose different, sometimes mutually exclusive, explanations rather than committing to a single one.

For example, the resurrection of the body at the end of a transmigratory cycle is suggested as the most likely reason for mummification. Yet at the same time the mummy is understood as giving the deceased the form of Osiris, to which the deceased earn the right through a successful judgment that allows them to avoid the purgatory transmigration (and hence presumably the resulting resurrection of the body). This shows once again the increasing tension at this time between the growing importance and concreteness of the ethical judgment allowing access to the afterlife (or leading to damnation as the case may be) on the one hand and the purgatorial transmigration on the other.

Not coincidentally, this echoes tensions also found in contemporary discourses about the Christian afterlife (e.g., Rowell 1974; Wheeler 1994, esp. 68–83; Sharp 2006, 148–50). This background may well have contributed to the overall development in this period where metempsychosis is increasingly subsumed under a broader framework of judgment resulting in rewards and punishment, coming to play a role as a temporary purgatory. It may thus be no accident that the main writers on this subject were Protestants who would likely have regarded the notion of purgatory as at best superfluous and at worst potentially corrupting. As we saw above, Wilkinson makes this connection explicitly, so it is quite likely that this overall understanding of the role of metempsychosis, along with other reasons noted, would have contributed to making this idea seem increasingly redundant within the emerging model of the Egyptian afterlife.

Another development in the mid-nineteenth century of possible relevance is the increasing popularity of spiritualist movements emphasizing a belief in reincarnation (Sharp 2006). While quite frequently the motif of reincarnation was associated specifically with Egypt (e.g., Dobson 2022), the prevalence of such ideas in contemporary Europe would have changed their appeal as scholarly explanatory models. For example, it may be more than mere coincidence that one of the most explicit early rejecters of the idea of ancient Egyptian metempsychosis, French Egyptologist Gaston Maspero (1872, 340n1), himself took an interest in spiritualism and in particular in Madame Blavatsky's theories that had reincarnation of souls as a central element (David 1999, 64–66).

Lepsius's Book of the Dead

The Prussian scholar Karl Richard Lepsius (1810–84; cf. Lepper and Hafemann 2012), widely credited as the founder of German Egyptology, would later go on to produce another monumental expedition-based description of Egypt. In 1842 he published a seminal work on the ancient Egyptian composition hitherto known as the "funerary ritual," for which he coined the term still in use, the Book of the Dead (*Todtenbuch*) (Lepsius 1842; cf. Assmann 2012, 80–83; Willems 2023). The main focus of Lepsius's book is documenting an extensive manuscript in the Egyptian Museum in Turin, dividing the manuscript into its constituent parts or "chapters," as the subdivisions of the Book of the Dead are still known. In addition to this philological work, Lepsius includes an introduction in which he lays out the cultural importance and distinguishing features of the Book of the Dead, especially as they appear in the Turin manuscript. Lepsius initially presents his basic understanding of the significance of the funerary papyrus by noting that the Egyptians would give such scrolls to the deceased "for the soul's long journey" in order that they might serve as a "passport" (*Paß*) securing their positive reception at "the many gates in the heavenly regions and dwellings [*himmlischen Gegenden und Wohnungen*]" (Lepsius 1842, 3).

To justify his new name for the composition, Lepsius notes that it does not have the content one might expect if it were a ritual manual along the lines assumed by Champollion and others as implied in their designation as "funerary ritual." Instead of ritual instructions, hymns, and prayers, Lepsius stresses that the deceased is presented as acting, and that thus the texts and images "concern only him and his encounters [*Begegnisse*] on the long wandering [*Wanderung*] after the earthly death" (Lepsius 1842, 3). Lepsius correspondingly understands the manuscript as detailing the movements and experiences of the deceased, on the one hand, and on the other his prayers to the various gods he meets. In other words, Lepsius's closer study of the texts and images of the Book of the Dead consolidates the assumption that the composition as a whole details the events in the afterlife, just as earlier scholars such as Jomard had conjectured simply based on the weighing of the heart scene, interpreted as the final judgment of the deceased.

Nonetheless, Lepsius takes care to note that the book is apparently not a firmly delineated, progressive account of the travels of the soul. Instead, the individual chapters are separate compositions of varying importance, all in one way or another relating to the "future of the soul [*Zukunft der Seele*])" (Lepsius 1842, 4).

Conceptually, Lepsius's German text offers a productive ambiguity. The standard term for transmigration of souls, *Seelenwanderung*, is used of the journey of the deceased, but the literal meaning is simply "wandering of the soul," which may thus refer simply to the soul's traveling from one place to another, or entering a new, heavenly body in the beyond, rather than necessarily being reincarnated in different worldly bodies (as widely discussed during the late eighteenth and early nineteenth centuries; e.g., Sawicki 2002, 47–51). Thus, without the component "soul" (*Seele*), Lepsius uses the word "wandering" (*Wanderung*) simply of the long journey undertaken after death (Lepsius 1842, 3). This means that Lepsius is able to remain somewhat agnostic regarding the specific dogma of transmigration despite drawing on its terminology. Thus he characterizes the purpose of the first fifteen chapters of the book as dealing with "the appearance in light, i.e., the transfiguration [*Verklärung*]) of the deceased, the end goal of the entire transmigration/wandering of the soul [*Endzwecke der ganzen Seelenwanderung*]" (Lepsius 1842, 8). The notion of *Verklärung* (from the verb *klären*, "make/become clear") is used as a gloss of Lepsius's translation of the title of the Book of the Dead as whole, *Erscheinung im Lichte* ("appearance in light"), but at the same time he is no doubt conscious of the theological usage of the term to designate the "transfiguration" of Christ as described in the synoptic gospels (Luke 9:28–36; Mark 9:2–9; Matthew 17:1–8). In the Egyptian case, Lepsius notes a slight mismatch between the previous assumption that the book described the afterlife journey and the details observed in the manuscript. The "transfiguration" is depicted in the form of the deceased's ultimately leaving the tomb alive, but "none of the intervening phases [*Zwischenstationen*] have found pictorial expression but are only briefly and partially touched upon in the individual chapters of the text" (Lepsius 1842, 8).

It is worth noting at this point that Lepsius would go on to articulate this eschatological vision even more explicitly in a subsequent book on the earlier textual tradition of the Book of the Dead (Lepsius 1867). He notes that the expression "day" in the indigenous title of the Book of the Dead as "coming out by day" refers to

> "the Day of Resurrection, of Judgment, of Justification," etc., in the ordinary temporal usage, without allusion to the light of the subterranean Re, or of the clarity of the future life as opposed to the earthly darkness, or to a "luminous form of the soul" [*Lichgestalt der Seele*] and similar un-Egyptian ideas. It is the well-known, self-evident day, *dies illa* that everyone should remember above all others and that therefore is not specified further. (Lepsius 1867, 7)

Here an Egyptian expression can serve to demonstrate that resurrection, judgment, and justification are inherently Egyptian ideas, unlike more exotic, and ultimately more culturally specific, notions that other scholars had proposed as central Egyptian dogma during the decades around the middle of the nineteenth century.

Returning to his earlier publication of the Turin manuscript, in his brief overview of the chapters, Lepsius establishes a new central vignette in the repertoire of illustrations of the Egyptian afterlife by connecting it, as with the weighing of the heart decades earlier, to existing ideas and expectations. As we have seen in previous chapters, a recurring challenge to interpretations of the Egyptian afterlife had been that, rather surprisingly, ancient images did not appear to depict the blessed existence analogous to the Greek Elysian Fields that scholars had deduced to be the aim of the beliefs in postmortem rewards and punishment, though earlier scholars had tentatively identified this theme in scenes of the tomb's owner engaged in agricultural work and other activities. Through his scrutiny of the texts and images of the Turin manuscript, Lepsius confirmed this connection in his interpretation of what in his new numbering corresponded to Book of the Dead chapter 110 (fig. 9), in which the owner of the book is shown carrying out a number of agricultural and cultic tasks in a stylized watery landscape. In what has become another long-lived and popular interpretation, Lepsius (1842, 13) provides the following reading and contextualization of the scene:

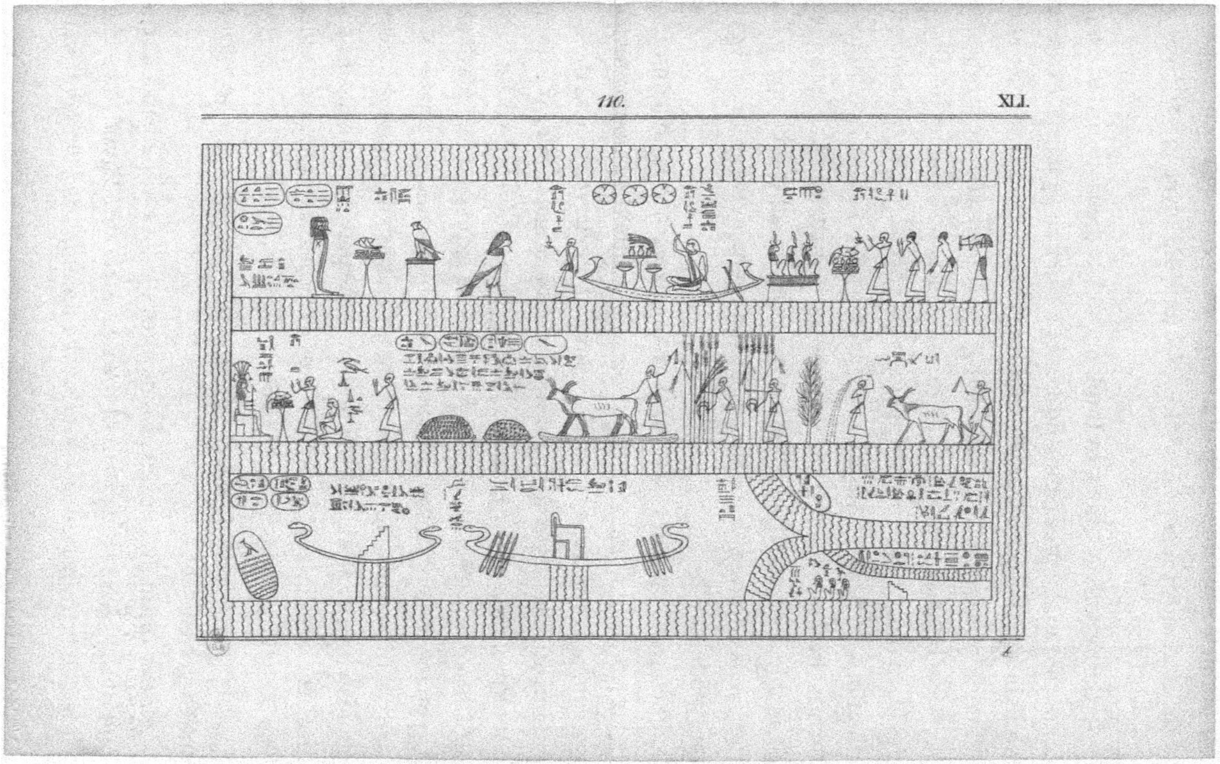

110. XLI.

Fig. 9: Vignette from Book of the Dead chapter 110 as reproduced by Lepsius. Karl Richard Lepsius, *Das Todtenbuch der Aegypter*, pl. 41. Bibliothèque nationale de France.

> This no doubt has a historical connection with the Greek conception of the Elysian Fields and Islands of the Blessed, which they like the Egyptians located in the far west, flushed or even entirely surrounded by the ocean, where the blessed souls of humans continued their earthly lives according to their individual inclinations, only liberated from all worldly toils [*Mühsal*]. Later they associated a judgment of the dead with it under the auspices of Saturn, the Egyptian Seb [Geb].

In this way the vignette to Book of the Dead chapter 110 becomes connected to the preexisting notion of a carefree paradisial existence while in turn becoming an illustration of what the Egyptian afterlife actually looked like, something that had otherwise been missing. Precisely because it was missing from the classical sources relating to Egypt, in describing how each person lives according to their own inclinations, Lepsius seems to be drawing on Greek and Roman ideas such as the *Aeneid* (6, 653). In this way the vignette can also be used as a tangible demonstration of the frequent idea in earlier scholarship that the Greeks derived their descriptions of the underworld from Egyptian models.

The establishment of the vignette of chapter 110 as an icon of the Egyptian afterlife paradise thus follows exactly the same pattern as the similar construction of the weighing of the heart scene as the Last Judgment: a well-established abstract notion originally derived from a reinterpretation of classical authors, or extrapolation from them based on Christian expectations was found to be expressed in a particular Egyptian scene based on the scholar's iconographic expectations. As soon as this connection was accepted, the image-cum-interpretation could in turn stand alone to demonstrate the prevalence of the original idea. The afterlife paradise could thus join the Last Judgment as ideas that were firmly illustrated in ancient sources, while the specific historical process leading to this interpretation was quickly downplayed and forgotten.

Not surprisingly, Lepsius also devotes significant space to a discussion of the "divine judgment of the deceased," the Egyptian heading for which he translates as "Book of the redemption [*Erlösung*] in the hall of the double Justice [*Gerechtigkeit*]" (Lepsius 1842, 13), providing another example of the gradual co-optation of indigenous terminology by paraphrasing, or even translating, it with Christian theological terminology. The following detailed iconographic analysis is mostly descriptive, though his interpretation surfaces occasionally, as when Lepsius refers to the heart of the deceased on the balance as "the criterion of his earthly way of life [*Lebenswandel*]" (Lepsius 1842, 14). He translates the caption to Ammut and notes, apparently with implicit approval, that earlier scholars had compared this figure to the Greek Cerberus.

While he notes that the number of attendants (*Beisitzer*) of Osiris illustrated is the same as the number of judges given by Diodorus, he contrasts the former as "underworldly judges" (*unterirdische Richter*) (Lepsius 1842, 14), without detailing the relation between the ritual judgment and that taking place in the beyond. The role of the judges is also couched in Christian terms such as making each of them responsible for "punishing a particular sin [*Sünde*]." Lepsius does, however, note the particularity of the speech situation, pointing out that

> This is thus not a confession of sins [*Sündenbekenntniß*] as preparation for a merciful reception [*einer gnädigen Aufnahme*] among the blessed, but one's own justification [*Rechtfertigung*] before the judge adjudicating according to strict justice, upon which the acquittal [*Lossprechung*] depends. (Lepsius 1842, 15)

The distinction between his contemporary Christian beliefs and ancient Egyptian ones is thus couched in theological terms of the difference between a reliance on divine grace versus reliance on a juridical framework of transgression of laws, with the analogy to the difference between Protestant notions of salvation through divine grace alone (*sola gratia*) versus Catholic reliance on good works probably not being entirely coincidental.

At the end of his overview of the contents of the Book of the Dead, Lepsius offers some remarks on the work's overall significance. Struck by the wealth of detail in the text, he suggests that one could in principle extract "an entire heavenly geography of the Egyptians" from the text and images, and he notes that the book accordingly contained "everything that relates to their conceptions about the life of the soul after death" (Lepsius 1842, 16).

It is remarkable that the papyrus in Lepsius's study was able to completely live up to the conjecture Jomard made before the decipherment of hieroglyphs, according to which he expected its texts and images to contain a description of the soul's journey through the underworld. This makes it possible to take a step further than the identification of conventional ideas such as the judgment of the dead in ancient Egyptian imagery and instead use the remainder of the contents to flesh out aspects of the afterlife not mentioned, or mentioned only vaguely, in the classical sources. This is the case notably with the vignette to chapter 110, understood to depict the rewards of a carefree paradisial existence that previous scholars had deduced logically. It is also worth noting how the vocabulary remains distinctly Christian even when, as with the "negative confession," it is used to emphasize minor contrasts between Christian (and especially Protestant) practices and Egyptian religion. Indigenous terms are now also co-opted, as when the notion of "redemption [*Erlösung*]" is used in translating the heading accompanying the weighing of the heart scene.

Another noteworthy development crystallizing clearly in Lepsius's work is the growing tendency to understand the ancient Egyptian afterlife in concrete terms similar to prevalent nineteenth-century modes of thinking about life after death. McDannell and Lang enumerate four key features of this new conception developing from the mid-eighteenth century (McDannell and Lang 1988, 183; for the German context more specifically, see Sawicki 2002; Weir 2008; Pangburn 2014). First, for the righteous the heavenly existence begins immediately after death without the notion of a period of sleeping or first spending time in purgatory. This idea was the slowest to be taken up in the ancient Egyptian model, because for most scholars it would become compatible only once the central notion of metempsychosis was abandoned during the third quarter of the nineteenth century. Second, rather than a contrast to life on earth, heaven came to be seen as "a continuation and fulfillment of material existence" (McDannell and Lang 1988, 183; cf., e.g., Wheeler 1994, 130–33; Sawicki 2002, 41–42). This is seen especially clearly with

Lepsius's interpretation of the "Elysian Fields," but as we saw above, earlier nineteenth-century scholars similarly held a rather "material" vision of the Egyptian afterlife. The vignette of Book of the Dead chapter 110 also fit popular expectations about heaven in additional ways corresponding to McDannell and Lang's third and fourth points: the remarkably active conception of existence in heaven, with the righteous "experiencing spiritual progress and joyfully occupying themselves in a dynamic, motion-filled environment. The journey to God does not end with admittance to heaven but continues eternally" (McDannell and Lang 1988, 183; cf., e.g., Wheeler 1994, 131–32; Sharp 2006, 148–49; Sparn 2007, 21–23; Pangburn 2014, 786–87), as well as a focus on social relationships in the afterlife (cf. Wheeler 1994, 120–21, 132–33; Jalland 1996, 271–76; Rugg 1999, 213–15; Pangburn 2014, 784–85), which is not mentioned explicitly by Lepsius but very likely is how the presence of additional human figures in the vignette was understood.

While aspects of McDannell and Lang's overall model can certainly be nuanced in places according, for example, to various social groups and contexts of writing (e.g., Jalland 1996, 266–71), as indicated by the references in the previous paragraph it has been generally confirmed by subsequent studies of nineteenth-century conceptions of the afterlife in different nations and denominations. These changes of the understanding of the afterlife in Christian traditions (and Christian-derived ones such as spiritualism; cf. Sawicki 2002; Sharp 2006) help explain how expectations around initiatory journeys in the vein of Terrasson could combine with an increasing familiarity with ancient Egyptian religious iconography to form attractive and comprehensible models of the Egyptian afterlife that, while seemingly arising directly from the imagery itself, were both novel and at the same time firmly rooted in the frameworks developed over the previous centuries. In particular, this update meant that the overall features of the Egyptian afterlife could continue to correspond to the understanding in contemporary mainstream (especially Protestant) Christianities.

As noted above Lepsius's interpretation of the "Elysian Fields" vignette can be seen as mirroring the earlier establishment of the weighing of the heart vignette as the Egyptian Last Judgment. Just as in that previous interpretation, Lepsius established a fit between strong expectations (in this case of relatively recently developed intuitions about the afterlife as opposed to the long-standing idea of postmortem judgment) that first allowed him to identify and interpret the importance of the image and then, immediately afterward, to use it to demonstrate that the Egyptians did in fact believe in the concept projected onto them, even if in this case the eighteenth- to nineteenth-century origins of the general model of the afterlife are brought out clearly by its difference from earlier concepts. At the same time, the emphasis on concrete imagery interpreted literally established a contrast to contemporary German Protestant thought, where the afterlife, increasingly referred to more abstractly as the "Beyond" (*Jenseits*) from the 1830s and 1840s, tended to be understood in a more metaphorical sense in both text and image (Sparn 2007; Weir 2008).

Apart from his publication of the Turin manuscript and his later work on the textual tradition of the Book of the Dead (Lepsius 1867), Lepsius did not have Egyptian religion as a main focus in his research (Assmann 2012). The same year his *Todtenbuch der Ägypter* was published, Lepsius left for a multiyear expedition to Egypt (1842–45) commissioned by King Friedrich Wilhelm IV of Prussia. The published work, *Denkmaeler aus Aegypten und Aethiopien* (Monuments from Egypt and Ethiopia; Lepsius 1849–56) was a major contribution to the knowledge of the ancient monuments in the tradition of the *Description de l'Égypte*. Only the plates were published right away, as Lepsius never wrote the planned text volumes with commentary that might have provided further details about his understanding of aspects of Egyptian mortuary religion following his lengthy study of the monuments. The text volumes that were eventually published from 1897 to 1913 were written by major scholars of that time based on the notes of Lepsius and other expedition members, but they are highly focused on description and documentation over interpretation, let alone those of Lepsius himself from several decades earlier. As such, the *Denkmaeler*, despite its undisputed status as a milestone in early Egyptology, has little to offer for our present concerns.

Lepsius's study of the Book of the Dead almost immediately became an important benchmark for identifying chapters and comparing textual traditions in catalogs, publications, and interpretations of Book of the Dead manuscripts in other collections (e.g., Hincks 1843, esp.

22–32). The rapidly spreading understanding of the Book of the Dead as a literal description of the soul's fate in the afterlife, now seemingly vindicated by a detailed study of a lengthy manuscript, did not necessarily lead to an overt sidelining of the model of metempsychosis. In his two-volume *History of Our Western Philosophy* (*Geschichte unserer abendländischen Philosophie*), German philosopher Eduard Röth (1807–58) argued in favor of the indebtedness of pre-Socratic philosophy to "eastern" ideas, more specifically Egyptian and Zoroastrian ones. In his bid to rehabilitate the advanced and sophisticated character of Egyptian beliefs, Röth uses the time-honored strategy of drawing mainly on Platonic and Hermetic models applied to ancient Egypt, thereby establishing a clear continuity with Greek thought. While he acknowledges the value of the Book of the Dead for reconstructing Egyptian beliefs (Röth 1846, 124) and draws on its illustrations as depictions of the afterlife, in practice his overall approach has more in common with those found in the eighteenth century or even earlier by prioritizing classical writings, with only the occasional confirmation in the newly available Egyptian sources.

Correspondingly, his model is one where the souls of the deceased are judged in the underworld, with those souls that were found "fully cleansed and purified" being allowed to ascend to the higher regions to lead a blessed existence forever among the pure gods and spirits (Röth 1846, 178). By contrast, souls that were not sufficiently purified had to undergo a "state of atonement" (*Büssungszustand*) on earth in the body of a human, animal, or even plant, according to the degree and nature of their sins. To Röth it is the initial journey through the underworld to the place of judgment that is mainly described in the Book of the Dead, while the parts following chapter 125 and the weighing of the heart are understood as showing the ascent of the virtuous soul to the gods (Röth 1846, 178–79). Because the Book of the Dead was naturally focused on the positive outcome, the fate of the damned souls is not depicted or described. For this Röth draws on the well-established identity of the pig in the Book of Gates judgment scene as the newly assigned body of a wicked soul. To harmonize Herodotus's notion of a three-thousand-year cycle with this general ethical framework, Röth supposes that it was possible to shorten the period of atonement by leading "a holy and virtuous life." This means that there was no concept of eternal punishment, as the entire purpose of life on earth was to purify the soul in preparation for its ultimate return. Röth (1846, 180–81) can thus conclude that there is a complete logical consistency between the doctrine of metempsychosis and the notion of postmortem rewards and punishments when understood within this framework.

Even when metempsychosis was thus taken as fundamental for Egyptian mortuary religion as Röth's interpretation shows, it still played a rather marginal role as a temporary process of purgation, and if the Book of the Dead described only the fate of the blessed, one would thus not expect to find metempsychosis described there. The result is that although the tenor of Röth's discussion differs from more mainstream contemporaries owing to his centering of the language of metempsychosis, at the higher level of abstraction of the overall model, the differences turn out to be superficial.

A scholarly consensus was thus emerging in the 1840s, and several of the works discussed above enjoyed significant influence whereby the ideas were disseminated widely, helped along by the fact that scholars like Rosellini and Wilkinson based their ideas on, and were thus largely compatible with, older literature and traditionally accepted ideas while seemingly anchoring them firmly in newly available ancient evidence. These models were not, however, accepted unquestioningly by all scholars of the time. An example of critical reception of the new interpretations is found in the work of English historian and classicist John Kenrick (1788–1877; cf. Kennedy 2006) exemplifying what David Gange terms the "unorthodox Egyptology" of midcentury Britain (Gange 2013, 95–120).

As a Unitarian inspired by historical-biblical criticism, Kenrick was critical of what he viewed as a corruption of Christianity, whereby original Christian ideas had become overlaid with ancient Greek (and thus pagan) philosophical tenets. As a central example, as a Unitarian Kenrick was strongly convinced of the human nature of Christ, understanding the prevalent interpretation of him as divine as being an intrusive, pagan idea (Kennedy 2006, 134–37). Notably, he saw Egyptian religion as having undergone a similar fate of being circumscribed by Greek philosophy in an effort to systemize its teachings—ultimately in vain, because such systemizing was foreign to the multitude of ideas commingling in ancient Egyptian thought (Kennedy 2006, 282–84).

The first volume of his general historical survey *Ancient Egypt under the Pharaohs* (1850) ends with chapters devoted to questions of religion, a significant part of which deals with topics connected more specifically to mortuary religion (Kenrick 1850, 472–509). Kenrick begins this discussion by noting the universal nature of ideas about a future life, proposing that such beliefs originate in the impossibility "for man not to conceive of himself as composed of two elements, a corporeal and a spiritual principle, to which a different destiny is assigned, when their temporary union is dissolved by death" (Kenrick 1850, 472). Having thus established the innate nature of belief in the soul and its continuance after death, he goes on to present a brief overview of such ideas in different ancient cultures before turning to Egypt more specifically. Kenrick argues that the great expenditure on tombs and their decoration can be explained only with reference to Servius's idea of the soul's remaining attached to the body as long as the latter remains intact, whereas the complete detachment of the soul or its transmigration through animals could not explain Egyptian burial practices (Kenrick 1850, 475–76). Tomb decoration and grave goods would then imply that the soul could be "kept in a state by which its living condition was closely imitated" (Kenrick 1850, 477).

This does not fit readily with Herodotus's description of metempsychosis, and consistent with his interests in close, critical reading of Herodotus, Kenrick offers an exegesis of the passage arguing that Herodotus meant the soul would begin its transmigration upon death, not only when the body had decayed. He also points out that Herodotus does not imply that transmigration could function as reward or punishment, nor that its purpose is purgatorial. He likewise points out that the idea of the soul's returning to its divine origin at the end of transmigration is an idea found only in later writers, not in Herodotus's own work. Keeping thus to a very strict reading of Herodotus (already presented in germinal form in Kenrick's textual commentary; Kenrick 1841, 161–62), he notes that this cannot, however, have been a part of the popular religion, but rather was "a refinement of sacerdotal philosophy," in contrast to the popular belief in a transcendent afterlife, which he characterizes with a free paraphrase of Diodorus as "the hope that the deceased may dwell in peace and happiness under the protection of Osiris in the invisible world." Correspondingly, he emphasizes that it is "very rare" to find evidence of metempsychosis in the monuments, and he explicitly questions the conventional interpretation of the weighing scene from the Book of Gates on contextual grounds, noting wryly that it would be "very strange, however, that the sepulchre of a king should exhibit his soul as condemned to such a degradation, and we may therefore doubt whether the relation of this to the judgement-scene has been rightly apprehended" (Kenrick 1850, 479–80).

If Herodotus thus makes no implication of judgment in his description of the Egyptian belief in metempsychosis, Kenrick proposes that "it could hardly exist among the Greeks without being combined with punishment and reward," so that he does not follow the standard practice of projecting such ideas in Pindar, Plato, and the Hermetic writings back onto the Egyptians themselves, but rather understands them as Greek innovations (Kenrick 1850, 479–84). On the other hand, the "popular conception of the state of the dead, as subjected to the judgement of Osiris and existing in the invisible world, which the Egyptians called Amenthe, must have acknowledged a retribution for the conduct during life" (Kenrick 1850, 484), a notion he demonstrates with the conventional illustration of the weighing of the heart vignette from the Book of the Dead. In line with his contemporaries, he understands the book as a whole as describing the deceased's "adventures after the soul has left the body" (Kenrick 1850, 485) and briefly describes a few of the episodes based on the published sources, especially Lepsius's *Todtenbuch*. His interpretations also largely follow Lepsius, including the "Elysian Fields" of chapter 110, where the deceased is depicted "offering to the inhabitants of the celestial regions, embarking on the heavenly waters, ploughing, sowing, reaping and threshing" (Kenrick 1850, 486).

Not only is the fate of the damned not described in the Book of the Dead, but Kenrick assumes that the very fact of mummification meant the person who thus received the image and name of Osiris had been approved by the god—"just as among ourselves, every one who receives Christian burial is assumed to die in peace with the Church and in the hope of a happy immortality" (Kenrick 1850, 487). Ultimately Kenrick regards it as futile to attempt to reconcile the three different ideas of transmigration, rewards and punishment, and the soul's remaining with the embalmed body in the tomb with additional ideas like the more specific scenarios depicted in the royal tombs or the ritual related by Porphyry. Here as well he sees a parallel in Christian afterlife dogmas that were increasingly debated during his own time (cf. Rowell 1974):

> Not only is a future state of retribution the universal belief of Christendom, but this belief is founded upon express revelation; yet how variously has it been conceived! A millennium on earth, purgatory or the sleep of the soul between death and the general resurrection, the eternal suffering, final extinction or final restitution of the wicked—these are only some of the diversities of opinion to which this doctrine has given rise. (Kenrick 1850, 489)

Kenrick thus takes the idea of the distinction between priestly and popular beliefs even further and acknowledges a potential multitude of partly contradictory ideas, which makes it much less incumbent on him to attempt to reconcile them all. In doing so, he also goes beyond merely paralleling individual Egyptian tenets with their Christian counterparts by also proposing a larger-scale analogy in the different dogmatic schisms that had characterized Christianity, both historically and in his contemporary society.

In the last chapter of the volume, Kenrick discusses the practicalities of embalming, drawing on the range of information available including the classical authors, modern "mummy studies" like Pettigrew's, and pictorial representations of the process of embalming published by Rosellini. In discussing the following funerary ceremonies, he cites Diodorus's description of the judgment ritual before the burial without connecting it to the afterlife judgment previously discussed, and he interprets the depiction of the mummy being touched with an adz—which he understands "symbolically expresses *approbation*" following Rosellini—as the only reflection this custom has found in the monuments (Kenrick 1850, 500).

Kenrick's main contribution is thus on the one hand the return to the strict letter of the Herodotus passage on metempsychosis, leading him to reject later ideas of reincarnation as reward or punishment as Greek innovations. On the other hand, he takes a step further than the conventional idea of distinct popular and elite religious beliefs in acknowledging a potential range of ideas coexisting in ancient Egypt, so that it is not merely unnecessary, but might actually be misguided, for modern scholars to attempt to reconcile them into a single cohesive doctrine.

Egyptian Religion as the Dawn of Morality

A prominent figure in the international discussions about ancient Egypt during the 1850s and 1860s was the German diplomat and historian Christian Karl Josias von Bunsen (1791–1860; cf. Foerster 2001). An advocate of German higher criticism, Bunsen argued in favor of a controversial interpretation of Egyptian chronology according to which the newly available Egyptian monuments were understood to support the chronology found in classical authors as opposed to the traditional biblical understanding of the earth as being no more than six thousand years old (Gold 2019, 218–21).

For all his nonconformity in questions of chronology and stances on method, Bunsen's discussion of ancient Egyptian mortuary religion in his major work *Egypt's Place in Universal History*, published in German from 1845 and translated into English from 1848, largely follows the ideas of the prominent scholars of the 1840s. He begins his discussion of the topic by stating that the Egyptian belief in the immortality of the soul was "mentioned by all Greek writers from Herodotus to Aristotle" in addition to being "brilliantly confirmed by the monuments" (Bunsen 1860, 639; German version Bunsen 1857, 544). To Bunsen the centrality of the doctrine of metempsychosis is confirmed by the prevalence of animal worship, as he rejects various utilitarian explanations of the practice, noting instead that it stems ultimately from "that consciousness of the divinity of nature which is implied in all the religious consciousness of the old world" (Bunsen 1860, 640; 1857, 545–46). He sees the Egyptian religious beliefs in this regard as fundamentally a mixture of African "feticism" with a "spiritual root" of Asiatic origin ingraining "a consciousness of moral responsibility and a belief in the personal indestructibility of the soul" (Bunsen 1860, 640; 1857, 546). As such, Bunsen is unusually explicit about the principles he—and no doubt more implicitly other writers of both this and earlier periods—saw as underlying Egyptian religion. To Bunsen the combination of these ideas is what leads to the familiar picture of a moral judgment after death resulting in the potential punishment of being condemned to life in an animal's body.

Bunsen explains the rationale behind mummification along the lines of Wilkinson and Rosellini as a belief in the resurrection of the body. He understands the transmigration through animals as a purgatory punishment, with the result that the soul will have been justified on its return to the original body. Bunsen regards it as possible that this may happen in "a higher or lower state," with the German original adding one further possibility that, while echoing writers of the earlier decades, is not explained further and is omitted from the English translation: that of "resting [*ruhen*] in Osiris" (Bunsen 1857, 548). The practice of mummification thus becomes something more than merely preserving the body, though that is certainly a central part of its motivation:

> Man justified is one with God, the eternal Creator, self-created. His bodily organ therefore is holy. This doctrine we may now read in every page of their sacred books. Thence the popular notion in Egypt, that, unless its old human envelope was preserved, the soul would be subject to disturbances and hindrances in performing its destined course. (Bunsen 1860, 641–42; 1857, 548)

After presenting this general framework, Bunsen turns to what he regards as two detailed expressions of these ideas, first the familiar Book of the Dead scene of the weighing of the heart, and second the Late Egyptian *Tale of Two Brothers*, newly made available in French Egyptologist Emmanuel de Rougé's rendering (Rougé 1852) as one of the first lengthy ancient Egyptian compositions to be translated.

Bunsen's discussion of the weighing of the heart begins on familiar ground by quoting the passage from Porphyry, whose affinity with the "negative confession" in the Book of the Dead had been firmly established through textual study. However, Bunsen is able to reach a new level of detail, going well beyond the preliminary remarks Rosellini offered on the subject, by drawing on the full translation of a Book of the Dead manuscript by Keeper at the British Museum Samuel Birch, which would appear in the fifth volume of the English version of *Egypt's Place in Universal History* (Bunsen 1867, 123–333, discussed further below). Bunsen does not address the contextual disparity between the prayer Porphyry presents as being part of a funerary ritual and the Book of the Dead scene which he understands as illustrating events in the beyond, introducing a lengthy quotation of the beginning of the text by presenting it as "a speech addressed by the soul of the deceased to Osiris and the forty-two judges assisting him in the tribunal of Hades" (Bunsen 1860, 644; this information is not present at this point in the German version, Bunsen 1857, 550–51).

In keeping with his purpose of elucidating Egypt's place in universal history, Bunsen's interests in the text quickly converge on the idea of ethical commandments rather than the specific afterlife setting. Thus he notes the similarity between the "negative confession" and Mosaic law but also notes that "the self-justifying conscience clung to external works, and to the self-satisfaction and self-righteousness connected with them" (Bunsen 1860, 646; 1857, 552), contrasted implicitly to the pious recognition of one's own sins and reliance on divine grace—a theological distinction already present in Lepsius, as noted above. Bunsen goes on to discuss brief passages from two other chapters of the Book of the Dead, notably chapter 85, where "the moral, and therefore Biblical, character is very prominent," and in which he sees a reference to going to the place of punishment as a "direct reference to the migration of the soul" (Bunsen 1860, 647; 1857, 552).

The uneasy status of morals in Egyptian religion makes Bunsen suppose that the evident "longing for the world to come" is formed by an innate "feeling of terrestrial existence being a burthen, of the life in the body being a prison-house." Nonetheless, he also admits that there must have been higher-minded individuals whose ideas point forward to a purer religion characterized by "a longing after sinlessness, after the life in God, a longing compatible with a happy life on earth" (Bunsen 1860, 647–48; 1857, 553). In this way Bunsen is able to use the Book of the Dead at a new level of detail to pinpoint the precise position of ancient Egyptian religion in the evolution of religious ideas ultimately leading to the pinnacle of Protestant Christianity—for which Bunsen's ideal was in fact a return to the spirit, and even architecture, of the early church (Foerster 2001, 284–87).

While the discussion of the Book of the Dead is thus focused primarily on identifying similarities with Christianity that can be understood as precursors, the discussion of the *Tale of Two Brothers* (cf. Wettengel 2003; Hollis 2008) focuses on the more exotic details of metempsychosis. Bunsen understands this story as being based profoundly on the doctrine of transmigration of souls:

> The hero may die as often as the author pleases; it seems even that he may become a tree for a considerable period. At last, however, the supremacy of the moral government of the world is shown in his case as in the history of Job. Evil is punished; the Good Principle is victorious; the hero becomes a man again, and his daughter attains a high destiny. (Bunsen 1860, 649–50; 1857, 555–56)

The discussion of this "new" source of knowledge of Egyptian metempsychosis quickly gives way to more general considerations, returning to topics such as animal worship and the preservation of the body, the rationales behind which as understood by Bunsen have already been discussed, illustrated with a few further passages from the Book of the Dead (Bunsen 1860, 650–53; 1857, 556–58).

The interest in Bunsen in the present connection lies primarily in the way he relates Egyptian religion to Christianity and to other religions to show the types and stages of religious belief and practice. In doing so, he shows the similarities and differences between the emerging understanding of Egyptian religion on the one hand and Christian models on the other, thereby also making unusually explicit a certain type of motivation for interpreting Egyptian religion in this framework in the first place. Specifically, to Bunsen "the faith in a moral government of the world, in personal moral responsibility, in a personal divine judgment" (Bunsen 1860, 649; 1857, 555) are the redeeming features that not only make Egyptian religion understandable, but also make it relevant to situate it in a universal history. Correspondingly, at this early point when a full translation was only just becoming available, these are also the aspects that are singled out in Bunsen's somewhat selective quotations from the Book of the Dead, in turn shaping the impression of that work as a whole.

An early reaction to Bunsen's first volumes, written by Emmanuel de Rougé (1811–72) who would go on to become curator of Egyptian antiquities at the Louvre as well as Champollion's successor as professor of Egyptian archaeology at the Collège de France, is worth discussing here because of the prominent place it gives to mortuary religion and the Book of the Dead. In a series of articles, Rougé responded to a wide range of issues raised by the three first volumes of Bunsen's work that had appeared by 1846. While this did not include the detailed analysis of Egyptian mortuary religion discussed above, nonetheless the Book of the Dead and its interpretation is the very first topic Rougé takes up after a brief overview of the contemporary state of scholarly knowledge of ancient Egypt and the principal sources on ancient Egyptian history and culture (Rougé 1846, 435). The immediate motivation for this discussion is Bunsen's suggestion, which Rougé cites with approval, that the Book of the Dead presents an extant example of the fabled books of Thoth in which the Egyptians codified all their knowledge.

Writing just a few years after Lepsius's publication of the Turin manuscript, Rougé essentially adopts his overall understanding of the Book of the Dead as detailing "the journey of the soul after death in the infernal regions that the Egyptians named Amenti (land of the setting sun)" (Rougé 1846, 435). This journey involves "trials" (*épreuves*) including battles with various creatures and gates that need to be passed, but there are also longer stays during which the deceased works celestial fields where he must complete a certain number of harvests and offer up the results to the celestial Nile. A prominent place is taken by the "great scene of judgment," the text of which contains "a long list of sins [*péchés*] for which the deceased claims to be free" to finally arrive at the "luminous spheres" to worship the sun, forming together a "curious transmigration of souls" (Rougé 1846, 436).

Rougé quickly moves on to other topics in his response to Bunsen's opus, but his brief notes on the Book of the Dead contain in a seminal form many of the key ideas that he would develop in much more detail in his 1860 study devoted to this work (see chapter 8 below). Of particular interest is his reception of Lepsius's ambiguous use of the notion of "wanderings of the soul." As noted above, Rougé regards the Book of the Dead as fundamentally describing a journey of the soul, and he sums up the contents as a "transmigration of souls." He does not, however, make any mention of actual reincarnation in new bodies, and as we will see below, this idea also does not play any significant role in his later, more detailed exposition. As such, his use of the notion of "transmigration" shows a weakening of its meaning similar to that found in Lepsius, but now without the linguistic ambiguity of the German *(Seelen)wanderung*. This detail is admittedly a small point, yet it is symptomatic of the increasing tendency to understand the soul's postmortem fate as a journey replete with trials and obstacles instead of a series of reincarnations.

Conclusion

The steadily growing prominence of the Book of the Dead as a source for understanding ancient Egyptian mortuary religion is characteristic of the decades after Champollion's decipherment examined in this chapter. The tentative predecipherment hypothesis, that if the weighing of the heart scene showed the Last Judgment, probably the rest of the Book of the Dead dealt with other episodes in the afterlife, seemed to be steadily vindicated. From Champollion's analysis of the weighing scene at the Dayr al-Madīnah temple, to Lepsius's facsimile and initial analysis in distinct parts of the Turin manuscript, to Birch's eventual complete translation of a Book of the Dead into English, the trajectory of the gradual exploration of the book served to shape an unprecedented consensus about the details of Egyptian mortuary religion. Despite disagreements on such adjacent topics as the relation between Christianity and ancient Egyptian religion, the wider place of Egypt in universal history, or the evolution of morality, scholars came to agree on an overall understanding of Egyptian mortuary beliefs combining well-established ideas of judgment, rewards, and punishments with the newer notion of a journey fraught with trials, and the increasingly prominent idea that all of this was conveniently described and illustrated in the Book of the Dead.

In the course of this consensus building, the notion of metempsychosis that had long been held a central tenet of Egyptian religion was increasingly marginalized. Originally used to establish the belief in post-mortem rewards and punishment, metempsychosis started to look less pivotal now that such ideas could seemingly be derived directly from the ancient Egyptian sources, notably the vignettes of Book of the Dead chapters 110 and 125. By contrast, other than the established reading of the judgment scene in the Book of Gates, metempsychosis seemed to be much less prominent in the vignettes of the Book of the Dead, leading scholars like Lepsius and Rougé to subtly co-opt the traditional terminology of transmigration of souls to refer to the simpler notion of the soul's fraught pilgrimage after death to reach the place of judgment or eternal reward that they saw illustrated in the Book of the Dead. Once it was marginalized, it took a relatively small step to jettison the notion of metempsychosis entirely, especially in a cultural milieu that regarded classical authors in general, and Herodotus in particular, with increasing skepticism (e.g., Gange 2020; Greene 2023; Haziza 2023).

EIGHT

Emergence of the Modern Paradigm: 1860–1885

During the previous decades, and especially after Lepsius's *Todtenbuch* was published in 1842, the study of ancient Egyptian mortuary religion had become inextricably linked to study of the Book of the Dead, which, as detailed in chapter 7, had come to be understood as containing a literal description of ancient Egyptian beliefs about the afterlife, not as clearly articulated doctrines, but rather as a detailed description of the concrete experiences of the soul in the afterlife. While Lepsius occasionally returned to the Book of the Dead throughout his career (Assmann 2012, 80–87), he never published the envisaged full translation and study, and it was only during the period covered by this chapter that significant new progress was made in its exploration. An important contribution in this direction was Emmanuel de Rougé's French study of the "funerary ritual," published in 1860 as a series of articles in the *Revue archéologique* but cited here in their anthologized monographic form printed the same year (Rougé 1860).

Taking as his point of departure Champollion's understanding that "the beliefs of the Egyptians concerning the fate of the soul after death were the essential topic of the book" (Rougé 1860, 5), Rougé goes on to provide an updated overview of the contemporary understanding, as well as enumerating the difficulties in the text that delayed its translation even two decades after Lepsius's publication of the Turin papyrus. Among these one is worth singling out, as it relates directly to the mismatch between the expectations from the text that had become prevalent and its observable contents. Thus Rougé notes with some frustration:

> The Egyptians only ever expound their doctrines under the, for us very thick, veil of symbols and allegories, the key to which can only be grasped after long, specialized studies. . . . The patient worker will often be compensated for his efforts by disentangling, through all these detours, the traces of an eminently elevated doctrine on great topics which have always preoccupied the man of avid religious beliefs, curious about his origin and anxious about his future destiny. (Rougé 1860, 8)

The tension expressed here is a natural consequence of the established expectation that the Book of the Dead should hold doctrinal contents on the afterlife, but Rougé is unusually candid about this problem. He also points out how this tension concerning the text can be resolved: the researcher should aim to arrive at the underlying afterlife doctrines through the effort of interpreting the text, which does not express these directly. It is also evident, however, that if this interpretive effort fails, it is simply a failure to penetrate the "veil" covering the doctrinal contents, not an indication that the mode of seeking such contents in the text is questionable in the first place. This method forms a crucial step in subsuming the details of the book's contents under the expectations formed before the decipherment of hieroglyphs, and in fact it has made this conventional approach to Egyptian funerary texts all but immune to criticism or alternative modes of reading to this day (cf. Nyord 2020).

Despite the difficulties, Rougé is able to identify a set of core religious tenets in the Book of the Dead, including the "unity of a self-existent supreme being, his eternity, his omnipotence, and the eternal generation in God; the creation of the world and all the living beings attributed to this supreme God; the immortality of the soul, completed by the dogma of punishments and rewards [*le dogme des peines et des récompenses*]" (Rougé 1860, 8–9). Not surprisingly at this point these beliefs thus not only turn out to have been assumed well before the access to Egyptian texts and images, but also to have clear correlates in the Christian framework within which they were first formulated. Here as well Rougé is more explicitly reflective than most authors in noting this similarity and questioning whether the Egyptians might have adopted these ideas from the Hebrews. Ultimately he rejects this idea on chronological grounds and concludes that the doctrines are part of a traditional wisdom, "the adoption of which seems to go back to the first cradle of the Egyptian people" (Rougé 1860, 9).

Rougé defends Champollion's original designation of the Book of the Dead as the "funerary ritual" against the criticism Lepsius leveled toward it. Not only do many of the chapters clearly describe different stages of the funerary ceremony while others are spoken by priests during rituals, but, de Rougé argues, the parts where it is ostensibly the deceased owner himself who speaks would certainly in practice have been recited by others on behalf of the deceased. Together these observations vindicate Champollion's designation, which de Rougé thus reinstates (Rougé 1860, 9–10). However, he does not question or otherwise discuss how this ritual understanding relates to the doctrinal contents the interpretive effort should seek to unveil.

After this introductory discussion, the second part of the study turns to the titles of the individual chapters given in Lepsius's edition, for which Rougé provides a translation with brief commentary on the accompanying vignettes (Rougé 1860, 10–36). In several places his comments reveal parts of his more general understanding of Egyptian mortuary religion, which makes them worth singling out here. Speaking of the first part of the book, chapters 1–15, he notes that they form a separate whole, ending with the vignette of chapter 15, described as "the sight of the light that was the *pleroma,* or the goal of the entire underworldly pilgrimage [*pèlerinage infernal*]" (Rougé 1860, 12), where the use of the word *pleroma* indicates his understanding within a doctrine of emanation and the individual soul's return to the world soul along the lines of earlier authors inspired by Platonism. Further on, he connects the danger of having one's head cut off and "dying a second time," mentioned in the titles of chapters 43 and 44 to the judgment of the dead, since "reprobates [*réprouvés*] were convicted to a second death; Horus is represented cutting off the heads of the convicted" (Rougé 1860, 17).

By contrast, chapters 54–65 are devoted to "the favors which await virtuous souls" (Rougé 1860, 18), and chapters 76–88 similarly concern "the different types of transformation that the virtuous soul could choose at will during the course of its underworldly journey" (Rougé 1860, 20). Although he describes it briefly, he does not give the conventional identification of the vignette of chapter 110 with the Elysian Fields, nor does he provide any other interpretation of its significance, noting merely that the vignette shows "a region where the deceased plows, sows, harvests, sails, and worships various deities" (Rougé 1860, 24). As I noted in the previous chapter, he had expressed elsewhere (Rougé 1846, 436) the idea that the farmwork depicted was a temporary task to be completed by the deceased rather than the paradisial destination as increasingly interpreted. Chapter 125, on the other hand, is described in conventional terms as "the famous scene of the Psychostasia and judgment," and the accompanying text is noted as containing "the entire basis for the moral and civil justice of the Egyptians" (Rougé 1860, 25).

If the exact way Rougé understands the practical function of the book as a whole is somewhat unclear, he notes that the sequence of chapters starting with chapter 127 are informational in nature, because they "have as their goal the instruction of the soul concerning the nature of the denizens of the various heavenly regions that it must traverse" (Rougé 1860, 26). Similarly, the description of various localities in chapters 144–50 signifies that "the knowledge of the mystical names of these places and their guardians was to safeguard [*garantir*] [the soul] against the afflictions of these dreaded spirits [*genies redoutés*]" (Rougé 1860, 29).

In the third part of the study Rougé translates and comments on the lengthy chapter 17. The detailed discussion focuses mainly on individual words and mythological expressions, however, and on the whole it does not offer much additional insight into his understanding of the nature of the Egyptian afterlife beyond demonstrating how detailed readings of the texts, and not just their overall themes, can be fitted into the general framework. They do not necessarily yield a consistent picture regarding salient questions like the fate of the soul and the precise sequence of seemingly incompatible ideas. Thus, for example, different chapters seem to provide quite different pictures, as Rougé describes it toward the end of his study:

> The soul, rejuvenated in the bosom of Isis, is admitted in the cycle of the stars that follow *Sothis* and *Sahu* (Orion). Several chapters contain hymns dedicated to this divine resurrection; we will cite in the first instance chapter 64, of which we have prepared a translation. There is no longer any question of change or of metempsychosis for the glorified soul: "Eternity becomes the course of life!," says the text of chapter 109 to the osiris. The destiny of the body of the elect is not mentioned in chapter 17; we know, however, that it must be associated with the favor of the resurrection. According to chapter 154, the divine light had granted him the grace of being preserved from corruption: We see, in chapter 89, the soul that comes to wake up its mummy on the funeral bier, and the god promises them that they will never be separated again. (Rougé 1860, 81–82)

Beyond listing them side by side, Rougé makes no attempt to reconcile these different ideas, and in this passage and elsewhere he seems to regard them as dealing simply with complementary aspects of the overall dogma. As the examples show, although it requires a certain interpretive agility, Rougé is nonetheless able to fit all the various themes, text formats, and speech situations attested in the different parts of the text into the overall framework of the journey of the soul through the afterlife, with the seemingly pleasant or desirable parts being rewards of virtuous souls and the threatening or violent parts being punishments accorded to the sinners, while the passages not obviously falling into either category were simple descriptions of beings and events encountered in the afterlife. Like previous scholars such as Lepsius, Rougé conveys a sense of unity through the terminology. As exemplified in the quoted passage, the goals and themes of the chapters are paraphrased, or even translated, by Christian terms like "resurrection," "soul," "eternity," "grace," and so on. Reducing the individual mythological motifs to such overarching concepts makes them more easily commensurable both with each other and with the overall interpretive model.

Similarly, various visual elements of iconography can be interpreted in fairly generic terms as "a symbol of life reborn from death" (Rougé 1860, 19) or "symbols of new creation which gives the soul eternal life" (Rougé 1860, 34). The overall result is cohesive and in many ways intuitively satisfying, succeeding as it does in bringing the entirety of the ancient text into the preexisting interpretative framework. Indeed, because of the long-term success of this way of reading the Book of the Dead (cf. recent anthologies on the topic like Scalf 2017 or Lucarelli and Stadler 2023), Rougé's text in many respects reads as very "modern." It is worth noting, however, that given the capacious nature of the concept of the "afterlife journey" and the interpretive work done by the paraphrase in Christian theological terms, it is difficult to imagine any text or image of a ritual or mythological nature that it would not have been possible to fit into the scheme. As a hypothesis on the nature of the text, then, Rougé's framework is methodologically somewhat specious.

Universality and Historical Critique

With the nearly complete avoidance of the concept of metempsychosis and the corresponding prevalence of Christian terminology and models, the similarity between the emerging consensus on Egyptian mortuary religion and Christian eschatological beliefs was becoming increasingly difficult to overlook. Because of its apparently robust rooting in extant ancient Egyptian sources, this comparison did not generally prompt skepticism toward the prevailing interpretation but instead tended to lead in one of two main directions for the scholars who observed it explicitly. As we saw in previous chapters, to some writers (Bunsen, for example, and before him Maillet), it had offered a comforting affirmation of the universality of Christian-style belief in personal salvation and the afterlife, with the scholars' own contemporary beliefs as the pinnacle, based as they were on divine revelation.

Others who had less confidence in contemporary mainstream Christianity could make exactly the opposite inference: Rather than affirming the value and superiority of Christian dogma, the similarity between the mid- to late nineteenth-century model of the Egyptian afterlife (and religion more generally) to certain Christian teachings could be used to show the latter's historical rooting in fundamentally pagan ideas. A notable example of this line of thinking is found in the writings of Unitarian scholar Samuel Sharpe (1799–1881; cf. Clayden 1883; Gange 2013, 107–11). Like contemporary Unitarian John Kenrick,

Sharpe interpreted ancient Egypt in terms amenable to his criticism of orthodox Christian positions, but he was also a highly popular narrator of Egyptian history with less overtly polemic aims.

Sharpe had written a lengthy popular history of ancient Egypt (Sharpe 1846) that would appear in six editions as well as several editions in German translation. The book did not have ancient Egyptian religion as a main focus, though the later parts do show a marked interest in the early development of Christianity. Thus in that earlier work he mainly follows Wilkinson in connecting images of the funeral procession in Theban tombs with later Greek ideas (understood as adopted from the Egyptians) about the river Styx, Charon, and so on. Also along the lines suggested by Wilkinson, he briefly notes that the tombs were intended to "keep the embalmed bodies safe and undisturbed till the day of judgment" (Sharpe 1846, 18; cf. 356), and elsewhere he proposes that penal labor in Egyptian mines provided Egyptian priests with the inspiration for "the punishment of the wicked souls in the next world" (Sharpe 1846, 47). Sharpe shows his interest in Christian heresies by noting how disagreement over the nature of the resurrection was sometimes rooted in these ancient Egyptian beliefs (Sharpe 1846, 106, 478, 523–24)—an idea developed in much more detail in his later work.

Almost two decades later, in a book titled *Egyptian Mythology and Egyptian Christianity with Their Influence on the Opinions of Modern Christendom* (Sharpe 1863), Sharpe presented his polemic argument in its fullest form. He lays out the premises and overall thesis in the work's preface, where he states that "most of the so called Christian doctrines, that have no place in the New Testament, reached Europe from Egypt, through Alexandria." Correspondingly, the aim of the book is "not only to explain the Mythology of Egypt, but to show the extraordinary readiness with which its religious opinions were copied by the neighbouring nations" (Sharpe 1863, viii). As we can see from the wording, Sharpe's aims are far from neutrally descriptive. Rather, he aims specifically to show that the particular doctrines of mainstream Christianity that he disagrees with as a Unitarian are the ones derived from pagan Egypt—thereby, through what we have called the *reductio ad Aegyptum* argument, demonstrating their fallacy. More specifically, he targets "principal doctrines known to be common to Egyptian

Mythology and modern orthodoxy, as distinguished from the religion of Jesus," including "the Trinity, the two natures of Christ, and the atonement by vicarious sufferings" (Sharpe 1863, ix).

Sharpe's aims are thus much broader and more fundamental than just Egyptian mortuary religion, and I will restrict my focus here to topics that directly relate to this theme. Proceeding from a description of Egyptian burial practices, especially as exemplified by the pyramids and the rock tombs of the Valley of the Kings, Sharpe notes briefly that these demonstrate "the care taken by a great king to save his earthly body unhurt and undisturbed against the day of resurrection" (Sharpe 1863, 44), and later he elaborates on the underlying belief and its implicit similarity to and contrast with Christianity in noting the Egyptians' "wish for immortality or a life hereafter, and the belief that it could be obtained with the help of this earthly body and not without it" (Sharpe 1863, 45). This also fits well with the by now conventional interpretation of the Book of the Dead as "containing an account of the events which will befal the deceased in the next world, in his passage through trials and difficulties to a state of final bliss" (Sharpe 1863, 47).

As for his contemporaries, the theme of judgment holds an especially central importance for Sharpe. He understands the relevance of the judgment of the deceased's conduct in this life as fixing "his reward or punishment in the next," and as being both depicted in the Book of the Dead and "enacted by the priests as part of the funeral ceremony" (Sharpe 1863, 50), albeit without elaborating on the relationship between the earthly ritual and the actual judgment in the beyond. In Sharpe's interpretation Ammut takes on several roles, as "the wicked Typhon, as an hippopotamus, the Cerberus of the Greeks, accuses him to the judge, and demands that he shall be punished" (Sharpe 1863, 50–51). Like other authors before him, Sharpe is apt to note the didactic value especially of the ritual performance of the judgment:

> Those who were too uncultivated to listen to a sermon might thus learn wisdom from what they saw with their eyes, and this ceremony was a forcible method of teaching the ignorant multitude that a day of judgment awaits us all after death, and that we should so regulate

> our lives that when weighed in the great balance they may not be found wanting. (Sharpe 1863, 51)

By using the pronoun "we," Sharpe signals that he regards the description as having universal validity—in other words, that this is an aspect of a teaching shared by the Egyptians that he does accept. By the same method applied previously, however, he goes on to contrast more specific aspects, in particular that the Egyptians apparently brought "sin-offerings" to sway the assessors' judgment. Similarly, the four sons of Horus often depicted in the weighing of the heart scene are understood as intercessors or advocates on behalf of the deceased—and may even themselves be offered up as an "atoning sacrifice" to increase the chances of a favorable verdict (Sharpe 1863, 51–52). Although he presents these descriptions in a neutral way, elsewhere in the book their polemic relevance is made clear, namely that Sharpe opposes the doctrines of atonement and intercession in Christianity. To him these tenets thus form part of the ideas that the Egyptians superstitiously added to the otherwise wholesome notion of postmortem judgment, in turn strongly encouraging their identification in the ancient sources even if it requires somewhat idiosyncratic interpretations, as in the case of the four Sons of Horus.

Although earlier authors, such as Kenrick, had begun to doubt this interpretation, Sharpe cites the Book of Gates scene of the pig in the version in the tomb of Sety II as evidence of the Egyptian doctrine of metempsychosis in the traditional fashion. Conforming to his understanding of mummification as indicating a belief in bodily resurrection, he understands the human body at the end of Herodotus's transmigration of souls as being the soul's return to its "old dwelling" (Sharpe 1863, 53). He does not address the tension between Herodotus's description of an automatic sequence of animal species on the one hand and the notion that the nature of the animal in which the soul is incarnated is a reward or punishment depending on the judgment verdict. Only later in Egyptian history, "perhaps not till after their intercourse with the Greeks," did the Egyptians entertain the possibility of a purely spiritual resurrection (Sharpe 1863, 54). The importance of this distinction lies in the fact that Sharpe opposed the mainstream Christian notion of resurrection in the flesh and thus approved of this Egyptian development, though for the same reason he does not see it as characteristic of original Egyptian beliefs (cf. Clayden 1883, 217–19).

As had become customary, Sharpe discusses the Book of the Dead as the most direct source of knowledge about what the ancient Egyptian afterlife was like. He understands the sequence of chapters as given in the Turin manuscript published by Lepsius as a sequential narrative of the soul's destiny:

> The roll of papyrus buried with the mummy often describes the funeral, and then goes on to the return of the soul to the body, the resurrection, the various trials and difficulties which the deceased will meet and overcome in the next world, and the garden of paradise in which he awaits the day of judgment, the trial on that day, and it then shows the punishment which would have awaited him if he had been found guilty. (Sharpe 1863, 64)

Sharpe goes on to discuss each of these episodes in more detail based on the vignettes in ways largely corresponding to their interpretation by Lepsius and Rougé. One innovation is the last part of the narrative concerning the punishment of the guilty. This relates to the depiction of the lake of fire shown in the vignette to chapter 126 and thus immediately after the weighing of the heart (fig. 10). Sharpe elaborates his understanding of this as "the lake of fire into which the wicked are to be thrown, and the gods of punishment, the Cabeiri, with swords in their hands" (Sharpe 1863, 65). The Greek Cabeiri seem to be brought in here mainly because of their association with fire, but the chief inspiration for the interpretation of the Egyptian scene is clearly the Book of Revelation, where a "lake of fire" is mentioned repeatedly in chapters 19–21 as a place of utter destruction of evildoers. A similar innovation serving to bring out further details connecting to Christian beliefs is the understanding of the tree goddess sometimes depicted in Book of the Dead vignettes as "the tree of life . . . , one of the trees in the paradise which the deceased enters" (Sharpe 1863, 66). Because he understands

Fig. 10: Vignette from Book of the Dead chapter 126 as reproduced by Lepsius. Karl Richard Lepsius, *Das Todtenbuch der Aegypter*, pl. 51. Bibliothèque nationale de France.

the Book of the Dead as a sequential narrative, Sharpe needs to introduce the ambiguity that sometimes the deceased arrives in paradise and awaits the day of judgment there, while sometimes going to paradise is the reward for being acquitted in the judgment, apparently depending on the order of the vignettes in different manuscripts.

As I have noted throughout this summary, many of the details where Egyptian beliefs could be paralleled with Christian ones, especially in the cases where Sharpe introduces new interpretations along these lines, are meant specifically to further Sharpe's overall argument. Thus he sees Egyptian influence through "Gnosticism" attaching itself in Alexandria to the pristine teaching of Jesus, and these ideas are precisely the ones he previously identified in his ostensibly descriptive overview of pharaonic religion. For example, in the Epistle to the Hebrews, which Sharpe sees as containing such Alexandrian influences,

> Jesus is no longer the Teacher of a new Religion, as in the Gospels, but he acts as a mediator or advocate before the judge on behalf of mankind . . . and as we have seen the Egyptian lesser gods [i.e., the Sons of Horus in the weighing of the heart scene] acting . . . not as a mediator to persuade the sinner to repent, but to persuade the Judge

> to forgive the sin. And his death is no longer that of a martyr to the great cause of regenerating his fellow creatures, but it is somewhat of an atoning sacrifice, made to propitiate the Judge. (Sharpe 1863, 89)

In this way many of Sharpe's innovations in the interpretation of Egyptian imagery and religious practices become understandable when he traces the intrusion of similar ideas into Christianity in later times. In other words, Sharpe builds strategically on the already established commonalities between the interpretation of Egyptian mortuary religion and contemporary Christianity in order to trace the pedigree of specific theological doctrines as a way of criticizing them. Although, as we have seen throughout this book, the parallelism between ancient Egyptian religion and Christianity had less to do with ancient ideas and practices than with the contexts that had shaped the modern understanding, somewhat ironically his overall argument led Sharpe to further emphasize these parallels and produce additional, even more specific ones. Whether or not individual readers were convinced of the historical connection he argued, the more general effect was thus a further approximation between the beliefs and terminologies of the two religions.

The Book of the Dead in English

As I mentioned in the previous chapter, the year 1867 saw an important milestone in the study of ancient Egyptian mortuary religion, with the first full translation of the Book of the Dead by Samuel Birch (1813–85), Keeper of Egyptian and Assyrian antiquities at the British Museum. The translation appeared in the fifth, supplementary volume of the English translation of Bunsen's *Egypt's Place in Universal History* (Bunsen 1867, 123–333) along with various other groundbreaking sections, including other contributions by Birch on Egyptian grammar and lexicography.

Birch includes both Champollion's and Lepsius's designations of the work, labeling it in the title to his contribution as "The Funereal Ritual, or Book of the Dead," although he notes that it is not strictly a ritual, but "consists of several Hermetic works divided into separate chapters" (Bunsen 1867, 125). Correspondingly, he notes that what he takes to be

Champollion's idea about the later, fixed sequence of chapters of the Book of the Dead as "a mythical description of the progress of the soul in the future state" does not hold up to closer scrutiny, but that the order may instead have been decided based on the age of the compositions, judging especially from a group of chapters toward the end of the sequence (chapters 162–65), which he sees as filled "with foreign barbaric names and of mystical import" and thus "evidently of a later age" (Bunsen 1867, 126). Birch's description begins by focusing on the age of the different parts of the composition and the various media in which it is transmitted before moving on to questions of style and the many variant readings found in copies of the same texts.

When discussing the contents of the book, Birch notes the central role of the god Thoth both as speaker and occasionally explicitly as author, which is why he uses the term "Hermetic" (Hermes being the conventional Greek interpretation of the Egyptian Thoth) to refer to the text (Bunsen 1867, 133). He correspondingly regards the text as containing secrets of sacred theology, although

> their real purport was widely different. To the soul they assured a passage from the Earth; a transit through the Purgatory and other regions of the dead; the entrance into the Empyreal Gate by which the souls arrived at the presence of the Sun; the admission into the Bark or orb of the Sun, ever traversing in brilliant light the liquid ether; and protection from the various Liers-in-wait, or adversaries, who sought to accuse, destroy, or detain it on its passage or destiny. (Bunsen 1867, 134)

Birch does not make it clear precisely how he understands the text to ensure the soul's access to these various stages of the journey, but later wording indicates that he thinks it is the esoteric knowledge of the cosmos contained within that is capable of saving the soul. Following this, he moves on to lay down some fundamental principles of Egyptian belief arising from his detailed work with the texts as well as the overall context within which he understands them. The goal for the Egyptian was not to die again in Hades, with the first "death" happening at birth when the soul was "imprisoned in the human form" (Bunsen 1867, 134).

Introducing an idea that would prove highly influential, Birch noted that instead of being merely the combination of a body and a soul, to the Egyptians the human being consisted of at least five "distinct principles": the *ba*, "soul"; the *akh* or *khu*, "intelligence"; the *ka*, "existence"; the *khaba*, "shade"; the *kha*, "body"; and the *sah*, "mummy." In the future state the soul and body are separated, though the soul "still continue[s] to revisit the body." However, the separation between body and soul is not made consistently, and "the deceased is often described as if existing as a mortal even in Hades." Finally, Birch sees allusions to the soul's ultimate absorption into the Deity in references in the Book of the Dead to "becoming a God" and other similar expressions. He explicitly notes that these transformations were "future" and are thus different from "the transmigrations of the soul during its terrestrial existence," which Birch thus seems to consider part of the overall system (as indeed does Bunsen, as we saw above), even though he mostly discusses the Book of the Dead in terms of a transcendent afterlife (Bunsen 1867, 135).

Further elucidating his understanding of the religion of the Book of the Dead, Birch notes that the preservation of the body, and especially the heart, forms a significant theme in the text, and he sees this purpose also behind the placement of amulets and other items with the mummified body. He notes that "in some mysterious manner the immortality of the body was deemed as important as the passage of the soul." While he admits that much remains uncertain, he states that "the great facts" in relation to the soul "are its trials and justification" and notes that it is its "*gnosis*, or knowledge of celestial and infernal mysteries," that allows the soul to triumph (Bunsen 1867, 135–36).

Following this general introduction to the religious framework, Birch goes on to characterize the contents of the individual chapters or groups of chapters. For the most part the purpose of the chapters is merely translated or paraphrased from Egyptian expressions without connecting the themes to the overall framework within which the Book is understood. The several exceptions to this, where Birch treats a theme in more detail and discusses its significance within the wider context, are thus the most interesting for present purposes.

One such case is the group of chapters (chapters 22–26; Bunsen 1867, 139–40) relating to the "Reconstruction of the deceased," where various body parts are preserved, the heart being the most important. Birch connects this to the "mystical destruction of Osiris, and the discovery and readjustment of his limbs by Isis." He also notes in this connection that rather than focusing on the entire body, those parts singled out are "the recipients of the intellectual rather than of the sensuous impressions, the mental devisers of sin, and the agents of intellectual existence," seemingly hinting that he understands the "reconstruction" as having a moral significance beyond the purely corporeal one. The next group (chapters 27–42) similarly deals with parts of the body, but now in the context of their being in danger of being "taken away by the Typhonian animals in Hades." Birch notes that some of the chapters seem to indicate that the deceased does get eaten but "escapes alive through the bellies of these monsters" (Bunsen 1867, 140).

A later group of chapters (chapters 71–75; Bunsen 1867, 142–43) relate to what Birch calls "the Manifestation and Exit of the soul from earth." In particular, the first of these chapters seeks to save the soul from "the seven mortal sins, which lie in wait at the balance ready to destroy the heart of the deceased or arrest his further progress," while the next was meant to "expedite the passage of the soul from earth, its entrance into Elysium, its reception of the mystical food of the Gods, by virtue of which the spirits of the blest become invested with a divine nature." In discussing the following group of chapters for "the Transformations or genesis of the soul," he emphasizes once more that these transformations are not those of the transmigration of the soul, but should rather be understood as "the absorption of the soul into the Soul of the Earth or Universe" (Bunsen 1867, 143).

Of the next group of chapters, Birch's brief discussion of chapter 110 is worth singling out. As we saw above, this chapter and its accompanying vignette had come to be understood as a representation of the Elysian Fields, and Birch too designates the represented region as Elysium, noting that it consists of two parts, one showing the sowing, reaping, and offering of grain, and the other showing "the transport of the food of the West." Birch also sees a theme of judgment here, since the depiction shows "various pits or pools fatal to the reprobate or Unjustified" (Bunsen 1867, 145).

Not surprisingly, Birch devotes considerable space to the summary of chapter 125 concerning the judgment in the Hall of the Two Truths. He describes the address to Osiris and the "Forty-Two Demons of the Dead, each of whom presides over and avenges some particular sin or fault." Birch distinguishes between faults that are of a "general nature, such as are common to all codes of morals and religion," and those that are of a more "local character, and refer to neglect of particular formulæ, or sacrifices of a special nature" (Bunsen 1867, 146). In the vignette of the weighing of the heart, Birch points out that "one of the penalties or rewards of the future state is the metempsychosis, *meskhen*," in a rare proposal of an ancient Egyptian term and iconographic element corresponding to this idea from the classical authors. To Birch, the "most remarkable" part of the text is not the negative confession that Bunsen emphasized, but rather the much more rarely cited (even today) "mystical address of the Door and Hall of Truth itself" (Bunsen 1867, 146). Lending itself much less well to a reading of the chapter as focusing on an ethical judgment, but aligning well with Birch's focus on the Book of the Dead as salvific *gnosis*, this part of the chapter demonstrates the "mystery of names, the knowledge of which was a sovereign virtue, and which at a later period degenerated into the rank heresy of the Gnostics and the magic of enchanters." He notes similarly that "mystical names" of architectonic elements as used in masonic mysteries thus "are actually found in Egyptian mysteries, so far as can be gathered from the obscure hints on subjects so removed from popular knowledge or philosophical speculation" (Bunsen 1867, 147).

The group of chapters 144–49 contains "descriptions of the mystical house of Osiris in the Aahenru, or Elysium; where each staircase or pylon has a name written on the door, a demon inhabitant with a secret or mystical name, and a demon doorkeeper," and the deceased must know all the names to be able to pass through. Birch connects these places with the "Infernal Purgatory" represented in a version of the Book of Caverns, where the sounds heard in each of the caverns (or "halls," as Birch translates the word) are described. Comparing these regions with "the cold Hades of Homer, or the hotter Hell of a Dante or a Milton," Birch notes that it remains unclear if "they were of a purgatorial nature, or the wicked were detained there" (Bunsen 1867, 152–53).

In many ways Birch presents a full-fledged "modern" mode of reading the Book of the Dead, because the expectations of the texts had been laid out in so much detail before they were actually translated, and because these expectations have remained largely the same to this day. The clear dangers or obstacles alluded to in some of the chapters are understood as literal threats the deceased encounters in the underworld, while other chapters simply have their stated purposes and themes paraphrased under the assumption that they were similarly needed in the afterlife. Texts that explicitly relate to festival celebrations or otherwise have instructions that seem to contradict the reading as descriptions of the afterlife are simply set aside as less central than compositions like chapters 110 or 125, which have the added advantage of having instructive vignettes that can serve as illustrations of beliefs that had been assumed for centuries by Birch's time, and as such had become established as cornerstones long before accompanying texts were translated. As we saw above, this mode of reading the Book of the Dead as a whole thus follows the assumption first suggested in the beginning of the nineteenth century, and because of the malleable nature of ancient beliefs about the afterlife, the texts could (and can) be fitted into this framework without any cause for revising the general model.

Birch's contribution is also instructive in relation to the declining importance of metempsychosis. While he invokes the idea several times in his introduction, it is mostly in connection with the transformation chapters' being related *not* to transmigration, but rather to another aspect of the Platonic doctrine of emanation, namely the absorption into the universal soul. As I noted above, metempsychosis had for some time been reduced to merely an instrument of rewards and punishment resulting from postmortem judgment, and this is in fact the one connection where Birch invokes the idea in a positive sense. However, since the Book of the Dead (and other Egyptian compositions) had offered several other candidates for illustrating the expected rewards and punishments, it would by now be quite easy to get rid of the idea of metempsychosis entirely without noticeably changing the overall model. Additionally, if another way of explaining the transformation chapters could be found, even that last aspect of the more general doctrine of emanation would be redundant, and it could be done away with altogether as an explanatory framework for Egyptian mortuary religion.

For most authors of this time, as for Birch, the notion of metempsychosis had thus outlived its usefulness despite its central status in conventional interpretations. As we saw in previous chapters, the idea had been embraced for centuries in part simply because Herodotus described it in such straightforward terms, but also, and especially, because it could be used—when complemented by Plato or the Hermetic writings (or both)—to establish the expected idea of postmortem rewards and punishments through differential treatment of different souls. Since the early decades of the nineteenth century, however, this slot in the model of the Egyptian afterlife had begun to be filled by the more static notion of a journey of the soul as conveniently described and illustrated in a literal way in the funerary papyri. Although the Book of the Dead did in some chapters speak about transformation into gods and animals, by the 1870s the framework had shifted to one where even such ideas could instead be incorporated as means of empowering or satisfying the soul of the deceased in its afterlife journey. Accordingly, in 1872, as I noted above, Gaston Maspero could make short work of the entire notion of metempsychosis in a ten-line footnote as a simple misunderstanding by foreign and late commentators (Maspero 1872, 340n1)—notably without requiring significant reinterpretation of the remaining parts of the conventional model.

Other parts of the Hermetic writings saw a temporary rehabilitation in the studies of the Book of the Dead during this period, however. This is especially true of passages concerning the interplay between the various parts of the human being, a topic that was of considerable interest and to which the Book of the Dead could lend itself well, as we saw above in the case of Samuel Birch. Thus, for example, in Lepsius's newly established *Zeitschrift für ägyptische Sprache und Alterthumskunde*, Egyptologist Théodule Devéria includes in his discussion of the first chapter of the Book of the Dead a passage from the tenth Hermetic tractate (cf. Copenhaver 1992, 34), in a translation in which he has inserted the hieroglyphic words he understands as corresponding to the concepts in the Greek text, with Greek *nous*, "mind, intelligence" corresponding to Egyptian *akh*, and so on (Devéria 1870, 62–64). Similarly, Maspero, despite his explicit disavowal of the doctrine of metempsychosis as noted above, takes a similar approach to conceptions of the human being (Maspero 1872, 338–40). This represented a brief acceptance in certain quarters of mainstream scholarship of ideas that during the nineteenth century had otherwise become associated with more esoteric writers like German historian of philosophy Eduard Röth (e.g., Röth 1848, 176–81).

In Maspero's case his parallel reading of the Hermetic writings and the Book of the Dead leads to a somewhat idiosyncratic model that still, however, stays well within the boundaries and conceptual framework of the established understanding (Maspero 1872, 338–40). Drawing on the Hermetic writings (and the Western esoteric tradition they had helped inspire), Maspero sees the human being as consisting of a divine intelligence, clothed in *soul* as its first step of manifestation. In order to enact its will upon matter, it uses the intermediary agent of *spirit* or *breath*, which is able to permeate the body. In turn, when the human being dies the spirit withdraws to the soul, and intelligence is freed from its covering, leaving the soul behind. Although this system, derived directly from the Hermetic texts, is thus significantly more complicated than conventional interpretations, the remainder of Maspero's model is familiar. The soul is judged by weighing the heart (understood as the conscience) on the balance, and intelligence is compelled to carry out the sentence. The wicked souls are punished by centuries of torment, during which they cause illness and madness among humanity before returning to nonexistence through the "second death." The just souls must go through a number of additional trials and battles, armed with enhanced powers and knowledge. Owing to the Hermetic backdrop, Maspero sees the goal of this journey slightly differently than most other authors do, but similarly to Rougé, he understands the work in the Field of Iaru (the "Elysian Fields" of earlier authors) not as the blessed existence in itself, but rather as an additional trial to overcome. Instead, Maspero invokes the blessed fate of the virtuous soul in exalted terms:

> The end of its ordeals approaches, the shadows gradually dissipate, the day of blessed eternity is dawning and penetrating it with its brightness; it mingles with the company of the gods and walks with them in the adoration of the perfect Being [*l'Être parfait*]. There are

> two choirs of gods, one wandering, the other fixed; this is the last degree of the glorious initiation of the soul. At this point the soul becomes all intelligence: it sees God face to face and is immersed [*s'abîme*] in him. (Maspero 1872, 340)

Maspero's interpretation is of interest for illustrating the potential for variation within the emerging model. The framework of rewards and punishment had long been established beyond doubt, and the idea of the Book of the Dead as a description of the trials of the soul after death was more recently so. Within this fairly rigid system, it was still possible to suggest different understandings of the blessed eternal existence itself, and similarly also to imagine the punishment of the sinners in different ways. Because of its wording derived from the Hermetic writings, Maspero's interpretation thus seems to be something of a departure from convention, and indeed this direction was rejected by most subsequent scholars (e.g., Brugsch 1872, 66, hinting not only at an underlying French-German rivalry, but also more explicitly a difference of opinions regarding how advanced as thinkers the ancient Egyptians really were). However, on closer scrutiny, the differences turn out to be relatively superficial and merely fill in the open slots in the overall model in a way slightly different from the more conventional Christianity-inspired interpretation that would ultimately prove more successful. Indeed, in his later works Maspero abandons the technicalities derived from the soul conceptions of the Hermetic writings in favor of a less rigid scheme where the Egyptians do not consistently distinguish between their many terms for "that which survives of man" after death (Maspero 1887, 269). Characteristically, this change could be made without notable consequences for the understanding of the overall model and the general contents of the Book of the Dead.

Mortuary Rituals

The Book of the Dead thus continued to loom large in discussions of ancient Egyptian mortuary religion during this period owing to the understanding that it provided direct insight into the Egyptians' afterlife beliefs (Gange 2013, 209–13), but it was not the only source used.

Increasingly, discussion split into two parts, one dealing with the reconstruction of the soul's journey as apparently related in the Book of the Dead, while another dealt with more practical questions of rituals, mummification, and so on. Even if it became more and more difficult to connect these two themes directly as the afterlife was understood in increasingly transcendent terms, their juxtaposition was thought to provide a complete picture of the mortuary beliefs.

An example of this approach is the Hibbert Lectures given in 1879 by British Egyptologist Peter Le Page Renouf (1822–97). Inaugurated the previous year by historian of religions Max Müller, the lecture series was meant to tackle broad theological issues, and correspondingly Renouf titled his lectures "The Origin and Growth of Religion as Illustrated by the Religion of Ancient Egypt" (Renouf 1880). Like many other scholars of the time, Renouf saw Egyptian religion as fundamentally monotheistic and considered this character present from the earliest times, noting that the "sublimer portions are demonstrably ancient; and the last stage of the Egyptian religion, that known to the Greek and Latin writers, heathen or Christian, was by far the grossest and most corrupt" (Renouf 1880, 91). It is within the model implied by this development that Renouf understands the various aspects of Egyptian religion, including mortuary religion.

In the first of the two lectures devoted to this subject, Renouf begins by establishing the universality of a "belief in the persistence of life after death" (Renouf 1880, 124). More specifically, in ancient Egypt he sees "an entire system of notions wonderfully (indeed, almost incredibly) similar to those entertained by our Indo-European ancestors" (Renouf 1880, 126–27). His following description of Egyptian tombs and their inscriptions and imagery is peppered with Egyptian terms such as the "notion of everlasting life, *ānch t'cta* [*ꜥnḫ ḏt*]" (Renouf 1880, 127) that he cites from the inscription on a coffin in the British Museum made for the reburial of King Mycerinos of the Fourth Dynasty long after his death. Describing the motifs of daily life found in Egyptian tomb decoration, he notes that "all these representations are really subordinate to one end, and that is the worship of the departed" (Renouf 1880, 130), concluding that the imagery depicts the sacrifices for the deceased for the perpetuation of which an endowment was established. Along the same lines, he notes that the "greatest importance was attached to the permanence of the tomb, to the continuance of the religious ceremonies, and to the prayers of passers-by" (Renouf 1880, 134).

While this part of the discussion is almost entirely devoid of references to salvation, the afterlife, and such, Renouf does mention that the "lustral water offered upon earth to the dead had its counterpart in the other world" (Renouf 1880, 141), and he notes a "remarkable coincidence" according to which Hindus believed that Brahmans without a son to perform the funeral rites "could not enter into heaven" (Renouf 1880, 142). These indications give a sense that he understands the fate of the soul in the afterlife as being dependent on the mortuary cult, even if he does not elaborate on this. Renouf goes on to discuss the Egyptian concept of the *ka*, which he understands as referring fundamentally to the "image" of a deceased person (147–52; cf. Nyord 2019 for this theory), and to broader conceptions of the soul, which the Egyptians understood "to be provided with a material form and substance" enabling it, for example, to eat and drink (Renouf 1880, 153). The rest of the chapter discusses various textual examples of interactions with the gods and the divinity of the king, which need not occupy us here.

In the following lecture Renouf turns to "the religious books of Egypt," among which he focuses especially on the Book of the Dead. Citing the disagreements over the designation of the work by Champollion, Lepsius, and Rougé, he ends up siding with Rougé at least as far as the idea that the words put in the mouth of the deceased in the text would have been spoken on his behalf by participants in the ritual (Renouf 1880, 172–73). After discussing the problems with the interpretation of the work and the ongoing efforts by Swiss Egyptologist Eduard Naville (1844–1926) to collect a synoptic edition (Willems 2023), he turns to the topic of the "Beatification of the Dead," which he understands as "the main subject of every chapter" and corresponding fundamentally to "everlasting life promised to the faithful" (Renouf 1880, 179), which he discusses in each of three "aspects" (Renouf 1880, 179). The first of these is "enjoying an existence similar to that which he had led upon earth." As implied by this wording as well as his note that the deceased receives fields "in the lands of Aarru and Hotep," this does not actually take place on earth but is a bodily existence in the beyond where all physical needs are met (Renouf 1880, 180–81). The second "aspect" is transformation, since the deceased "has the range of the entire universe in every shape and form that he desires" (Renouf 1880, 181). The basis of this idea is the twelve "transformation chapters" of the Book of the Dead, though he understands these as providing merely a nonexhaustive list of the unlimited options available to the deceased. He notes how this notion of free transformation has given rise to the misunderstanding "through a confusion between Egyptian notions and either Pythagorean or Hindu notions" whereby the belief in metempsychosis had erroneously been ascribed to the ancient Egyptians, "even by scholars who might have known better" (Renouf 1880, 182–83). He regards metempsychosis with the attendant notion of renewed life on earth as a form of punishment for sins as being entirely a development of "previously existing Hellenic modes of thought," with no antecedent in Egyptian religion. More generally, Renouf rejects any notion of expiation:

> If the judgment in the Hall of Law is favourable, the departed comes forth triumphantly as a god whom nothing can harm; he is identified with Osiris and with every other divinity. The nether world, and indeed the universe at large, is full of terrible and hostile forces; but through his identification with the great gods and his uttering words of power in their name, he passes unhurt in any direction that he pleases. (Renouf 1880, 183–84)

This point leads directly to the third and last aspect of beatification, the identification with Osiris and other gods. As seen in the quotation, Renouf regards this as fundamentally a way to empower the deceased against the obstacles encountered in the next world as related in the Book of the Dead. With the rejection of metempsychosis, Le Page Renouf is seemingly left without a clear fate for the sinners who do not share in the "beatification" described by the Book of the Dead. However, he proposes that this can be inferred indirectly from the kind of threats the empowered deceased is portrayed as overcoming. The chief way for souls to achieve salvation is still "the conformity of their conduct with the standard of law by which they are judged by Osiris in the

Amenti," although they are also protected by "amulets and talismans" as well as "the knowledge of religious formulas (such as the chapters of the Book of the Dead) or of divine names" (Renouf 1880, 191). With these considerations, Le Page Renouf thus takes up the problem going back as far as Lepsius of the purpose of the Book of the Dead for the Egyptians (as opposed to modern scholars, for whom it was understood to offer useful, literal descriptions of the ancient Egyptian afterlife). The problem is thus partly resolved by assuming a primacy of the judgment on ethical merits while accordingly amulets and ritual knowledge encoded in funerary texts play a secondary role, seemingly in the quite concrete sense that the knowledge of formulas and names could empower the deceased to defeat opponents and obstacles, and that that knowledge could in turn be imparted by a written document.

Not only is the moral element the more significant in Renouf's understanding, as a concept it is also vastly superior to the power of knowing and repeating names, which he characterizes as "rubbish . . . only worthy of the spells of vulgar conjurors." He explores the moral doctrine in the conventional way by turning to the text of chapter 125 of the Book of the Dead and its accompanying vignette of the weighing of the heart, before turning to brief summaries of other Book of the Dead chapters that had been made the subject of detailed studies in the recent scholarship (Renouf 1880, 196–200).

Ostensibly, then, Renouf's model is based almost exclusively on ancient sources, from texts of various types and genres to tomb decoration and funerary papyri. This makes his discussion another example of a late nineteenth-century analysis that reads as quite "modern"; and in completely sidestepping classical authors and the most overt Christian terminology alike, his approach represents a turning point. And yet his model of Egyptian mortuary religion remains deeply rooted in previous approaches, albeit in ways that are becoming less and less obvious with the changing terminology.

First, his understanding of the Book of the Dead as providing a literal, perhaps even narratively sequential, description of the soul's fate in the afterlife was completely conventional, and as we have seen in the previous chapters was very much dependent on the Christian soteriological framework that continued to structure it. The Christian terminology was thus largely bypassed (apart from the occasional, albeit central, exception like "beatification"), but the overall framework of individual salvation and eternal life, along with more specific entailments such as funerary papyri containing literal descriptions of the afterlife, remained.

Second, the pivot of Renouf's understanding is the underworld judgment on moral merits leading to the reward of salvation and eternal life or to punishments that are less specific. As we saw above, he explicitly regards this as the most valuable aspect of Egyptian mortuary religion as judged through late nineteenth-century Christian eyes, though he also sees this intermingled with superstitious practices, and in fact his negative wording, "No one could pass to the blissful dwellings of the dead who had failed at the judgment" (Renouf 1880, 194), indicates that he understands judgment as a necessary, but not sufficient, requirement for salvation. The reason for this, as we saw above, was to make room for the role of amulets and the knowledge imparted to the deceased by the Book of the Dead itself, but it is also likely that we see an underlying idea here made more explicit in later authors connecting the cult of the dead discussed in a separate chapter with the soteriology extracted from the Book of the Dead.

As I noted above, Renouf understands the deceased as being in some way dependent on the offerings made in the cult. Although he does not elaborate on this, a very logical entailment of salvation and eternal life depending on the cult performed by the living is that the deceased needed a steady stream of offerings to sustain existence—an idea incidentally quite compatible with Renouf's description of one aspect of beatification's being a life similar to that led on earth. We thus see an incipient step toward another, hitherto largely residual, category of evidence being claimed by the overall soteriological model: that relating to the mortuary cult.

Syntheses of the Egyptian Afterlife

The year 1885 saw the publication of two general introductions to ancient Egypt written by scholars who would go on to become hugely influential well into the twentieth century, owing not only to their central societal and academic positions in their time and to the practice of reprinting their books continuing to the present day, but also to their ability to couch ancient Egyptian evidence in terms and models both understandable and attractive to contemporary readers. As such, these two books, complemented with considerations of how the ideas expressed there develop further in the authors' later works, can be used as convenient examples of the mature model of the ancient Egyptian afterlife that would set the agenda for the next century and more.

As a recent graduate in Semitic languages from the University of Cambridge, Ernest Alfred Wallis Budge (1857–1934) had been appointed as assistant in the newly established Department of Oriental Antiquities of the British Museum in 1883 and almost immediately began what would become a long and prolific publishing career. An early landmark publication was his *Dwellers on the Nile* (Budge 1885).

Initially Budge introduces the Book of the Dead as a required part of the funerary equipment, because "it was considered of the greatest importance that the deceased in his journey and wanderings through the nether world should possess the mystic power imparted by the magic words, formulæ, and prayers of the book, which was supposed to be of divine origin" (Budge 1885, 149). While he makes the most of the Book of the Dead as a source of knowledge of the afterlife in a later chapter (see below), he also draws on more conventional ideas deriving ultimately from the classical authors, as when he notes that the Egyptians "believed that the soul would revisit the body after a number of years," and that this was the reason it was necessary to preserve the body "if its owner wished to live for ever with the gods" (Budge 1885, 156–57).

After brief discussions of practices of mummification based on the classical authors and examples of mummified bodies from the British Museum, Budge turns to the Book of the Dead in more detail. Drawing heavily on Renouf's Hibbert Lectures, in Budge's paraphrase the three complementary "aspects of beatification" discussed there have now become a sequential scheme describing how "the religious man gained everlasting life; first living in Hades as he lived upon earth, then passing through whatever transformations he wishes, and finally being identified with Osiris, the god of the dead" (Budge 1885, 168). He apparently at the same time understands the Book of the Dead as largely sequential in its structure, as he sees the various threats to the deceased, including "the attack of devils" as preceding "the great and final judgment" (Budge 1885, 172–75).

Again following Renouf, Budge notes that there is no place of probation, and that thus the deceased passing the judgment successfully becomes "identified with Osiris, in whose shape his mummy was made, and he roams through the fields of bliss at pleasure" (Budge 1885, 177). At the end of the chapter, Budge reiterates Renouf's characterization of Egyptian mortuary religion as a mixture of high-minded morality with base superstition, his wording precisely echoing that of the earlier scholar, while expanding the metaphor: "Still, underneath the heap of rubbish which gathered round their religion, there lie grains of truth and lofty morality which are worth picking up even by the civilised nations of to-day" (Budge 1885, 178).

As the juxtaposition of Budge with Renouf quickly reveals, Budge's thoughts on mortuary religion and the Book of the Dead in particular are largely derivative of that scholar's. Apart from the influential nature of Budge's oeuvre for well over a century, the interest of *Dwellers on the Nile* for present purposes lies in its demonstration of the after all relatively flexible nature of the model on individual details. Thus it is easy for Budge to bring back the ideas Renouf avoided about the return of the soul to the well-prepared body as a necessity for salvation. Similarly, the overall idea that the funerary papyri can be mined for concrete beliefs about the afterlife makes it possible to change the order, to reinterpret Renouf's "aspects" as a sequence of states attained one after the other, and, as in previous nineteenth-century contributions, to characterize the actual blessed existence itself as one finds most compelling (since it does not have to be found in the text itself). These capacious possibilities for "reading" the Book of the Dead (and eventually also similar texts in the funerary tradition) was an important reason the framework could continue unquestioned through the following century and more. Between the possibilities of understanding individual parts of a text as empowering the deceased for the afterlife in one way or another, avoiding threats in the afterlife, illustrating worship of entities encountered in afterlife, or simply describing the existence there for less specific purposes, there was little that could not be fitted into the mold.

The same year Budge's *Dwellers on the Nile* was published saw another broad introduction to ancient Egypt by a future giant of the emerging generation: *Aegypten und aegyptisches Leben im Altertum* (*Egypt and Egyptian Life in Antiquity*), by Adolf Erman (1854–1937; cf. Schipper 2006). Erman was appointed to the chair in Egyptology in Berlin and the directorship of the Egyptian Museum there in the same year and would go on to become one of the most influential scholars of Egyptian language and religion of his generation.

Within his 1885 work, Erman devotes one chapter to religion and one to "the dead" (*die Toten*). The latter in particular takes up the themes relevant to the present discussion. Erman makes a familiar distinction in stating from the outset that he will focus less on the "confused conceptions" (*verworrenen Vorstellungen*) of the Egyptians concerning life after death and more on the relations between the living and the dead in practice. Despite this evaluation, Erman nonetheless finds it necessary to begin with a discussion about the "fate [*Schicksal*] of the dead" (Erman 1885, 2:413). As indicated by his wording cited above, Erman makes the fundamental assumption that the Egyptians did not have clearly conceived ideas about what happened to the soul after death, but that they held a number of concrete, apparently contradictory, beliefs:

> One thought that the deceased was to be sought in the sky amongst the stars, others that he sat in the trees among the birds, and yet others thought that he must actually be where his bones lay in the ground. One moment it was thought that it gave him particular pleasure to appear in one shape after another, today as a heron, tomorrow as a scarab, and the day after as a lotus flower on the water. The next he dwells in the Realm of Light, the *Duat*, where the gods dwell, and wanders with the previously deceased *on the beautiful roads on which the transfigured wander*. (Erman 1885, 2:413–14; emphasis in the original)

While this vagueness and confusion seem like a stark departure from the clear articulation of Egyptian dogmas in the previous literature, it is in fact a natural consequence of the old and well established idea that the Book of the Dead with all its heterogeneous contents should be read as a literal description of the afterlife. As we saw above, Renouf had sought to group the many ideas found there into three complementary "aspects," with the precise interconnection between them not made clear, while Budge had reinterpreted (or misunderstood) this as a sequence of states, albeit not one reflected in the order of the chapters of the book. But as Erman points out, the ideas attestable in the Book of the Dead and other texts and images relating to the dead are in fact significantly more variegated than these three categories suggest. Erman's conclusion that it was full of mutually contradictory ideas was a logical consequence of a close reading of the text along with the long-accepted premise that the Book of the Dead should be read as a literal description of the afterlife (and without having too high expectations for the intellectual rigor of the ancients). While Renouf, and Budge with him, had seen Egyptian religion as a mixture of noble morality with superstition and magic, Erman's low opinion of the spiritual life of the ancient Egyptians gave him no qualms about blaming these apparent contradictions squarely on their confusion and lack of consistency.

Renouf had already pointed out the centrality of the Egyptian entity known as the *ka*, and Erman assigns it a pivotal place in the interaction with the dead. Proposing translations like "spirit" (*Geist*) and "image" (*Bild*), Erman understands the *ka* as living on after death and needing a statue that preserves the individual features (*Züge*) of the deceased that are no longer present in the corpse. The *ka* similarly has to be supplied with its favorite household goods (*Hausrat*), and first and foremost it needs to be sustained by food and drink served at the offering slab in the tomb, "for if this does not happen, the deceased is plagued by hunger and thirst" (Erman 1885, 2:414–15). To Erman this basic model explains the main practices attested in ancient Egyptian funerary culture: "for their [sc. the conceptions of the *ka*] sake did they mummify corpses, build indestructible tombs, establish endowments for maintaining mortuary offerings, keep statues and goods in the tombs—in short, do everything by which knowledge of their people has been conveyed to us" (Erman 1885, 2:415).

This explanation, which would prove highly influential and is still often repeated in more or less the same form, mixes conventional ideas with more novel ones in a complex way. The assumption that grave goods were placed in tombs for use by the soul of the deceased had been around for centuries, so it was merely a question of mapping the Egyptian entity *ka* onto this idea. The notion of statues as substitutes for the body in a sense followed quite naturally from Maspero's and Renouf's idea of the *ka* as denoting fundamentally an image (cf. Nyord 2019), along with the much older idea of the anxiety over the preservation of the body in a lifelike state. As noted above, the idea that the soul of the deceased needed to be sustained by food was largely implicit in Renouf's discussion, but it is in a sense a logical consequence of the combination of the simple fact that food was being offered with the long-standing assumption that the objective of every practice of Egyptian mortuary religion was the salvation of the soul of the deceased. As food was evidently necessary for this goal, it must have meant that the soul (now with the co-opted indigenous designation *ka*) needed food to sustain itself. This shift in deductive logic sidelines the earlier explanation of food offerings along more explicitly Christian lines as expiatory sacrifices, since the food is given a much more direct role to play as a condition for the salvation and eternal life of the soul.

Along with these fundamental ideas about the soul, another basic concept was that of the deceased's imitating the mythological fate of Osiris, who was brought back to life (*neu zum Leben erwachen*), which in turn motivated a wide range of mythological imagery assimilating the deceased with this god (Erman 1885, 2:416). This concept in turn motivated the "imagination" (*Phantasie*) to people the realm of Osiris with "terrible demons" (*schreckliche Dämonen*) like those attending the judgment of the dead. Erman's description here is essentially similar to that of his contemporaries in speaking of "confessing sins" (*Sünde bekennen*) and so on, but whereas Renouf and Budge saw this as evidence of a lofty moral principle under layers of superstition, Erman thus sees it more condescendingly as evidence of the lively imagination the Egyptians brought to bear on their religious conceptions (Erman 1885, 416–18).

After this discussion of the beliefs motivating Egyptian burial practices, Erman turns to the evidence of funerary architecture as it changed through the ages, after first pointing out that burials of the type exemplified by extant monumental tombs would have been the privilege of a very small proportion of the populace. This part of the chapter focuses mainly on the outward description, which is however interspersed occasionally with proposed motivations, for example, "the tomb is not only to provide protection for the dead body, but is also at the same time the place where one can bring offerings for the *ka* of the deceased and recite the necessary formulae" (Erman 1885, 420). Of particular interest for elucidating Erman's understanding is his discussion of the various types of grave goods and other funerary practices. Although, as I noted above, he understands funerary texts as offering literal descriptions of the afterlife, he nonetheless sees their actual deposition in tombs as being mainly for ritual reasons, noting that apparently it was believed that "these formulae, the so-called *transfigurations* [*Verklärungen*], the rattling off [*Herbeten*] of which is so useful for the deceased, would have the same effect when given to him in written form" (Erman 1885, 425).

He interprets the use of heart scarabs in direct connection with the weighing of the heart, as the "sinful [*sündige*] heart" was replaced by the sacred symbol of the scarab, along with an instruction to the real heart not to stand up as witness. By contrast, the reason for removing the other organs during mummification was connected with the worry that the deceased would experience hunger and thirst, for which the digestive organs were seen as responsible—echoing in a reinterpreted form ideas like those present in Plutarch and Porphyry. He correspondingly understands the main role of the four sons of Horus, in whose shapes the jars containing the removed organs were often made, as "protecting the dead against hunger" (Erman 1885, 427). Other practices were likewise aimed at staving off the "much-feared danger of hunger" (*vielgefürchtete Hungersgefahr*) as backup for the actual mortuary offerings and the magical formulas. This is true not only of wooden replicas of food offerings placed in tombs, but also of "models" of people engaged in various kinds of food production (cf. fig. 1), and indeed other activities apparently benefiting the deceased in the afterlife through "the magical power of wooden figures" (*magischen Kraft hölzerner Figuren*). From being primarily an explanation of the role of the *ka* and the rationale of the cultic sacrifices, the fear of hunger has thus been elevated to a pivotal concept in Egyptian funerary culture, capable of explaining a wide range of findings while also tinting the overall psychological nature of the model.

Erman's thought process is in a sense quite logical. Proceeding from the old and unquestioned assumption that every element of Egyptian funerary culture aimed at the salvation of the soul to achieve eternal life, it seems reasonable to assume that each constituent part of the grave goods is aimed at warding off a concrete threat against this goal, especially given Erman's evaluation of the ancient Egyptians' "unpleasant cast of mind" (*unerfreulichen Geistesrichtung*) (Erman 1885, 429). Thus, as I noted above, the fundamental idea that the Egyptians feared hunger in the afterlife was based on the food offerings' being presented and the assumption that this was supposed to ensure eternal life and thus apparently had to go on forever–a requirement bound to present practical challenges. This means every element of grave goods and tomb decoration that in one way or another seems to deal with the theme of food could be understood as meant to ensure a steady food supply by "magical" means. Having established that, it seems natural that other concrete dangers in the afterlife can be deduced in a straightforward fashion from other types of grave goods, such as amulets offering protection against more or less clearly articulated fears. In this way a large amount of additional evidence from Egyptian burial practices that has hitherto played a relatively withdrawn role in interpretations of religious beliefs can now be brought in line with the established understanding by assuming afterlife challenges that each is supposed to address.

With Erman's framework, the stage was set for the next century and more of studies of ancient Egyptian mortuary religion. The ease with which new evidence could be incorporated into this model is shown not only by his treatment of "new" categories of grave goods, as just discussed, but especially strikingly by the way Erman was able to incorporate the newly published body of texts from the royal pyramids of the late Old Kingdom into his new, more detailed analysis in his *Egyptian Religion* (*Die ägyptische Religion*) from 1905. The Pyramid Texts being of fundamentally the same nature as the Book of the Dead, they lent themselves easily to illustrating Erman's main point concerning the contradictory and imaginative nature of Egyptian beliefs about the afterlife. Indeed, it is difficult to imagine textual contents that could *not* have corroborated this capacious hypothesis.

While explicit and specific Christian terminology is thus generally on the decline during the later decades of the nineteenth century, the overall model always allowed for individual authors to bring it back in, because of the straightforward compatibility of the underlying schemes. Thus, for example, French archaeologist François Lenormant (1837–83) in his broad history of the ancient world explained the curious fact that according to the conventional understanding of the Book of the Dead even the virtuous soul seemingly had to go through a series of arduous trials by reference to a sort of original sin, reasoning that "as a human [*en sa qualité d'homme*] he had by necessity been a sinner [*pécheur*]" (Lenormant 1869, 529). Similarly, the old notion that the god Osiris was a deified human could still be understood to decidedly Christlike effect (as it had been much earlier; for example, by Thorlacius) by writers wanting to make Egyptian religion particularly relatable to contemporary readers:

> The Egyptians of every period in which they are known to us believed that Osiris was of divine origin, that he suffered death and mutilation at the hands of the powers of evil, that after a great struggle with these powers he rose again, that he became henceforth the king of the underworld and judge of the dead, and that because he had conquered death the righteous also might conquer death. (Budge 1899, 41)

Note how this description almost sentence by sentence parallels the section of the Apostles' Creed dealing with Jesus Christ. As we saw above, far from being radical and divergent reinterpretations, such overtly Christianizing interpretations merely made explicit parts of the conventional framework that were increasingly overwritten by appropriated indigenous sources and terminology.

Conclusion

In the preface to the 1907 English translation of Adolf Erman's book on Egyptian religion, the British Egyptologist Francis Llewellyn Griffith noted among the strong motivations for translating the book for a wider English-speaking audience the Egyptian religion's "early recognition of a high moral principle, its elaborate conceptions of life and death, and its connection with the development of Christianity" (Erman 1907, v). In other words, the very expectations that had informed European study of ancient Egyptian religion for more than four hundred years had now gained a seemingly sound empirical basis. Just as important, they had been formulated in a way capacious enough to incorporate any new texts and images that might appear as so many literal descriptions of the Egyptian afterlife, and archaeological finds as equipment needed in that afterlife, from which the challenges they were supposed to help against could in turn be deduced. A framework had been established that would determine Egyptological interpretations of ancient Egyptian mortuary religion down to the present day.

CONCLUSION

Where Do We Go from Here?

Perhaps the most striking feature of European engagement with ancient Egyptian mortuary religion is how relatively little it changed over the past several hundred years in spite of the massive political, social, economic, religious, and intellectual changes that period experienced. From the point of view of modern expectations it is particularly striking how seamless the transition was between "speculative" and "empirical" approaches during the nineteenth century. Where modern disciplinary histories of Egyptology have tended to assume a Copernican revolution at the "birth of Egyptology" around 1822, recent work outside the field has tended to emphasize the slow and incremental nature of such changes (e.g., Gange 2013), and this examination has very much corroborated this view concerning the interpretation of Egyptian mortuary religion.

One of the earliest and longest-lived ideas about ancient Egyptian culture is the notion that corpses were mummified to preserve them for eternity. This idea crystallized as far back as the medieval period at the intersection of several observations and interests. First, and no doubt a prime contributor to the longevity of this idea, mummified bodies—especially unwrapped ones—could be directly observed as preserving bodily features of people embalmed millennia earlier. It was as logical a move for the medieval observer as it is for modern ones to conflate this *effect* of mummification with the ancients' *purposes*. An originally separate line of observation ultimately pointing in the same direction had to do with the specific materiality of mummified bodies, particularly their suffusion with the black, gumlike substance that reminded early observers of mumia, the medically efficacious asphalt from which "mummies" would gain their name. The healing properties of such mumia seemed to align logically with the ancient Egyptians' purpose of using it to preserve dead bodies, though the primary interest to Europeans initially lay rather in the possibility of harvesting this efficacious substance. A further line of thought coinciding with this idea was the burgeoning European interest in embalming for the specific purpose of preserving bodies, whether for practical purposes of bringing the bodies of important persons dying abroad home to be buried or, later on, for more theologically motivated reasons related to the interrelation between body, soul, and resurrection. The result of these intersecting lines was the firm establishment in European thought of the idea that the ancient Egyptians embalmed bodies for their long-term preservation (which could easily be extended to eternal preservation when contexts required).

A momentous change in the engagement with ancient Egypt took place in the late fifteenth and early sixteenth centuries, when a number of pertinent classical texts became available to European scholars. For mortuary religion in particular, passages of specific and long-lasting interest came from Herodotus on mummification, ritual mourning, and metempsychosis, and from Diodorus on mummification and the ritual judgment of the deeds of the deceased. Herodotus's discussion of Egyptian beliefs about the soul could be complemented by passages from Plato and the Hermetic writings (both understood to have direct relevance to ancient Egyptian religion), and the practice of mummification could be connected to religious ideas through a short passage from Servius on the soul's dependence on an undecayed body for its survival. The passages were largely taken at face value at this early stage, with Servius helping to bridge a gap in Herodotus where beliefs in the soul and practices of mummification remain unconnected. Similarly, Diodorus tended to be understood in a straightforward fashion as describing a ritual judgment determining the right to burial. Slightly more marginal writers like Plutarch and Porphyry offered seemingly small details, which could however be used to bridge another gap between the technical description of embalming procedures in other writers and the question of underlying beliefs that was often at the forefront of the minds of early modern and later European observers.

The seventeenth century saw ancient Egyptian culture deployed increasingly in wider diachronic arguments concerning universal history. The established framework for understanding Egyptian mortuary religion based on the classical authors was at once robust enough for this prevalent feature of the ancient culture to figure prominently into such discussions and left room for flexibility in serving specific purposes. Given the interests of scholars at the time, contemporary religion or society was most often the ultimate subject of such historical arguments, so that the deployment of Egypt tended to be a matter of emphasizing either the similarities or the differences between particular aspects of that culture and the corresponding phenomena in contemporary European society or through history. Thus, for Henri de Sponde's argument at the end of the sixteenth century concerning the universal importance of burial rites and hence intervening in contemporary debates about the rights of Protestants to be buried in Catholic cemeteries, it was the cross-cultural importance of undisturbed and uninfringed burial that was of interest. This argument could be furthered by assuming that the Egyptians had also believed in the resurrection of the body as a reason for stressing the sanctity of burials, and similarly Diodorus's ritual determination of the right of burial could underline the connection between this right and a just life.

While arguments like those of Sponde stressing the continuity of Egyptian beliefs with Christianity tended to avoid or redirect the notion of metempsychosis, for scholars interested in establishing discontinuity and in "othering" ancient Egyptian religion, the notion of metempsychosis was particularly useful. This is the case notably with a scholar like Athanasius Kircher, who sought to distinguish traditions in ancient Egyptian religion of antediluvian wisdom compatible with Christianity from competing superstitious corruptions. Metempsychosis naturally belonged to the latter category, and Kircher could emphasize its otherness by drawing parallels to numerous non-Egyptian traditions seen as destinations to which these ideas diffused from their Egyptian origin. In contrast to Sponde, ideas like Diodorus's postmortem judgment that could have more readily established similarity to Christianity recede into the background.

Many of the seventeenth-century reconstructions of Egyptian mortuary religion can be understood within this general framework of deploying a strategic selection from the established set of classical authors to emphasize similarities or differences compared with contemporary Christianity depending on the place accorded to ancient Egypt in the model of universal history argued by a given author. One important idea that emerged during this process is that of the moral or ethical dimension of Egyptian mortuary religion, either through an emphasis on reincarnation in more or less noble animals based on Plato or the Hermetic writings, or through an increasing approximation of Diodorus's ritual judgment with the Christian Last Judgment, initially mainly in the sense that they both serve as strong motivators for a virtuous life on earth.

During the course of the century, three strands of thought converged to establish an even closer association between ancient Egypt and the notion of postmortem judgment leading to rewards and punishments. The first, and arguably the instigating framework, was a basic Christian expectation that a people expending so much energy on burial practices must have been intensely occupied with postmortem salvation, and that there must thus have been a sense of rewards and punishments after death. This idea could be supported by, and in turn itself support, slight reinterpretations of central passages from Herodotus and Diodorus. Thus the second strand of thought comes from a reading of Herodotus where the transmigration of souls is not an automatic sequence through all types of animals; rather, the nature of the body into which the soul transmigrates is a result of the soul's behavior in this life. While going against Herodotus's wording, such an interpretation could find support in Plato and the Hermetic writings, and it seemed natural to assume a procedure of formal judgment along Christian lines for determining this outcome. Third, Diodorus's description of a legal procedure determining the deceased's right to be buried could also be reinterpreted as (or in some cases doubled to include) a procedure of judgment in the afterlife. While Diodorus explicitly rejects such an interpretation as a Greek misunderstanding of the Egyptian ritual, with mutual support from the other two strands it often came to be seen as another independent piece of evidence supporting Egyptian afterlife judgment.

A long-standing debate involving many of the most important scholars writing on the topic of ancient Egyptian mortuary religion during the seventeenth and early eighteenth centuries is the relation between the religion of Moses and that of the ancient Egyptians. In line with earlier approaches, contributions to this debate tended to emphasize either continuity or discontinuity, on the one hand between Egyptian religion and Judaism, and on the other between Judaism and Christianity, leading to a number of permutations (cf. also Assmann 1997b).

The notion of an ancient Egyptian mystery tradition with trials and initiations became one of the most influential ideas about the culture during the eighteenth century. First introduced to a wider audience by Jean Terrasson's novel *Séthos*, the notion of Egyptian initiation was closely entangled with mortuary religion from the very beginning, as illustrated by Terrasson's locating the title character's initiation in a secret underground complex under the Great Pyramid, the funerary nature of which was otherwise well established by this point. Not only did this help cement a prevalent new understanding of a difference between exoteric and esoteric religions in ancient Egypt (Jan Assmann's *religio duplex*; Assmann 2014), with a corresponding interest from Freemasons and other societies in reconstructing and replicating the secret rituals, it also introduced the new idea of initiatory trials as an important motif in Egyptian religion, and more specifically, in combination with prevalent understandings of mortuary religion, the notion of the soul undergoing such trials after death.

Alongside these intellectual developments, the eighteenth century also saw travelers increasingly adopting new Enlightenment-inspired approaches to a more precise and systematic recording of ancient Egyptian monuments for publication. Although travelers like Carsten Niebuhr did not necessarily have a specific interest in ancient Egyptian mortuary religion, for scholars back in Europe who did, the material they made available made it possible to gradually adopt more empirical approaches. A prevalent example of such an encyclopedic approach is the work of Georg Zoëga, who combined most of the knowledge available on the eve of the eighteenth century from classical authors, objects in European collections, and previous scholars and travelers into a single comprehensive model. This resulted in a postmortem scenario in which the soul resides in the underworld, where it enjoys a blessed existence until the body decays, after which it begins a cycle of transmigration through different animals, ending with a new human body. To Zoëga this complicated picture was the result of a compromise between priestly and more popular ideas. An important consequence of his engagement with available imagery is that, drawing on earlier more sporadic examples, he enshrined a tradition of attaching interpretations to specific Egyptian iconography, notably the weighing of the heart scene understood as the postmortem judgment that scholars had long presumed the Egyptians to believe in.

The new "empirical" focus thus started before the Napoleonic invasion in 1798, but the vast material made available through the *Description de l'Égypte* was quickly deployed to connect Egyptian monuments to the traditional interpretations. A notable and long-lasting effect of this is that specific motifs in Egyptian imagery soon became inextricably linked to themes in the traditional interpretation. Notably this was true of Book of the Dead vignettes of the weighing of the heart, which became connected with the conventional notion of an Egyptian Last Judgment (helped along both by the prevalence of the psychostasis motif in European depictions of the Christian Last Judgment and by the fact that the number of attendant figures in the papyri corresponded to the number of assessors in some versions of Diodorus's description of the judgment ritual, which had come to sometimes be interpreted as taking place in the afterlife). The version of the weighing scene in the Book of Gates in the tomb of Ramesses VI, which was reproduced in the *Description*, became a similar illustration of the concept of transmigration of the soul, with its depiction of a pig being chased away from the presence of Osiris. Both scenes were frequently referred to and thus gained an ambiguous double status as being at once demonstrations of the conventional reading of the classical authors and convenient illustrations that could be used to communicate the details to contemporary readers independent of the classical texts (much in the way the Book of the Dead scene is still used today in teaching and outreach, but also in more specialized academic discourse).

Against this background, the decipherment of hieroglyphs in 1822 at first played a surprisingly secondary role for understanding Egyptian mortuary religion. For example, as the significance of the weighing of the heart scene had already been widely accepted, the translation of the captions from a monumental version by Champollion, and a little later of the statements of the "negative confession" by Rosellini, could very easily be fitted into this framework. For larger questions, such as that regarding beliefs in the resurrection of the body, as well as the general relation between the different parts of the concept (judgment, transmigration, transcendent afterlife, etc.), neither the newly available artifacts and images nor the inscriptions gradually being translated offered any direct input, as for example James Prichard remarked with a mixture of disappointment and relief (Prichard 1838, xii–xiii).

A ramification of the identification of the weighing of the heart scene as depicting a Last Judgment was that it became a natural supposition that the rest of the Book of the Dead and other funerary compositions similarly depicted situations of the afterlife, an interpretation greatly helped along by the associations with trials and tests derived from the framework of Egyptian initiation. Meanwhile, Christian (at first mostly Protestant) expectations of the afterlife were changing profoundly, making themes like journeys, activities, and experiences expected in the afterlife in a way that had not been the case before the mid-eighteenth century. This overall understanding had the convenient side effect of having the images (and in time the accompanying texts) of the funerary papyri offer precisely the kind of detailed knowledge about the fate of the soul that scholars had been intensely interested in, but on which the classical sources had been mostly silent. Thus, in the seminal publication of a comprehensive Book of the Dead manuscript from Turin in 1842, Karl Richard Lepsius could present it as basically a full description of the fate of the soul after death, leading to its transfiguration as the ultimate goal of the soul's journey—though he also, slightly incongruously, suggested its simultaneous function as a sort of passport to the afterlife.

If the first half of the nineteenth century was thus still characterized by a certain excess of ideas that one could fit together in various ways, the midcentury began to see efforts that would streamline and simplify this profusion, especially by sidelining the idea of metempsychosis. The new empirical evidence from ancient Egyptian monuments certainly contributed to this, though not as the straightforward result of a lack of empirical evidence for transmigration of souls that a modern observer might imagine. Rather, an important factor was that the idea of metempsychosis had gradually grown conceptually redundant. A first step toward this had been taken much earlier when a notion of rewards and punishments through the nature of the body in which the soul was incarnated had been added to Herodotus's description. As long as the classical authors had remained the main source of information, this had been a crucial way to project an element of postmortem judgment with rewards and punishments onto Egyptian religion. As imagery from the Book of the Dead and the royal tombs from the Valley of the Kings presented other methods that could be understood as the punishment of sinners, this key function of metempsychosis was no longer needed. The ideas continued to coexist for a while, either as competing priestly and popular doctrines, as occurring in a sequence, or with metempsychosis as a temporary purgatory forming a subsidiary part of the model. However, such parallel treatments only tended to demonstrate further the redundancy of metempsychosis at this time when the ethical basis of the Egyptian Last Judgment could be more simply demonstrated and illustrated in other ways, and the parallelism with purgatory may well have contributed to this impression of redundancy to the predominantly Protestant scholars of the time. Correspondingly, largely without explicit debate, metempsychosis all but disappeared from discussions of Egyptian religion by the 1870s, leaving only the framework of ethical postmortem judgment, rewards, and punishments that it had originally helped to support.

With the loss of metempsychosis, the traditional main instrument of "othering" Egyptian mortuary religion had disappeared, so that what was left was a system remarkably similar to Christianity—not surprisingly, since it was constructed from Christian expectations and concepts in the first place. For this reason, while earlier authors had emphasized such similarities to demonstrate either historical continuities or human universals, the parallels between Christianity and Egyptian religion in the late nineteenth century became particularly striking. While this could be used as grist for universalists' mill just as it had been in previous centuries, it also offered more specific polemical possibilities. One of the most striking examples is Samuel Sharpe's argument that orthodox Christianity had taken over many of its core concepts from Egyptian religion, a point he used to further his own Unitarian ideas, which avoided exactly the theological concepts he could trace back to ancient Egypt. As this particular argument had no use for metempsychosis, Sharpe ended up sidelining this concept, and in so doing he ultimately contributed to bringing the understanding of Egyptian religion even closer to that of contemporary Christianity.

Another aspect of Egyptian mortuary religion that became clear from the encounter with Egyptian monuments since the early nineteenth century was the importance of the ancestor cult, with its emphasis on sacrifices, especially of food and drink. Initially understood in very general terms along the lines of similar memorial celebrations in Greek and Roman religious practices, the offering cult soon became subsumed under the general soteriological framework. Early understandings of this practice interpreted it on the model of Catholic expiation as a temporary measure, but as the conceptual model was simplified, the offering cult too came to be understood as one of the many requirements for achieving ultimate salvation: since the ancient Egyptians wanted eternal life, they apparently believed this could be achieved only by a steady stream of food and drink. Scholars naturally realized the paradox inherent in eternal life's being contingent on continued practices among one's descendants, but rather than questioning whether this was indeed the Egyptians' aim, instead a wide range of burial practices, from tomb imagery and inscriptions to grave goods, came to be understood as "magical" ways to remedy this inherent weakness in the system.

The last decades of the nineteenth century, still sometimes referred to as the "Golden Age of Egyptology," saw the final crystallization of the overall model that remains dominant in modern Egyptology. The specifically Christian theological vocabulary might be very explicit (e.g., Budge) or more toned down (e.g., Erman), but the model's continuity with previous decades—and indeed centuries—remains clear either way. With the notion of metempsychosis completely sidelined, the overall goal of Egyptian mortuary religion was now understood as a quest for eternal life, defaulting to understanding this as taking place in a transcendent realm, which was described directly and literally in the images and texts of the Book of the Dead (and later also the Pyramid Texts) and decoration of tomb walls. The various liminal situations found in the texts and images were thus straightforwardly understood as so many threats to the salvation of the soul, with the weighing of the heart as a central, readily understandable, and thus eminently teachable example of this. The result of this mode of reading the Book of the Dead was the understanding that the Egyptians apparently believed they could sidestep the requirements for an ethical life through the magical means of various grave goods, including the Book of the Dead itself.

As the summary of this development shows, and as demonstrated in more detail throughout this book, ancient Egyptian ideas and practices were always narrowly circumscribed by the conceptual frameworks brought to bear on them by European scholars, even in the more "othering" approaches. By the time indigenous texts and concepts came to play a role in the interpretation, the overall framework had already been strongly entrenched in European thought. While this could in principle have led to a tension between evidence and framework, as seen especially in the previous two chapters, the framework was at once intuitive enough that it would take very robust counterevidence to shake it in the least, and capacious enough that just about any text or image could be fitted into the personal, transcendent, and eternal afterlife posited.

If one of the recurring observations has been that interpretations of the Egyptian afterlife became shaped in fundamental ways by "Christian" ideas, we have also seen just what multifarious results this general source of inspiration could lead to. This underscores an important point in the history of European ideas, here as formulated by Kocku von Stuckrad (2010, 14): "It is not that Christian Europe never existed; instead, Christianity in Europe has always been diverse and comprised many forms of beliefs and practices that populated the minds of believers (and non-believers)."

It is no surprise, then, that "Christian" inspirations could lead to very different, even directly opposite views depending on time, place, and stances on such questions as the reformation of the church, the place of Egypt in universal history (including whether Egypt is primarily aligned to Christianity, "othered," or a combination), and the precise discursive ends for which ancient Egypt was deployed. Nonetheless, in aggregate the core concepts and vocabulary shared across such internal divisions contributed greatly to the stability of European thought about ancient Egyptian mortuary religion. Whether one argued for or against, for example, an ancient Egyptian belief in the resurrection of the body, the fundamental terms of the interpretation were established and delineated by the application of this Christian concept. That the Christian notion in itself was open to different interpretations (and indeed different degrees of commitment by European scholars), while certainly playing a role, nonetheless tended to dwindle in the encounter between ancient Egyptian evidence and Christian conceptual frameworks. The effect of framing Egyptian religion in terms of a binary question of adherence (or not) to a specific Christian doctrine tended to overshadow more specific dogmatic questions of precisely how that tenet was understood by the interpreter, and with what degree of conviction. On the other hand, such dogmatic details could frequently play a role for the specific interpretations or arguments a given scholar arrived at. But in terms of the general discourse (e.g., Foucault 1978)—what could meaningfully be expressed or discussed about ancient Egyptian religion—the very application itself of Christian categories had a much more significant and formative effect.

This is also the time to address what may be perceived as an "elephant in the room" throughout this book. As laid out in the introduction, the overarching stance has been an effort to sidestep the usual question of how far the different interpretations analyzed were "correct" by modern standards. The reason for this was twofold. First, judging ideas developed in the past by modern standards would introduce significant anachronism through the notion of a timeless and unchanging ideal of Egyptological research (which happens to coincide with that of the modern scholar). More specifically in the present case, as has been copiously documented in the preceding discussion, the "modern" ideas in this domain, far from emerging organically from an increasingly accurate objective engagement with the ancient sources as is usually assumed, are in fact themselves inextricably entangled with the historical developments explored here. This would make attempts to judge the historical ideas by the yardstick of how far they point forward to currently accepted notions a highly circular endeavor.

And yet, to the modern reader, Egyptologist or not, the tracking of these developments will inevitably raise significant questions regarding our current understanding. If, as the preceding discussion has indicated, our contemporary framework of understanding ancient Egyptian mortuary religion is the direct result of the nineteenth-century reception of early modern ideas, with ancient Egyptian sources eventually fitted into the framework rather than contributing fundamentally to its construction in any meaningful sense, surely that should have consequences for the authority of the contemporary model? Can we continue to speak confidently of the ancient Egyptian "afterlife beliefs" and "quest for immortality" knowing that these ideas can be traced back to the Renaissance, where they were constructed intuitively drawing on Christian concepts and a few passages from classical authors no longer regarded as authoritative in order speculatively to explain practices of burial and mummification that were known in very little detail?

The genealogy of the concepts explored here, in other words, strongly underscores that our core models and vocabulary are more European and Christian than ancient Egyptian. If this notion seems to run directly counter to even the most recent discussions of Egyptian mortuary religion, this is at least partly because a significant amount of research potentially capable of calling details of this framework into question has not been put to that purpose. It is worth mentioning some examples of such details to illustrate this. As we saw above, the afterlife hypothesis has a distinct need for dualistic concepts of body and soul, even if their close interrelation is often stressed to explain mummification. By contrast, neither of the Egyptian concepts of *ka* or *ba* enlisted since the nineteenth century as indigenous correlates to Western notions of the "soul" actually function as anything like the immortal and immaterial portion of a human being (*ba* concept, Žabkar 1968; *ka* concept, Nyord 2019). In fact the very idea that such Egyptian "aspects of the personality" are all on a par is itself the result of nineteenth-century deduction according to which Egyptian concepts of personhood could be modeled on the Christian body/soul distinction, just by adding the notion that the "soul" or "immaterial" component was split into multiple entities (cf. Gee 2009, 1–2). Similarly, for the Egyptians mummification did not aim to preserve the body in a lifelike state for eternity, but rather was a material part of the process of transforming the deceased into an ancestor (Nyord 2013; Riggs 2014). Funerary texts were not conveniently literal descriptions of the transcendent afterlife, but a complex and heterogeneous collection of ritual compositions with different origins and purposes alluding to a wide range of mythological and cosmological concepts (Podemann Sørensen 1996, 2013, 15–24 and 36–45; Smith 2017; Nyord 2020). More specifically, the Book of the Dead chapters accompanying the popular weighing of the heart scene do not bear out the notion of an Egyptian Last Judgment (Janák 2023), and its setting in Egyptian religion was not even exclusively mortuary (Lieven 2012, 263–64).

Similar ideas certainly did surface on occasion in much earlier scholarship. For example, Richard Pococke (1743), as well as occasional later scholars, understood the mummified body as an image of Osiris, making the aim of the practice imitating the god rather than preserving the body for eternity. Similarly, Jean-Pierre Rigord, also in the eighteenth century and hence well before the hieroglyphic writing could be read, understood funerary texts as being ritually efficacious rather than communicating information about the afterlife (Rigord 1704). However, such exceptional interpretations were universally sidelined by the conventional set of ideas which proved both more intuitive and easier to fit into an overall narrative.

Individually, such ideas can certainly be (and often are) ignored as insignificant details that need not trouble what has seemed like a robust framework. Yet if the very foundation of that framework is brought into question, as in this book, they appear in a very different light, as so many signposts toward a new understanding of ancient Egyptian mortuary religion sidestepping Christian-style soteriology. This sense of an approaching tipping point is highly characteristic of what Thomas Kuhn terms a crisis within a scientific paradigm, where anomalies reach a critical mass, eventually motivating a "revolution" rejecting the conventional framework (Kuhn 1962).

An important part of the reason it has taken so long to reach this point is no doubt the same as that for the ease with which new data could be fitted into the existing framework from the early nineteenth century forward: Within its overall soteriological outline, the framework is highly capacious, so that it is almost impossible to even imagine what kind of evidence from Egyptian tombs it would take to question or reject it (cf. Nyord 2018, 77–78). The heavily empirical discipline of Egyptology has thus not been well poised to critique the framework, since its problem is not that it cannot explain just about any detail one might encounter in ancient Egyptian funerary practices. By contrast, Egyptology does not have a strong tradition of historiographical or conceptual critique, which is precisely what would be needed to show the problematic nature of the model as a whole (resulting in the most pointed criticism of such frameworks coming from outside the discipline, not least the history of religions; e.g., Otto 2013; Podemann Sørensen 1996, 2013, 15–24 and 36–45).

As I noted in the introduction, it is not that the past scholars discussed here were "wrong" in any meaningful sense. In sometimes awe-inspiring feats of intellect and erudition, they synthesized the available evidence into comprehensible models capable of fitting ancient Egyptian religion into their and their readers' worldview, the success of which is amply demonstrated by the impact and longevity of their interpretations. These models were not, however, the direct reflection of indigenous concepts and motivations that they are usually taken to be, nor can we continue to assume the near-universality of central Christian concepts the way early modern and nineteenth-century scholars could do, and this is where contemporary Egyptology should part ways with these ideas. In modern terms they are very much the result of an ongoing conceptual colonization narrowly circumscribing how indigenous practices and categories could be understood. The scholars of the past did not fail to live up to some timeless universal ideal for objective Egyptology, but scholarly ideas and institutions have moved away from universalizing Christian concepts to increasingly privilege indigenous understandings instead. As seen throughout this book, for all its success in providing intuitive explanations, the Eurocentric "afterlife" framework was never well poised to do that.

If the underlying assumptions are thus no longer considered tenable, why have ideas about the Egyptian afterlife proved so tenacious and long-lived, even in recent decades? Part of the reason is no doubt that while they may no longer be current in (all) academic spheres, the intuitive expectation that there is a universal human longing for transcendent, eternal life for the individual (an idea that happens to usually be couched in Christian terminology) is still alive and well in many domains of modern, globalized existence. A little less obvious is that in addition to appealing naturally to modern and past observers alike, enormous efforts are continuously going into upholding the framework. Sociologist Bruno Latour has pointed out the vast amount of "work" required to extend facts beyond the social and material networks that first produced them (e.g., Latour 2000). This helps us understand the function of the endless numbers of seemingly redundant museum exhibitions, documentaries, and popular books, not to mention efforts in primary, secondary, and tertiary education, focusing on maintaining an awareness and appreciation of the Egyptian "quest for eternity," "longing for the afterlife," and such. To the individual documentary film director, curator, or educator, these activities may seem simply a way of communicating well-established ideas with a proven popularity, requiring a minimum of effort because the script, the labels, and the lectures have already been written many times over—just as the amount of repetition over the centuries in writings explored in this book is striking. But from a broader, sociological point of view, the effect of these concerted efforts is to keep the facts and explanations stable through time and space. If those efforts ceased, or if they changed their focus to a different set of "facts," chances are the ideas would quickly come to seem much less intuitive.

Where do we go from here? A new understanding of Egyptian mortuary religion, one in which indigenous concepts and categories are taken as a point of departure rather than being subsumed under an existing framework, will be the focus of a future book. But for the time being, one immediate effect of the results presented here should be a profound skepticism toward concepts and frameworks that are clearly drawing on Christian models and have the age to show it, while having no correlate in Egyptian concepts. It is best to avoid broad notions like "afterlife" or the overall framework of souls in need of salvation to achieve eternal life, or at the very least to support such notions with a strong, empirically based argument independent of their traditional entrenchment, which has been shown to derive from highly ethnocentric and historically contingent ideas. To return to Thomas Kuhn, the rejection of a paradigm is an exciting phase, opening the discipline to new ways of thinking about well-established evidence while also laying bare uncertainties and anxieties over the questioning of truths that have long been taken as certain.

To be a little more concrete, if the ancient Egyptian transcendent, personal afterlife has turned out to be something of a mirage, fortunately there are other aspects of Egyptian mortuary religion that are much more firmly entrenched in ancient data but have tended to play only a subsidiary role because they do not square easily with the soteriological framework. Notably, a workable first step would be to recenter the ritual practices of the cult as the site of encountering the ancestors in ancient life. Unless one assumes with the nineteenth-century scholars that funerary texts present literal descriptions of the afterlife, it is striking how little the Egyptians seemed occupied with the looming threat of damnation, to judge from other types of writing such as letters or literary texts (Nyord 2020).

One might object at this point that just because early to mid-nineteenth-century scholars had insufficient basis for their intuition that funerary papyri (and hence funerary texts more generally) should describe and depict a transcendent, personal afterlife, that does not in itself mean the interpretation is wrong. However, this objection still builds on a more fundamental assumption of the same model: that funerary texts are completely different in nature from other ritual texts from ancient Egypt. The circularity is evident if one recalls that the main classificatory criterion of such texts is that they are inscribed or deposited in tombs, with this context leading to their being read in an entirely different way from other, overtly similar ritual texts from the temple cult or private rituals for healing and protection (Podemann Sørensen 1996, 2013, 15–24 and 36–45; Smith 2017; Nyord 2020). A declaration claiming identity with a deity in a temple or healing context will be understood as a statement that has relevance solely within the ritual, while the same statement in a funerary text will be understood as a literal claim of the identity, or at least empowerment, of the deceased in the afterlife—a difference resulting solely from the historically contingent background explored in this book.

Turning instead to the well-established practices of the ancestor cult, we are in territory that is interpreted rather similarly in the conventional framework and in the new model outlined here. The difference is that whereas the traditional interpretation makes the cult a matter of providing the deceased with the necessities of the afterlife, the new model once again stresses the continuity with similar practices in other cultural domains of ancient Egypt. If both gods and ancestors were given very similar offerings and otherwise treated ritually in parallel ways, the only reason to understand them in fundamentally different ways is the historically contingent tradition of separating out the ancestor cult as dealing solely with soteriological concerns. As I noted above, recent research has tended to emphasize the continuities between these two spheres, but because of the entrenchment of the overarching model, scholars have been reluctant to draw the natural conclusion that the apparent split between temple, private, and ancestor rituals is to a significant extent the result of modern expectations.

Recentering the practicalities of the cult as the pivot of ancient Egyptian funerary culture (see also Weiss 2022) removes the apparent paradox in the traditional model between the transcendent afterlife assumed to be described by the funerary texts and the much more concrete concerns with help from beyond the grave often worded in explicitly quid pro quo terms in letters to the dead (Hsieh 2021) and addresses to the living in tombs (Shubert 2007), underscoring the mutual dependency between living and deceased members of the community. Such a view also helps us appreciate the deep embeddedness of the ancestor cult in local socioeconomic contexts against the (remarkably Protestant) concerns with ethics and faith as a means to achieve salvation that the conventional model projects onto the ancient Egyptians.

Such a perspective also allows us to take seriously a less monolithic view of the significant changes across the millennia-long history of ancient Egyptian culture. Notably, from about 600 BCE forward, the idea of the realm of the dead as a concrete, otherworldly place of habitation appears as a literary device in narratives such as *Papyrus Vandier* and *Setne and Si-Osire* (translations in Posener 1985 and Simpson 2003, 470–

89, respectively). The question of when and how such ideas arise has hardly been posed in previous scholarship because of the assumption that they always formed a central part of Egyptian religious thought. A rethinking like that suggested here raises the question whether such ideas arose within indigenous Egyptian thought or as a consequence of cultural interaction (the narrative in *Setne and Si-Osire* is clearly inspired by Greek mythology of the underworld as a place of poetic justice, for example), and of how much they influenced, and were in turn influenced by, religious practices and conceptions.

As a concrete example of the more practical interpretive results of reorienting our interpretation of Egyptian mortuary religion, let us return briefly to figurines of the kind discussed in the introduction. As we saw above, Erman (and following him the great majority of subsequent scholars) saw the main function of such figurines as securing the eternal life of the tomb's owner by providing a never-ending supply of food. Sidestepping this underlying soteriological model, the motif of food production (and other activities engaging the figurines) instead leads us back to similar imagery in two dimensions on tomb walls (Barker 2022). Accompanying inscriptions confirm that such activities take place in the "funerary domain," the social setting where the offerings for the ancestor cult are produced.

This social embeddedness means that figurines are not detached individuals potentially coming to life in the beyond. Rather, they depict processes already taking place and undertaken by descendants, household members, or specialists contracted to carry them out (Nyord forthcoming). Rather than being seen as "anonymous" servants, as they are often described, the figurines can be viewed as depicting concrete social and ritual responsibilities that would be emphasized by their ritual depositing in the tomb, quite likely to be understood as a pledge by the ritual participants. In turn, this helps us fit the figurines into well-attested ritual uses of images as connection makers rather than having to hypothesize that ancient Egyptians made such figurines and deposited them in tombs like Victorian toys that might come to life at night.

The work of extending trajectories in recent research to establish a new framework is just beginning (cf. also Nyord 2020). Without a clear understanding of the history of the conventional framework, it may even have seemed questionable to many whether such a new framework was needed at all. As this book has demonstrated, there is indeed an urgent need to rethink core concepts of Egyptology, a project with enormous promise for revitalizing the study of ancient Egyptian mortuary religion.

Acknowledgments

This book has been long in the making. Ideas about a critical historiography of prevalent thinking about the ancient Egyptian afterlife first started to crystallize during my time as Lady Wallis Budge Fellow at Christ's College, Cambridge, from 2010 to 2014, and funding provided by an internationalization grant from the Carlsberg Foundation and a grant from the Sir Isaac Newton Trust allowed me take on this project in earnest from 2014 to 2017. Since then the project has changed significantly in its scope. I initially imagined that I would simply need to trace contemporary ideas back to the early nineteenth century, before the conventional date for the "birth of Egyptology" in 1822, to show the need for a rethinking, but that merely raised a series of new questions. How had a consensus been established among European scholars well before the deciphering of hieroglyphs—to the point where Thomas Young could write confidently in 1819 of the "received opinion" that the ancient Egyptians believed in postmortem judgment and rewards and punishments in the afterlife—given that classical authors offer very little along those lines? The project evidently needed to expand in scope to include the seminal early modern period, while consequently it became most feasible to postpone the planned second part of the book presenting an Egyptological rethinking in reaction to the historiographical critique. The result is this book, presenting a genealogy of the contemporary Egyptological, as well as popular, notion of the ancient Egyptian afterlife over a sweeping time span from the late medieval period to the late nineteenth century, when the model appeared in something like its present form.

These changes in the conception of the book, along with the vicissitudes of postdoctoral existence, led to a rather lengthy gestation period, and accordingly over the years it has benefited significantly from discussions with colleagues in Egyptology and beyond—too many to name here. An important stimulus was offered by iterations of my seminar The Discovery of the Ancient Egyptian Afterlife at Emory University in the spring semester of 2019 and the fall semesters of 2020 and 2023. Each time I taught the seminar, the in-depth discussions brought new insights, and it has been a privilege to develop the manuscript and my ideas while exploring the issues with such engaged groups of students. It was a year as Samuel H. Kress Senior Fellow at the Center for Advanced Study in the Visual Arts at the National Gallery in Washington, DC, in 2022–23 that allowed me to complete the manuscript. I am very grateful to the deans and staff of the center as well as my cohort of fellows for a most stimulating and productive year by the National Mall. My thanks are also due to Kathleen Sheppard for reading through the manuscript and making a number of useful suggestions. I owe an intellectual debt that can be reflected only in part in the references to Jørgen Podemann Sørensen, whose undergraduate classes in the history of religions first made me aware of the significant problems with conventional Egyptological interpretations of the Egyptian funerary literature. I must further thank Karen Levine and Victoria Barry of the University of Chicago Press not only for taking on this unusual project in the first place, but for skillfully and patiently guiding me through the publication process. I also thank the two anonymous reviewers for helpful comments and suggestions as well as Alice Bennett for her efforts in tightening and polishing my language through her expert copyediting. This book is freely available in an open-access edition thanks to the generous support of Emory University and the Andrew W. Mellon Foundation. Last, but certainly not least, I owe a great debt of gratitude to my wife and daughter, without whose patience, support, and flexibility I would never have been able to complete this project.

References

Adler, William. 1983. "Berossus, Manetho, and '1 Enoch' in the World Chronicle of Panodorus." *Harvard Theological Review* 76 (4): 419–42.

Amin, Abbas. 2013. *Ägyptomanie und Orientalismus: Ägypten in der deutschen Reiseliteratur (1175–1663) mit einem kommentierten Verzeichnis der Reiseberichte (383–1845)*. Berlin: De Gruyter.

Anis, Muhammad. 1952. "The First Egyptian Society in London (1741–1743)." *Bulletin de l'institut français d'archéologie orientale* 50:99–105.

Anonymous. 1802. "Review of *De origine et usu obeliscorum, ad Pium Sextum pontificem maximum, auctore Georgio Zoega Dano*." *Critical Review* 36 (12): 494–508.

———. 1838. *A Visit to the British Museum: Containing a Familiar Description of Every Object of Interest in the Various Departments of That Establishment*. London: Chapman and Hall.

Ariès, Philippe. 1974. *Western Attitudes toward Death: From the Middle Ages to the Present*. Baltimore: Johns Hopkins University Press.

Arp, Urs. 2010. *The Birth of Orientalism: Encounters with Asia*. Philadelphia: University of Pennsylvania Press.

Ascani, Karen, Paola Buzi, and Daniela Picchi, eds. 2015. *The Forgotten Scholar: Georg Zoëga (1755–1809) at the Dawn of Egyptology and Coptic Studies*. Leiden: Brill.

Assmann, Jan. 1997a. "Ägypten als Argument: Rekonstruktion der Vergangenheit und Religionskritik im 17. und 18. Jahrhundert." *Historische Zeitschrift* 264 (3): 561–85.

———. 1997b. *Moses the Egyptian: The Memory of Egypt in Western Monotheism*. Cambridge, MA: Harvard University Press.

———. 2005a. *Death and Salvation in Ancient Egypt*. Ithaca, NY: Cornell University Press.

———. 2005b. *Die Zauberflöte: Oper und Mysterium*. Munich: Carl Hanser.

——— 2012. "Karl Richard Lepsius und die altägyptische Religion." In *Karl Richard Lepsius: Der Begründer der deutschen Ägyptologie*, edited by Verena M. Lepper and Ingelore Hafemann, 79–100. Berlin: Kadmos.

———. 2014. *Religio Duplex: How the Enlightenment Reinvented Egyptian Religion*. Cambridge: Polity Press.

Assmann, Jan, and Florian Ebeling. 2011. *Ägyptische Mysterien: Reisen in die Unterwelt in Aufklärung und Romantik. Eine kommentierte Anthologie*. Munich: Beck.

———. 2020. "The Mnemohistory of Egypt: Approaches towards the Understanding of Egypt in Intellectual History." In *Beyond Egyptomania: Objects, Style and Agency*, edited by Miguel John Versluys, 23–38. Berlin: De Gruyter.

Aufrère, Sydney H. 2021. "La réception de l'architecture monumentale égyptienne au prisme de *L'Antiquité expliquée* (1719–1724) de dom Bernard de Montfaucon: Une contribution à une histoire du regard égyptologique." *Égypte nilotique et mediterranéenne* 14:285–313.

Augstein, Franziska A. 1996. "James C. Prichard's View of Mankind: An Anthropologist between the Enlightenment and the Victorian Age." PhD diss., University College London.

Babbitt, Frank Cole. 1928. *Plutarch, Moralia*. Vol. 2. *How to Profit by One's Enemies. On Having Many Friends. Chance. Virtue and Vice. Letter of Condolence to Apollonius. Advice about Keeping Well. Advice to Bride and Groom. The Dinner of the Seven Wise Men. Superstition. Loeb Classical Library*, vol. 222. Cambridge, MA: Harvard University Press.

———. 1936. *Plutarch, Moralia*. Vol. 5. *Isis and Osiris. The E at Delphi. The Oracles at Delphi No Longer Given in Verse. The Obsolescence of Oracles. Loeb Classical Library*, vol. 306. Cambridge, MA: Harvard University Press.

Baber, Tessa T. 2016. "Ancient Corpses as Curiosities: Mummymania in the Age of Early Travel." *Journal of Ancient Egyptian Interconnections* 8:60–93.

Bachour, Natalia. 2016. "*Mūmiyā* als Arznei im arabischen und osmanischen Schrifttum." In *Muslim Bodies: Körper, Sexualität und Medizin in muslimischen Gesellschaften*, edited by Susanne Kurz, Claudia Preckel, and Stefan Reichmuth, 407–65. Berlin: LIT.

Baigent, Elizabeth. 2004. "Perry, Charles (d. 1780)." In *Oxford Dictionary of National Biography*, edited by Henry Colin Gray Matthew and Brian Howard Harrison. Oxford: Oxford University Press.

Barker, Georgia. 2022. *Preparing for Eternity: Funerary Models and Wall Scenes from the Egyptian Old and Middle Kingdoms*. Oxford: BAR.

Baschet, Jérôme. 1996. "Le sein d'Abraham: Un lieu de l'au-delà ambigu (théologie, liturgie, iconographie)." *Civilisation médiévale* 3:71–94.

Bates, Stephen. 2021. "Preparations for a Christian Death: The Later Middle

Ages." In *A Companion to Death, Burial, and Remembrance in Late Medieval and Early Modern Europe, c. 1300–1700*, edited by Philip Booth and Elizabeth Tingle, 72–105. Leiden: Brill.

Bednarski, Andrew. 2005. *Holding Egypt: Tracing the Reception of the "Description de l'Égypte" in Nineteenth-Century Great Britain*. London: Golden House.

Bednarski, Andrew, Aidan Dodson, and Salima Ikram, eds. 2021. *A History of World Egyptology*. Cambridge: Cambridge University Press.

Belon, Pierre. 1553. *Petri Bellonii Cenomani de admirabili operum antiquorum et rerum suspiciendarum præstantia: Liber primus. De medicato funere, seu cadauere condito, et lugubri defunctorum eiulatione: Liber secundus. De medicamentis nonnullis, seruandi cadaueris vim obtinentibus: Liber tertius*. Paris: Gulielmus Cauvellat.

Belzoni, Giovanni. 1820. *Narrative of the Operations and Recent Discoveries within the Pyramids, Temples, Tombs, and Excavations, in Egypt and Nubia; and of a Journey to the Coast of the Red Sea, in Search of the Ancient Berenice; and Another to the Oasis of Jupiter Ammon*. London: John Murray.

Bergin, Joseph. 2014. *The Politics of Religion in Early Modern France*. New Haven, CT: Yale University Press.

Bernabé, Alberto. 2013. "Orphics and Pythagoreans: The Greek Perspective." In *On Pythagoreanism*, edited by Gabriele Cornelli, Richard McKirahan, and Constantinos Macris, 117–51. Berlin: De Gruyter.

Betrò, Marilina, ed. 2010. *Lungo il Nilo: Ippolito Rosellini e la spedizione franco-toscana in Egitto (1828–1829)*. Florence: Giunti.

Betrò, Marilina, and Gianluca Miniaci, eds. 2013. *Talking along the Nile: Ippolito Rosellini, Travellers and Scholars of the 19th Century in Egypt: Proceedings of the International Conference Held on the Occasion of the Presentation of Progetto Rosellini, Pisa, June 14–16, 2012*. Pisa: Pisa University Press.

Blanke, Horst Walter. 1983. "Verfassungen, die nicht rechtlich, aber wirklich sind: A. H. L. Heeren und das Ende der Aufklärungshistorie." *Berichte zur Wissenschaftsgeschichte* 6, no. 1–4: 143–64.

Blumenbach, Johann Friedrich. 1865. *The Anthropological Treatises of Johann Friedrich Blumenbach*. London: Longman, Green, Longman, Roberts, and Green.

Boas, George. 1993. *The Hieroglyphics of Horapollo*. Princeton, NJ: Princeton University Press.

Bossuet, Jacques-Bénigne. 1681. *Discours sur l'histoire universelle a Monseigneur le Dauphin pour expliquer la suite de la Religion et les changements des Empires: Première partie: Depuis le commencement du Monde jusqu'à l'Empire de Charlemagne*. Paris: Sebastien Mabre-Cramoisy.

Bourget, Pierre du, and Luc Gabolde. 2008. *Le temple de Deir al-Médîna*. 2nd ed. Cairo: Institut français d'archéologie orientale.

Breguet, Marie. 2007. "L'Égypte dans l'imaginaire de Roucher: De l'égyptologie à l'égyptomanie." *Orages: Littérature et culture, 1760–1830*, 6:49–63.

Bret, Patrice. 2019. "Instruments of Knowledge and Power in a Colonial Context: Scientific Instruments during the French Occupation of Egypt, 1798–1801." In *Scientific Instruments between East and West*, edited by Neil Brown, Silke Ackermann, and Feza Günergun, 206–28. Leiden: Brill.

Browne, Elizabeth Saari. 2023. "Discernment or Devotion: Egypt and Sculptural Politics in Eighteenth-Century France." *Art History* 46 (2): 370–92.

Browne, Thomas. 1658. *Hydriotaphia: Urne-Buriall, or, A Discourse of the Sepulchrall Urnes Lately Found in Norfolk. Together with the Garden of Cyrus, or the Quincunciall, Lozenge, or Net-work Plantations of the Ancients, Artificially, Naturally, Mystically Considered. With Sundry Observations*. London: Hen. Brome.

Bruce, James. 1790. *Travels to Discover the Source of the Nile, in the Years 1768, 1769, 1770, 1771, 1772, and 1773*. Edinburgh: J. Ruthven for G. G. J. and J. Robinson.

Brugsch, Heinrich. 1872. "Das Todtenbuch der alten Aegypter." *Zeitschrift für Ägyptische Sprache und Altertumskunde* 10:65–72, 129–34.

Buchwald, Jed Z., and Diane Greco Josefowicz. 2010. *The Zodiac of Paris: How an Improbable Controversy over an Ancient Egyptian Artifact Provoked a Modern Debate between Religion and Science*. Princeton, NJ: Princeton University Press.

———. 2020. *The Riddle of the Rosetta: How an English Polymath and a French Polyglot Discovered the Meaning of Egyptian Hieroglyphs*. Princeton, NJ: Princeton University Press.

Budge, E. A. Wallis. 1885. *The Dwellers on the Nile, or Chapters on the Life, Literature, History, and Customs of the Ancient Egyptians*. London: Religious Tract Society.

———. 1899. *Egyptian Ideas of the Future life*. London: Kegan Paul, Trench, Trübner.

Bull, George. 1990. *The Pilgrim: The Travels of Pietro della Valle*. London: Hutchinson.

Bunsen, Christian Carl Josias. 1857. *Aegyptens Stelle in der Weltgeschichte: Geschichtliche Untersuchung in fünf Büchern. Fünften Buches, vierte und fünfte Abtheilung*. Gotha: Friedrich Andreas Berthes.

———. 1860. *Egypt's Place in Universal History*. Vol. 4, *Containing the Fifth Book, or, The Origines and Ages of the World*. London: Longman, Green, Longman, and Roberts.

———. 1867. *Egypt's Place in Universal History*. Vol. 5, *Containing the Epilogue, or Problems and Key, the Complete Hieroglyphic Dictionary and Grammar, a Comparison of Egyptian and Semitic Roots, the Book of the Dead, and a Select Chrestomathy of Historical Hieroglyphical Texts*. London: Longmans, Green.

Burke, Peter. 2013. "Images as Evidence in Seventeenth-Century Europe." *Journal of the History of Ideas* 64 (2): 273–96.

Burnett, Charles. 2003. "Images of ancient Egypt in the Latin Middle Ages." In *The Wisdom of Egypt: Changing Visions through the Ages*, edited by Peter Ucko and Timothy Champion, 65–99. London: UCL Press.

Burton, Anne. 1972. *Diodorus Siculus, Book 1: A Commentary*. Leiden: E. J. Brill.

Butterfield, David. 2015. "Lucretius in the Early Modern Period: Texts and Contexts." In *Lucretius and the Early Modern*, edited by David Norbrook, Stephen Harrison, and Philip Hardie, 45–68. Oxford: Oxford University Press.

Bynum, Caroline Walker. 1995. *The Resurrection of the Body in Western Christianity, 200–1336*. New York: Columbia University Press.

———. 2012. *Fragmentation and Redemption: Essays on Gender and the Human Body in Medieval Religion*. New York: Zone Books.

Caciola, Nancy Mandeville. 2016. *Afterlives: The Return of the Dead in the Middle Ages*. Ithaca, NY: Cornell University Press.

Cadet, Jean-Marcel. 1805. *Copie figurée d'un roleau de papyrus, trouvé à Thebes, dans un tombeau des rois*. Paris: Levrault, Schoell.

Cailliaud, Frédéric. 1823. *Voyage à Méroé, au Fleuve Blanc au-delà de Fazoql, dans le midi du royaume de Sennâr, à Syouah, et dans cinq autres oasis: Fait dans les années 1819, 1820, 1821 et 1822. Atlas II*. Paris: Rignoux.

Camille, Michael. 1999. "The Corpse in the Garden: *Mumia* in Medieval Herbal Illustrations." *Micrologus: Natura, scienze e società medievali* 7:297–318.

Campanelli, Maurizio. 2019. "Marsilio Ficino's Portrait of Hermes Trismegistus and Its Afterlife." *Intellectual History Review* 29 (1): 53–71.

Campbell, Stephen F. 1993. "Nicolas Caussin's 'Spirituality of Communication': A Meeting of Divine and Human Speech." *Renaissance Quarterly* 46 (1): 44–70.

Carol, Anne. 2023. "Tensions autour du cadavre: 'Révolutions' médicales, transitions funéraire en France." In *Transitions funéraires en occident: Une histoire des relations entre morts et vivants de l'antiquité à nos jours*, edited by Guillaume Cuchet, Nicolas Laboury, and Michel Lauwers, 439–52. Rome: École française de Rome.

Carré, Jean-Marie. 1932. *Voyageurs et écrivains français en Égypte*. Cairo: Institut français d'archéologie orientale.

Carruthers, William, ed. 2014. *Histories of Egyptology: Interdisciplinary measures*. New York: Routledge.

———. 2022. *Flooded Pasts: UNESCO, Nubia, and the Recolonization of Archaeology*. Ithaca, NY: Cornell University Press.

Castagnoli, Luca. 2019. "The *Phaedo* on Philosophy and the Soul." In *The Oxford Handbook of Plato*, 2nd ed., edited by Gail Fine, 182–205. Oxford: Oxford University Press.

Caussin, Nicolas. 1618. *De symbolica ægyptiorum sapientia*. Paris: Romanus de Beauvais.

Caylus, Anne-Claude-Philippe de Tubières de. 1752–67. *Recueil d'antiquités égyptiennes, étrusques, grecques, romaines et gauloises*. Paris: Desaint et Saillant (vols. 1 and 3), Duchesne (vol. 2), N. M. Tilliard (vols. 4-7).

Challis, Debbie. 2013. *The Archaeology of Race: The Eugenic Ideas of Francis Galton and Flinders Petrie*. London: Bloomsbury.

Chamoux, François, Pierre Bertrac, and Yvonne Vernière. 1993. *Diodore de Sicile: Bibliothèque historique, Livre I*. Paris: Les Belles Lettres.

Champion, Timothy. 2003. "Beyond Egyptology: Egypt in 19th and 20th Century Archaeology and Anthropology." In *The Wisdom of Egypt: Changing Visions through the Ages*, edited by Peter Ucko and Timothy Champion, 161–85. London: UCL Press.

Champollion, Jean-François. 1827. "Notice sur le Papyrus hiératique et les Peintures du cercueil de Pétamenoph." In *Voyage à Méroé, au Fleuve Blanc au-delà de Fazoql, dans le midi du royaume de Sennâr, à Syouah, et dans cinq autres oasis: Fait dans les années 1819, 1820, 1821 et 1822*, edited by Frédéric Cailliaud, 4, 22–54. Paris: Imprimerie royale.

———. 1833. *Lettres écrites d'Égypte et de Nubie, en 1828 et 1829*. Paris: Didot Frères.

Cherniss, Harold. 1957. *Plutarch, Moralia, Volume XII: Concerning the Face Which Appears in the Orb of the Moon. On the Principle of Cold. Whether Fire or Water Is More Useful. Whether Land or Sea Animals Are Cleverer. Beasts Are Rational. On the Eating of Flesh. Loeb Classical Library*, vol. 406. Cambridge, MA: Harvard University Press.

Ciampini, Emanuele Marcello. 2015. "*De origine et usu obeliscorum*: Some Notes on an Eighteenth-Century Egyptological Study." In *The Forgotten Scholar: Georg Zoëga (1755–1809) at the Dawn of Egyptology and Coptic Studies*, edited by Karen Ascani, Paola Buzi, and Daniela Picchi, 185–91. Leiden: Brill.

Clark, Gillian. 2000. *Porphyry: On the Abstinence from Killing Animals*. London: Bloomsbury.

Clayden, Peter William. 1883. *Samuel Sharpe: Egyptologist and Translator of the Bible*. London: Kegan Paul.

Clément, Raoul. 1960. *Les français d'Égypte aux XVIIe et XVIIIe siècles*. Cairo: Institut français d'archéologie orientale.

Cole, Juan. 2007. *Napoleon's Egypt: Invading the Middle East*. New York: Palgrave Macmillan.

Colla, Elliott. 2007. *Conflicted Antiquities: Egyptology, Egyptomania, Egyptian Modernity*. Durham, NC: Duke University Press.

Conti, Fulvio. 2023. "Entre utopie hygiénique, laïcité et mythe du progrès: La contribution italienne à la réinvention de l'idée de crémation dans l'Europe du

XIXe siècle." In *Transitions funéraires en occident: Une histoire des relations entre morts et vivants de l'antiquité à nos jours*, edited by Guillaume Cuchet, Nicolas Laboury, and Michel Lauwers, 453–69. Rome: École française de Rome.

Conybeare, F. C. 1912. *Philostratus, The Life of Apollonius of Tyana, the Epistles of Apollonius and the Treatise of Eusebius*. New York: William Heinemann.

Copenhaver, Brian P. 1992. *Hermetica: The Greek Corpus Hermeticum and the Latin Asclepius in a New English Translation, with Notes and Introduction*. Cambridge: Cambridge University Press.

Costa, Georges. 2005. "Le monument d'Henri de Sponde, évêque de Pamiers, à la cathedrale de Toulouse." *Mémoires de la Société archéologique du Midi de la France* 65:185–95.

Costaz, Louis. 1809. "Description des tombeaux des rois." *Description de l'Égypte, ou Recueil des observations et des recherches qui ont été faites en Égypte pendant l'expédition de l'armée française, publié par les ordres de sa Majesté l'Empereur Napoléon le Grand*, edited by Edme-François Jomard, Antiquités, Description, 1, 393–414. Paris.

Cudworth, Ralph. 1678. *The True Intellectual System of the Universe: The First Part; wherein, All the Reason and Philosophy of Atheism Is Confuted; and Its Impossibility Demonstrated*. London: Richard Royston.

Curran, Brian A. 2003. "The Renaissance Afterlife of Ancient Egypt (1400–1650)." In *The Wisdom of Egypt: Changing Visions through the Ages*, edited by Peter Ucko and Timothy Champion, 101–31. London: UCL Press.

———. 2004. "The Sphinx in the Piazza: Egyptian Monuments and Urban Spaces in Renaissance Italy." In *Artistic Exchange and Cultural Translation in the Italian Renaissance City*, edited by Stephen J. Campbell and Stephen J. Milner, 294–326. Cambridge: Cambridge University Press.

———. 2007. *The Egyptian Renaissance: The Afterlife of Egypt in Early Modern Italy*. Chicago: University of Chicago Press.

Dannenfeldt, Karl H. 1959. "Egypt and Egyptian Antiquities in the Renaissance." *Studies in the Renaissance* 6:7–27.

———. 1985. "Egyptian Mumia: The Sixteenth Century Experience." *Sixteenth Century Journal* 16 (2): 163–80.

Daussy, Hugues. 2016. "Huguenot Political Thought and Activities." In *A Companion to the Huguenots*, edited by Raymond A. Mentzer and Bertrand van Ruymbeke, 66–89. Leiden: Brill.

David, Elisabeth. 1999. *Gaston Maspero, 1846–1916: Le gentleman égyptologue*. Paris: Pygmalion.

Denon, Vivant. 1802. *Voyage dans la Basse et la Haute Égypte pendant les campagnes du Général Bonaparte*. Paris: P. Didot L'Ainé.

Derchain, Philippe. 1965. *Le tombeau d'Osymandyas et la maison de la vie à Thèbes*. Göttingen: Vandenhoeck und Ruprecht.

Devéria, Théodule. 1870. "A Monsieur Paul Pierret, Lettre sur le Chapitre 1er du Todtenbuch." *Zeitschrift für Ägyptische Sprache und Altertumskunde* 8:57–66.

Di Biase-Dyson, Camilla, and Birgit Grosskopf. 2019. "Johann Friedrich Blumenbach (1752–1840): Mumienforscher in vor-ägyptologischer Zeit." In *"Steinschrift und Bibelwort": Ägyptologen und Koptologen Niedersachsens*, edited by Janne Arp-Neumann and Thomas L. Gertzen, 93–98. Rahden: Marie Leidorf.

Dillon, John. 2014. "Plutarch and Platonism." In *A Companion to Plutarch*, edited by Mark Beck, 61–72. Chichester: Wiley Blackwell.

Dobrzeniecki, Karol. 2015. "Scales as a Symbol of Metaphysical Judgement from *Misterium Tremendum* to *Misterium Fascinosum*: An Analysis of Selected Works of Netherlandish Masters of Painting." *Santander Art and Culture Law Review* 1 (2): 259–74.

Dobson, Eleanor. 2022. *Victorian Alchemy: Science, Magic and Ancient Egypt*. London: UCL Press.

Doyon, Wendy. 2018. "The History of Archaeology through the Eyes of the Egyptians." In *Unmasking Ideology in Imperial and Colonial Archaeology: Vocabulary, Symbols, and Legacy*, edited by Bonnie Effros and Guolong Lai, 173–200. Los Angeles: Cotsen Institute of Archaeology Press.

Dufrenoy, Marie-Louise. 1975. *L'Orient romanesque en France 1704–1789*. Vol. 3. *L'idée de progrès l'Orient*. Amsterdam: Rodopi.

Duncan, John M. 2023. *Rhetorical Adaptation in the Greek Historians, Josephus, and Acts: Embedded Speeches, Audience Responses, and Authorial Persuasion*. Leiden: Brill.

Ebeling, Florian. 2007. *The Secret History of Hermes Trismegistus: Hermeticism from Ancient to Modern Times*. Ithaca, NY: Cornell University Press.

———. 2018. "Ägypten zwischen Pantheismus und Panentheismus: Gedächtnisgeschichtliche Spurensuche." *Aegyptiaca* 3:27–58.

———. 2022. "Freemasons and Platonism: The Allure of Egypt between Big Ideas and Small Details." In *The Allure of the Ancient: Receptions of the Ancient Middle East, ca. 1600–1800*, edited by Margaret Geoga and John Steele, 145–66. Leiden: Brill.

Edmonds, Radcliffe G., III. 2009. *Myths of the Underworld Journey: Plato, Aristophanes, and the 'Orphic' Gold Tablets*. Cambridge: Cambridge University Press.

El Daly, Okasha. 2005. *Egyptology: The Missing Millennium. Ancient Egypt in Medieval Arabic Writings*. London: UCL Press.

Emlyn-Jones, Chris, and William Preddy. 2017. *Plato, Euthyphro. Apology. Crito. Phaedo*. Loeb Classical Library, vol. 36. Cambridge, MA: Harvard University Press.

———. 2022. *Plato, Lysis. Symposium. Phaedrus.* Loeb Classical Library, vol. 166. Cambridge, MA: Harvard University Press.

Erman, Adolf. 1885. *Aegypten und aegyptisches Leben im Altertum.* Tübingen: H. Laupp'schen Buchhandlung.

———. 1905. *Die ägyptische Religion.* Berlin: Reimer.

———. 1907. *A Handbook of Egyptian Religion.* London: Archibald Constable.

Eurich, S. Amanda. 2008. "Between the Living and the Dead: Preserving Confessional Identity and Community in Early Modern France." In *Defining Community in Early Modern Europe,* edited by Michael J. Halvorson and Karen E. Spierling, 43–61. Burlington, VT: Ashgate.

Fairclough, H. Rushton. 1999. *Virgil, Eclogues. Georgics. Aeneid: Books 1–6.* Loeb Classical Library, vol. 63. Revised edition. Cambridge, MA: Harvard University Press.

Feingold, Mordechai. 2019. "'The Wisdom of the Egyptians': Revisiting Jan Assmann's Reading of the Early Modern Reception of Moses." *Aegyptiaca* 4:99–124.

Festugière, André Jean, and Arthur Darby Nock. 1954. *Corpus Hermeticum, Tome IV: Fragments extrait de Stobée (XXIII-XXIX); Fragments divers.* Paris: Société d'édition "Les belles lettres."

Finnegan, Rachel. 2019. *English Explorers in the East (1738–1745): The Travels of Thomas Shaw, Charles Perry and Richard Pococke.* Leiden: Brill.

———. 2021. *Richard Pococke's Letters from the East (1737–1740).* Leiden: Brill.

Fischel, Oskar. 1948. *Raphael.* London: K. Paul.

Foerster, Frank. 2001. *Christian Carl Josias Bunsen: Diplomat, Mäzen und Vordenker in Wissenschaft, Kirche und Politik.* Bad Arolsen: Waldeckischer Geschichtsverein.

Foucault, Michel. 1978. *The History of Sexuality.* Vol. 1. *An Introduction.* New York: Pantheon.

Fowler, Don. 2019. "The Virgil Commentary of Servius (revised by Sergio Casali and Fabio Stok)." In *The Cambridge Companion to Virgil,* edited by Fiachra MacGóráin and Charles Martindale, 88–94. Cambridge: Cambridge University Press.

Frandsen, Paul John. 2019. *Let Greece and Rome Be Silent: Frederik Ludvig Norden's Travels in Egypt and Nubia, 1737–1738.* Copenhagen: Museum Tusculanum Press.

Gange, David. 2013. *Dialogues with the Dead: Egyptology in British Culture and Religion, 1822–1922.* Oxford: Oxford University Press.

———. 2020. "Two Victorian Egypts of Herodotus." In *Herodotus in the Long Nineteenth Century,* edited by Thomas Harrison and Joseph Skinner, 154–78. Cambridge: Cambridge University Press.

Gascoigne, John. 1991. "The Wisdom of the Egyptians and the Secularisation of History in the Age of Newton." In *The Uses of Antiquity: The Scientific Revolution and the Classical Tradition*, edited by Stephen Gaukroger, 171–212. Dordrecht: Kluwer.

Gee, John. 2009. 'A New Look at the Conception of the Human Being in Ancient Egypt.' In *"Being in Ancient Egypt": Thoughts on Agency, Materiality and Cognition. Proceedings of the Seminar Held in Copenhagen, September 29–30, 2006*, edited by Rune Nyord and Annette Kjølby, 1–14. Oxford: Archaeopress.

Geoga, Margaret. 2022. "Ancient and Modern: Citational Practices and the Status of Ancient Egypt in Jean Terrason's *Séthos*." In *The Allure of the Ancient: Receptions of the Ancient Middle East, ca. 1600–1800*, edited by Margaret Geoga and John Steele, 185–229. Leiden: Brill.

Gertz, Sebastian Ramon Philipp. 2011. *Death and Immortality in Late Neoplatonism: Studies on the Ancient Commentaries on Plato's Phaedo*. Leiden: Brill.

Gertzen, Thomas L. 2020. "Some Remarks on the 'De-colonization' of Egyptology." *Göttinger Miszellen* 262:189–203.

Giehlow, Karl. 1915. "Die Hieroglyphenkunde des Humanismus in der Allegorie der Renaissance, besonders der Ehrenpforte Kaisers Maximilian I. Ein Versuch." *Jahrbuch der Kunsthistorisches Sammlungen des Allerhöchsten Kaiserhauses* 32:1–229.

Gieryn, Thomas F. 1983. "Boundary-Work and the Demarcation of Science from Non-science: Strains and Interests in Professional Ideologies of Scientists." *American Sociological Review* 48 (6): 781–95.

Gittings, Claire. 1999. "Sacred and Secular: 1558–1660." In *Death in England: An Illustrated History*, edited by Peter C. Jupp and Clare Gittings, 147–73. Manchester: Manchester University Press.

Godlewska, Anne. 1995. "Map, Text and Image. The Mentality of Enlightened Conquerors: A New Look at the *Description de l'Égypte*." *Transactions of the Institute of British Geographers* 20 (1): 5–28.

Godley, A. D. 1926. *Herodotus with an English Translation, in Four Volumes*. Vol. 1: *Books I and II. Loeb Classical Library*, vol. 117. Revised edition. Cambridge, MA: Harvard University Press/William Heinemann.

Goguet, Antoine-Yves. 1758. *De l'origine des loix, des arts, et des sciences; et de leurs progrès chez les anciens peuples*. Paris: Desaint et Saillant.

Gold, Meira. 2019. "Ancient Egypt and the Geological Antiquity of Man, 1847–1863." *History of Science* 57 (2): 194–230.

Gordon, Alexander. 1737. *An Essay towards Explaining the Hieroglyphical Figures, on the Coffin of the Ancient Mummy Belonging to Capt. William Lethieullier*. London: Author.

Graefe, Erhart. 1984. "Der Pyramidenbesuch des Guilielmus de Boldensele im

Jahre 1335 mit einem Anhang: Der Zeitpunkt des Aufbrechens der Chefrenpyramide im Mittelalter." *Studien zur Altägyptischen Kultur* 11:569–84.

Graepler, Daniel. 2007. "Archäologische Forschungsthemen Heynes." In *Das Studium des schönen Altertums: Christian Gottlob Heyne und die Entstehung der Klassischen Archäologie*, edited by Daniel Graepler and Joachim Migl, 45–72. Göttingen: Niedersächsische Staats- und Universitätsbibliothek.

Grafton, Anthony. 1983. "Protestant versus Prophet: Isaac Casaubon on Hermes Trismegistus." *Journal of the Warburg and Courtauld Institutes* 46:78–93.

———. 2018. "Annius of Viterbo as a Student of the Jews: The Sources of His Information." In *Literary Forgery in Early Modern Europe, 1450–1800*, edited by Walter Stephens and Earle A. Havens, 147–69. Baltimore: Johns Hopkins University Press.

Gray, Madeleine. 2021. "Deathbed and Burial Rituals in Late Medieval Catholic Europe." In *A Companion to Death, Burial, and Remembrance in Late Medieval and Early Modern Europe, c. 1300–1700*, edited by Philip Booth and Elizabeth Tingle, 106–31. Leiden: Brill.

Greaves, John. 1646. *Pyramidographia, or A Description of the Pyramids in Ægypt.* London: George Badger.

Greene, Margaret. 2023. "Herodotus, Ancient Egypt and the West: The Use of Herodotus' Histories to Construct Ancient Egypt in the *Edinburgh Review* throughout the Nineteenth Century." *Aegyptiaca* 7:55–80.

Greenhill, Thomas. 1705. *Νεκροκηδεια, or, The Art of Embalming; Wherein Is Shewn the Right of Burial, the Funeral Ceremonies, and the Several Ways of Preserving Dead Bodies in Most Nations of the World. With an Account of the Particular Opinions, Experiments and Inventions of Modern Physicians, Surgeons, Chymists and Anatomists. Also Some New Matter Propos'd Concerning a Better Method of Embalming than Hath Hitherto Been Discover'd. And a Pharmacopœia Galeno-Chymica, Anatomia Sicca Sive Incruenta, &c.* London: Author.

Grinevald, Paul-Marie. 2014. "Jomard et la *Description de l'Égypte*, 1777–1862." *Bulletin de la SABIX* 54:13–21.

Gurney, J. D. 1986. "Pietro della Valle: The Limits of Perception." *Bulletin of the School of Oriental and African Studies*, 103–16.

Hall, Edith. 1989. *Inventing the Barbarian: Greek Self-Definition through Tragedy.* Oxford: Clarendon Press.

Hamilton, Alastair. 2019. "Claude-Étienne Savary: Orientalism and Fraudulence." *Journal of the Warburg and Courtauld Institutes* 82:283–314.

Hamilton, William. 1809. *Remarks on Several Parts of Turkey. Part I: Ægyptiaca, or Some Account of the Antient and Modern State of Egypt, as Obtained in the Years 1801, 1802.* London: T. Payne/Cadell and Davies.

Harrison, Peter. 1993. "Animal Souls, Metempsychosis, and Theodicy in

Seventeenth-Century English Thought." *Journal of the History of Philosophy* 31 (4): 519–44.

Hau, Lisa Irene, Alexander Meeus, and Brian Sheridan. 2018. "Introduction." In *Diodoros of Sicily: Historiographical Theory and Practice in the Bibliotheke*, edited by Lisa Irene Hau, Alexander Meeus, and Brian Sheridan, 3–12. Bristol, CT: Peeters.

Haynes, Jonathan. 1986. *The Humanist Traveler: George Sandys's Relation of a Journey Begun An. Dom. 1610*. Vancouver: Fairleigh Dickinson University Press.

Haziza, Typhaine. 2023. "Ways of Seeing: Herodotus' Egypt in the History of Modern Reception." *Syllogos* 2:107–32.

Heeren, Arnold Hermann Ludwig. 1804. *Ideen über die Politik, den Verkehr, und den Handel der vornehmsten Völker der alten Welt: Zweiter Theil, afrikanische Völker. Carthager, Aethioper, Aegypter*. 2nd ed. Göttingen: Vandenhoeck und Ruprecht.

Heyne, Christian Gottlob. 1780. "Spicilegium Antiquitatis Mumiarum." *Commentationes Societatis Regiae Scientiarum Gottingensis: Historicae et Philologiae Classis* 3:69–98.

Hincks, Edward. 1843. *Catalogue of the Egyptian Manuscripts in the Library of Trinity College, Dublin*. Dublin: Andrew Milliken/Whittaker.

Hodgen, Margaret T. 1964. *Early Anthropology in the Sixteenth and Seventeenth Centuries*. Philadelphia: University of Pennsylvania Press.

Hollis, Susan Tower. 2008. *The Ancient Egyptian "Tale of Two Brothers": A Mythological, Religious, Literary, and Historico-political Study*. Oakville, CT: Bannerstone Press.

Hook, Larue van. 1945. *Isocrates in Three Volumes*. Vol. 3. *Loeb Classical Library*, vol. 373. Cambridge, MA: Harvard University Press/William Heinemann.

Horrox, Rosemary. 1999. "Purgatory, Prayer and Plague: 1150–1380." In *Death in England: An Illustrated History*, edited by Peter C. Jupp and Claire Gittings, 90–118. Manchester: Manchester University Press.

Hsieh, Julia. 2021. *Ancient Egyptian Letters to the Dead: The Realm of the Dead through the Voice of the Living*. Leiden: Brill.

Jalland, Pat. 1996. *Death in the Victorian Family*. Oxford: Oxford University Press.

Janák, Jiří. 2023. "Interrogation before Osiris: Judgment of the Dead or Immigration Interview?" In *In the house of Heqanakht: Text and Context in Ancient Egypt. Studies in Honor of James P. Allen*, edited by M. Victoria Almansa-Villatoro, Silvia Štubňová Nigrelli, and Mark Lehner, 450–62. Leiden: Brill.

Johnson, Aaron P. 2013. *Religion and Identity in Porphyry of Tyre: The Limits of Hellenism in Late Antiquity*. Cambridge: Cambridge University Press.

Jollois, Prosper, and Édouard du Terrage Devilliers. 1809. "Description du Temple de l'Ouest, ou du Temple d'Isis." In *Description de l'Égypte, ou Recueil des observations et des recherches qui ont été faites en Égypte pendant l'expédition de l'armée française, publié par les ordres de sa Majesté l'Empereur Napoléon le Grand*, edited by Edme-François Jomard, Antiquités, Description, 1, 161–73. Paris: Imprimerie impériale.

Jomard, Edme-François. 1809. "Description des Hypogées de la ville de Thèbes." *Description de l'Égypte, ou recueil des observations et des recherches qui ont été faites en Égypte pendant l'expédition de l'armée française, publié par les ordres de sa Majesté l'Empereur Napoléon le Grand*, edited by Edme-François Jomard, Antiquités, Description, 1, 305–92. Paris: Imprimerie impériale.

Jurman, Claus. 2022. *Pharaoh's New Clothes: On (Post)colonial Egyptology, Hypocrisy, and the Elephant in the Room*. Heidelberg: Propylaeum Fachinformationsdienst Altertumswissenschaften.

Kalfatovic, Martin R. 1992. *Nile Notes of a Howadji: A Bibliography of Travelers' Tales from Egypt, from the Earliest Time to 1918*. Metuchen, NJ: Scarecrow Press.

Karamanolis, George. 2014. "Porphyry and Iamblichus." In *The Routledge Companion to Ancient Philosophy*, edited by James Warren and Frisbee Sheffield, 610–25. New York: Routledge.

Kennedy, Alison Wilma Thomson. 2006. "John Kenrick and the Transformation of Unitarian Thought." PhD diss., University of Stirling.

Kenrick, John. 1841. *The Egypt of Herodotus: Being the Second and Part of the Third Books of His History. With Notes and Preliminary Dissertations*. London: B. Fellowes.

———. 1850. *Ancient Egypt under the Pharaohs*. London: B. Fellowes.

Khattab, Aleya. 1982. *Das Ägyptenbild in den deutschsprachigen Reisebeschreibungen der Zeit von 1285–1500*. Frankfurt am Main: Peter Lang.

Kircher, Athanasius. 1652–54. *Oedipus aegyptiacus, hoc est universalis hieroglyphicæ veterum doctrinæ temporum iniuria abolitæ instauratio. Opus ex omni Orientalium doctrina & sapientia conditum, nec non viginti diuersarum linguarum, autoritate stabilitum*. Rome: Vitalis Mascardi.

———. 1676. *Sphinx mystagoga, sive diatribe hieroglyphica, qua mumiæ, ex Memphiticis Pyramidum adytis erutæ, & non ita pridem in Galliam transmissæ, juxta veterum Hieromystarum mentem, intentionemque, plena fide & exacta exhibetur interpretatio ad inclytos abstrusiorumque cognitionum peritia instructissimos Galliæ philologos directa*. Amsterdam: Ex Officina Janssonio-Waesbergiana.

Kuhn, Thomas S. 1962. *The Structure of Scientific Revolutions*. Chicago: University of Chicago Press.

La Brasca, Frank. 1999. "'Hinc mel, hinc venenum': L'édition commentée du *De rerum natura* par Giovanni Nardi (1647)." In *Présence de Lucrèce: Actes du colloque tenu à Tours (3–5 décembre 1998)*, edited by Rémy Poignault, 381–98. Tours: Centre de Recherches A. Paganiol.

Lage, Julian zur. 2022. *Geschichtsschreibung aus der Bibliothek: Sesshafte Gelehrte und globale Wissenszirkulation (ca. 1750—1815)*. Wolfenbüttel: Herzog August.

Lane, Edward William. 1836. *An Account of the Manners and Customs of the Modern Egyptians, Written during the Years 1833, -34, and -35, Partly from Notes Made during a Former Visit to That Country in the Years of 1825, -26, -27, and -28*. London: Charles Knight.

Langer, Christian. 2017. "The Informal Colonialism of Egyptology: From the French Expedition to the Security State." In *Critical Epistemologies of Global Politics*, edited by Marc Woons and Sebastian Weier, 182–202. Bristol: E-International Relations.

———. 2023. "Egyptology: A Decolonial Investigation." *Archaeologies: Journal of the World Archaeological Congress* 19 (1): 39–59.

Lateiner, Donald. 1989. *The Historical Method of Herodotus*. Toronto: University of Toronto Press.

Latour, Bruno. 2000. "On the Partial Existence of Existing and Nonexisting Objects." In *Biographies of Scientific Objects*, edited by Lorraine Daston, 247–69. Chicago: University of Chicago Press.

———. 2005. *Reassembling the Social: An Introduction to Actor-Network-Theory*. Oxford : Oxford University Press.

Laurens, Henry. 1987. *Les origines intellectuelles de l'Expédition d'Égypte: L'Orientalisme Islamisant en France (1698–1798)*. Istanbul: Isis.

Lefkowitz, Mary. 2009. "Historiography and Myth." In *A Companion to the Philosophy of History and Historiography*, edited by Aviezer Tucker, 353–61. Chichester: Blackwell.

Lenoir, Alexandre. 1812. *Dissertation sur les deux questions suivantes: A-t-il existé un tribunal pour juger les rois d'Égypte après leur mort? Les pyramides d'Égypte étaient-elles destinées à servir de tombeaux aux rois?* Paris: Imprimerie de Chanson.

———. 1816. *Explication d'un papyrus égyptien, nouvelle édition, ornée de gravures, augmentée de notes instructives sur chaque sujet representé, de l'explication d'un autre papyrus conservé à la bibliothèque du roi, et d'une peinture découverte à Thèbes dans le tombeau des rois*. Paris: Imprimerie d'Hacquart.

Lenormant, François. 1869. *Manuel d'histoire ancienne de l'orient jusqu'aux guerres médiques*. Vol. 1. *Temps primitifs—Israélites—Égyptiens*. Paris: Maisonneuve.

Lepper, Verena M., and Ingelore Hafemann, eds. 2012. *Karl Richard Lepsius: Die Begründer der deutschen Ägyptologie*. Berlin: Kadmos.

Lepsius, Richard. 1842. *Das Todtenbuch der Ägypter nach dem hieroglyphischen Papyrus in Turin*. Leipzig: Georg Wigand.

———. 1849–56. *Denkmaeler aus Aegypten und Aethiopien: Nach den Zeichnungen der von seiner Majestät dem Koenige von Preussen Friedrich Wilhelm IV nach diesen Ländern gesendeten und in den Jahren 1842–1845 ausgeführten wissenschaftlichen Expedition*. Berlin: Nicolaische.

———. 1867. *Aelteste Texte des Todtenbuchs nach Sarkophagen des altaegyptischen Reichs im Berliner Museum*. Berlin: Wilhelm Hertz.

Letts, Malcolm. 1953. *Mandeville's Travels: Texts and Translations*. London: Hakluyt Society.

Levitin, Dmitri. 2013. "John Spencer's *De legibus hebraeorum* (1683–85) and 'Enlightened' Sacred History: A New Interpetation." *Journal of the Warburg and Courtauld Institutes* 76:49–92.

———. 2015. *Ancient Wisdom in the Age of the New Science: Histories of Philosophy in England, c. 1640–1700*. Cambridge: Cambridge University Press.

Lieven, Alexandra von. 2012. "Book of the Dead, Book of the Living. BD as Temple Texts." *Journal of Egyptian Archaeology* 98:249–67.

———. 2018. "Porphyrios und die ägyptische Religion im Lichte ägyptischer Quellen II: Der Magen als Sündenbock (*De abstinensia* IV.10.3–5)." In *Across the Mediterranean—Along the Nile: Studies in Egyptology, Nubiology and Late Antiquity Dedicated to László Török on the Occasion of His 75th Birthday*, edited by Tamás A. Bács, Ádám Bollók, and Tivadar Vida, 283–303. Budapest: Institute of Archaeology, Research Center for the Humanities, Hungarian Academy of Sciences and Museum of Fine Arts.

Lloyd, Alan B. 1975. *Herodotus Book II: Introduction*. Leiden: E. J. Brill.

Lorenz, Hendrik. 2019. "Plato on the Soul." In *The Oxford Handbook of Plato*, 2nd ed., edited by Gail Fine, 506–9. Oxford: Oxford University Press.

Lucarelli, Rita, and Martin Stadler, eds. 2023. *The Oxford Handbook of the Egyptian Book of the Dead*. Oxford: Oxford University Press.

Luraghi, Nino. 2006. "Meta-*historiē*: Method and Genre in the *Histories*." In *The Cambridge Companion to Herodotus*, edited by Carolyn Dewald and John Marincola, 76–91. Cambridge: Cambridge University Press.

Lüscher, Barbara. 2018. *Der sogenannte "Calendrier Égyptien" oder die Mumienbinden der Aberuerai (BN 89 + BN 229 / Louvre N. 3059 u.a.): Zur frühen Rezeptionsgeschichte eines späten Totenbuches*. Basel: Orientverlag.

Mackintosh-Smith, Tim. 2021. *A Physician on the Nile: A description of Egypt and journal of the famine years—'Abd al-Laṭīf al-Baghdādī*. New York: New York University Press.

Macpherson, Jay. 2004. "The Travels of *Sethos*." *Lumen: Selected Proceedings from the Canadian Society for Eighteenth-Century Studies* 23:235–54.

Manassa, Colleen. 2006. "The Judgment Hall of Osiris in the Book of Gates." *Revue d'Égyptologie* 57:109–50.

Manolaraki, Eleni. 2012. *Noscendi nilum cupido: Imagining Egypt from Lucan to Philostratus*. Berlin: De Gruyter.

Marchand, Suzanne. 2021. "Finding Truths among the "Lies": Fact-Checking Herodotus's Egypt in the Long Eighteenth Century." *History of Humanities* 6 (1): 269–93.

Marquet, Jean-François. 1987. "La quête isiaque d'Athanase Kircher." *Les études philosophiques*. 1987 (2/3): 227–41.

Marshall, Peter. 2002. *Beliefs and the Dead in Reformation England*. Oxford: Oxford University Press.

———. 2015. "After Purgatory: Death and Remembrance in the Reformation World." In *Preparing for Death, Remembering the Dead*, edited by Tarald Rasmussen and Jon Øygarden Flæten, 25–44. Göttingen: Vandenhoeck und Ruprecht.

Marshall, Peter K. 1997. *Servius and commentary on Virgil*. Binghamton, NY: Center for Medieval and Renaissance Studies.

Marsham, John. 1672. *Chronicus canon ægyptiacus, ebraicus, græcus et disquisitiones*. London: Thomas Roycroft.

Mascrier, Jean-Baptiste le, ed. 1735. *Description de l'Égypte, contenant plusieurs remarques curieuses sur la géographie ancienne et moderne de ce païs, sur ses monumens anciens, sur les mœurs, les coutumes, & la religion des habitants, sur le gouvernement & le commerce, sur les animaux, les arbres, les plantes, &c. Composée sur les mémoires de M. de Maillet, ancien consul de France au Caire*. Paris: Louis Genneau and Jacques Rollin.

Maspero, Gaston. 1872. "Le Papyrus de Neb-Qed." *Revue critique d'histoire et de littérature* 6 (2): 337–45.

———. 1887. "Bulletin critique de la religion égyptienne: Le Livre des Morts." *Revue de l'histoire des religions* 15: 265–315.

Matić, Uroš. 2018. "De-colonizing the Historiography and Archaeology of Ancient Egypt and Nubia, Part 1: Scientific Racism." *Journal of Egyptian History* 11 (1–2): 19–44.

———. 2023. "Postcolonialism as a Reverse Discourse in Egyptology: Decolonizing Historiography and Archaeology of Ancient Egypt and Nubia part 2." *Archaeologies: Journal of the World Archaeological Congress* 19 (1): 60–82.

McDannell, Colleen, and Bernhard Lang. 1988. *Heaven: A History*. New Haven, CT: Yale University Press.

McGeough, Kevin M. 2013. "Imagining Ancient Egypt as Idealized Self in Eighteenth-Century Europe." In *Eighteenth-Century Thing Theory in a Global Context: From Consumerism to Celebrity Culture*, edited by Ileana Baird and Christina Ionescu, 89–110. Farnham: Ashgate.

McManners, John. 1981. *Death and the Enlightenment: Changing Attitudes to Death among Christians and Unbelievers in Eighteenth-Century France*. Oxford: Oxford University Press.

Meyer-Zwiffelhoffer, Eckhard. 1995. "Alte Geschichte in der Universalgeschichtsschreibung der Frühen Neuzeit." *Saeculum* 46 (2): 249–73.

Milanese, Guido. 2016. "Italian Commentaries on Lucretius." In *Classical Com-*

mentaries: Explorations in a Scholarly Genre, edited by Christina S. Kraus and Christopher Stray, 195–215. Oxford: Oxford University Press.

Montagu, John. 1799. *A Voyage Performed by the Late Earl of Sandwich round the Mediterranean in the Years 1738 and 1739.* London: T. Cadell Jun. and W. Davies.

Montfaucon, Bernard de. 1722–24 [1719–24]. *L'antiquité expliquée et représentée en figures.* 2nd ed. rev. and corr. Paris: Florentine Delaulne, Hilaire Foucault, Michel Clousier, Jean-Geoffroy Nyon, Etienne Ganeau, Nicolas Gosselin, and Pierre-François Giffart.

Moore, Abigail Harrison. 2002. "*Voyage*: Dominique-Vivant Denon and the Transference of Images of Egypt." *Art History* 25 (4): 531–49.

Moser, Stephanie. 2006. *Wondrous Curiosities: Ancient Egypt at the British Museum.* Chicago: University of Chicago Press.

Moshenska, Gabriel. 2014a. "Thomas 'Mummy' Pettigrew and the Study of Egypt in Early Nineteenth-Century Britain." In *Histories of Egyptology: Interdisciplinary Measures,* edited by William Carruthers, 201–14. New York: Routledge.

———. 2014b. "Unrolling Egyptian Mummies in Nineteenth-Century Britain." *British Journal for the History of Science* 47 (3): 451–77.

Mosley, Derrick. 2021. "Sir John Marsham (1602–1685) and the History of Scholarship." PhD diss., University of Cambridge.

Muntz, Charles E. 2017. *Diodorus Siculus and the World of the Late Roman Republic.* Oxford: Oxford University Press.

Nardi, Giovanni. 1647. *Titi Lucretii Cari de rerum natura libri sex: Unà cum paraphrastica explanatione, et animaduersionibus.* Florence: Typis Amatoris Massæ Foroliuien.

Navratilova, Hana, Thomas L. Gertzen, Marleen De Meyer, Aidan Dodson, and Andrew Bednarski, eds. 2023. *Addressing Diversity: Inclusive Histories of Egyptology.* Münster: Zaphon.

Newmyer, Stephen T. 2014. "Animals in Plutarch." In *A Companion to Plutarch,* edited by Mark Beck, 223–34. Chichester: Wiley Blackwell.

Niebuhr, Carsten. 1774–78. *Reisebeschreibung nach Arabien und andern umliegenden Ländern.* Copenhagen: Nicolaus Möller.

Nielsen, Flemming A. J. 1997. *The Tragedy in History: Herodotus and Deuteronomistic History.* Sheffield: Sheffield Academic Press.

Noble, Louise. 2011. *Medicinal Cannibalism in Early Modern English Literature and Culture.* New York: Palgrave Macmillan.

Norden, Frederic Louïs. 1755. *Voyage d'Égypte et de Nubie.* Copenhagen: Imprimerie de la Maison Royale des Orphelins.

Nyord, Rune. 2009. *Breathing Flesh: Conceptions of the Body in the Ancient Egyptian Coffin Texts.* Copenhagen: Museum Tusculanum Press.

———. 2013. "Memory and Succession in the City of the Dead: Temporality in the Ancient Egyptian Mortuary Cult." In *Taming Time, Timing Death*, edited by Dorthe Refslund Christensen and Rane Willerslev, 195–211. Farnham: Ashgate.

———. 2018. "'Taking Ancient Egyptian Mortuary Religion Seriously': Why Would We, and How Could We?" *Journal of Ancient Egyptian Interconnections* 17: 73–87.

———. 2019. "The Concept of *Ka* between Egyptian and Egyptological Frameworks." In *Concepts in Middle Kingdom Funerary Culture: Proceedings of the Lady Wallis Budge Anniversary Sympoisum Held at Christ's College, Cambridge, 22 January 2016*, edited by Rune Nyord, 150–203. Leiden: Brill.

———. 2020. "On Interpreting Ancient Egyptian Funerary Texts." *Claroscuro* 19 (2): 1–23.

———. Forthcoming. "What Can an Image Do? Rethinking Wooden Funerary Models." In *Modelling Ancient Egypt: Papers of the 2019 Luxor University KunstModell-Project-Conference on Ancient Egyptian Models*, edited by Susanne Deicher, Heike Wilde, and Maria Keil, 9–42. Berlin: Kadmos.

O'Kane, Martin. 2007. "'The bosom of Abraham' (Luke 16:22): Father Abraham in the Visual Imagination." *Biblical Interpretation* 15:485–518.

Oldfather, Charles Henry. 1933. *Diodorus of Sicily in Twelve Volumes, I: Books I and II, 1–34. Loeb Classical Library*, vol. 279. Cambridge, MA: Harvard University Press.

Opsomer, Jan. 2012. "Plutarch on the Division of the Soul." In *Plato and the Divided Self*, edited by Rachel Barney, Tad Brennan, and Charles Brittain, 311–30. Cambridge: Cambridge University Press.

Otto, Bernd-Christian. 2013. "Zauberhaftes Ägypten—Ägyptischer Zauber? Überlegungen zur Verwendung des Magiebegriffs in der Ägyptologie." In *Ägypten—Kindheit—Tod: Gedenkschrift für Edmund Hermsen*, edited by Florian Jeserich. Vienna: Böhlau.

Pangburn, Kris. 2014. "The Religious Underpinnings of Early Prussian Liberalism: The Case of Wilhelm Grävel." *Central European History* 46:779–814.

Patillon, Michel, and Alain Philippe Segonds. 1995. *Porphyre, De l'abstinence, Livre IV*. Paris: Belles Lettres.

Pauw, Cornelius de. 1773. *Recherches philosophiques sur les égyptiens et les chinois*. Berlin: C. J. Decker.

Pearce, Susan. 2002. "Bodies in Exile: Egyptian Mummies in the Early Nineteenth Century and Their Cultural Implications." In *Displaced Persons: Conditions of Exile in European Culture*, edited by Sharon Ouditt, 54–72. Aldershot: Ashgate.

Perry, Charles. 1743. *A View of the Levant: Particularly of Constantinople, Syria, Egypt, and Greece, in Which Their Antiquities, Government, Politics, Maxims,*

Manners, and Customs, (with Many Other Circumstances and Contingencies) Are Attempted to Be Described and Treated on. London: T. Woodward, C. Davis, and J. Shuckburgh.

Pettigrew, Thomas Joseph. 1834. *A History of Egyptian Mummies, and an Account of the Worship and Embalming of the Sacred Animals by the Egyptians; with Remarks on the Funeral Ceremonies of Different Nations. And Observations on the Mummies of the Canary Islands, of the Ancient Peruvians, Burman Priests, &c.* London: Longman, Rees, Orme, Brown, Green, and Longman.

Piankoff, Alexandre. 1954. *The Tomb of Ramesses VI.* New York: Pantheon Books.

Pinch, Trevor J., and Wiebe E. Bijker. 1984. "The Social Construction of Facts and Artefacts: Or How the Sociology of Science and the Sociology of Technology Might Benefit Each Other." *Social Studies of Science* 14 (3): 399–441.

Places, Édouard des. 1982. *Porphyre, Vie de Pythagore, Lettre à Marcella.* Paris: Belles Lettres.

Pococke, Richard. 1743. *A Description of the East, and Some Other Countries.* Vol. 1, *Observations on Egypt.* London: W. Bowyer.

Podemann Sørensen, Jørgen. 1996. "Ritual Art: A Key to the Ancient Egyptian Book of the Dead." *Scripta Instituti Donneriani Aboensis* 16: 257–68.

———. 2012. "'The Eye of the World': An interpretation of the *Kore Kosmou* on its Egyptian background." Herme<neu>tica: New approaches to the text and interpretation of the *Corpus Hermeticum*, Princeton University. http://www.princeton.edu/~hellenic/Hermeneutica/PodemannPaper.pdf.

———. 2013. *Det gamle Ægyptens religiøse litteratur: Fra Pyramideteksterne til Hermes Trismegistos.* Højbjerg: Univers.

———. 2022. "'Tör De, mine Herrer, gjöre en Vandring med mig blandt Levninger af Döde': Thorlacius i Kongernes Dal—én måned før Champollions tydning." *Papyrus* 42 (2): 40–44.

Pommerening, Tanja. 2010. "*Mumia*: From Ozokerite to Cure-all." In *Mummies of the World*, edited by Alfried Wieczorek and Wilfried Rosendahl, 190–97. Munich: Prestel.

Pomplun, Trent. 2010. *Jesuit on the Roof of the World: Ippolito Desideri's Mission to Eighteenth-Century Tibet.* Oxford: Oxford University Press.

Posener, Georges. 1985. *Le Papyrus Vandier.* Cairo: Institut français d'archéologie orientale.

Poulouin, Claudine. 1995. "*L'Antiquité expliquée et représentée en figures* (1719–1724) par Bernard de Montfaucon." *Dix-Huitième Siècle* 27:46–60.

Prichard, James Cowles. 1813. *Researches into the Physical History of Man.* London: John and Arthur Arch and B. and H. Harry.

———. 1819. *An Analysis of the Egyptian Mythology: To Which Is Subjoined, a Critical Examination of the Remains of Egyptian Chronology.* London: John and Arthur Arch.

———. 1838. *An Analysis of the Egyptian Mythology, in Which the Philosophy and the Superstitions of the Ancient Egyptians Are Compared with Those of the Indians and Other Nations of Antiquity. To Which Is Added a Translation of the Preliminary Essay Prefixed by Professor A. W. von Schlegel to the German Edition of the Same Work*. London: Sherwood, Gilbert, and Piper.

Prochaska, David. 1994. "Art of Colonialism, Colonialism of Art: The *Description de l'Égypte* (1809–1828)." *L'Esprit Créateur* 34 (2): 69–91.

Quirke, Stephen. 2010. *Hidden Hands: Egyptian Workforces in Petrie Excavation Archives, 1880–1924*. London: Duckworth.

Raeburn, Gordon D. 2021. "The Reformation of Burial in the Protestant Churches." In *A Companion to Death, Burial, and Remembrance in Late Medieval and Early Modern Europe, c. 1300–1700*, edited by Christopher M. Bellitto, 156–74. Leiden: Brill.

Reetz, Katja. 2019. *Andreas Gryphius: Mumiae Wratislaviensis. Edition, kommentierte Übersetzung und Werkstudie mit ausführlicher wissensgeschichtlicher Einleitung*. Berlin: De Gruyter.

Reid, Donald Malcolm. 1997. *Whose Pharaohs? Archaeology, Museums, and Egyptian National Identity from Napoleon to World War I*. New York: Columbia University Press.

Renouf, Peter Le Page. 1880. *Lectures on the Origin and Growth of Religion as Illustrated by the Religion of Ancient Egypt. Delivered in May and June, 1879*. London: Williams and Norgate.

Richter, Daniel S. 2001. "Plutarch on Isis and Osiris: Text, Cult, and Cultural Appropriation." *Transactions of the American Philological Association* 131:191–216.

Riggs, Christina. 2014. *Unwrapping Ancient Egypt*. London: Bloomsbury Academic.

Rigord, Jean-Pierre. 1704. "Lettre de Monsieur Rigord Commissaire de la Marine aux journalistes de Trevoux sur une ceinture de toile trouvée en Egypte autour d'une mumie." *Mémoires pour l'Histoire des Sciences et des Beaux-Arts* 4:978–1000.

Rohbeck, Johannes 2002. "La philosophie de l'histoire chez Antoine-Yves Goguet: Chronique biblique et progrès historique." *Dix-huitième Siècle* 34:257–66.

Roos, Anna Marie. 2022. "The First Egyptian Society." In *Collective Wisdom: Collecting in the Early Modern Academy*, edited by Anna Marie Roos and Vera Keller, 261–288. Turnhout: Brepols.

Rosellini, Ippolito. 1836. *I monumenti dell'Egitto e della Nubia disegnati dalla spedizione scientifico-letteraria Toscana in Egitto. Parte seconda: Monumenti Civili, tomo III*. Pisa: Presso Niccolò Capurro.

———. 1838. *Breve notizia intorno un frammento di papiro funebre Egizio esistente nel Ducale Museo di Parma*. Parma: Stamperia Carmignani.

Roskam, Geert. 2017. *Plutarch*. Cambridge: Cambridge University Press.

Röth, Eduard. 1848. *Geschichte unserer abendländischen Philosophie: Entwicklungsgeschichte unserer spekulativen, sowohl philosophischen als religiösen Ideen von ihren ersten Anfängen bis auf die Gegenwart. Erster Band: Die ältesten Quellen unserer spekulativen Ideen*. Mannheim: Friedrich Bassermann.

Roucher, Jean-Antoine. 1797. *Consolations de ma captivité, ou correspondance de Roucher, mort victime de la tyrannie décemvirale, le 7 thermidor, an 2 de la République Française*. Paris: H. Agasse.

Rougé, Emmanuel de. 1846. "Examen de l'ouvrage de M. le chevalier de Bunsen intitulé Ægypteus [*sic*] Stelle in der Weltgefchichte [*sic*] (La place de l'Égypte dans l'histoire de l'humanité). Premier article" *Annales de philosophie chrétienne* 13 (78): 432–58.

———. 1852. "Notice sur un manuscrit égyptien, en écriture hiératique, écrit sous le règne de Merienphthah, fils du grand Ramsès, vers le XVe siècle avant l'Ère Chrétienne." *Revue Archéologique* 9 (2): 385–97.

———. 1853. "Mémoire sur l'inscription du tombeau d'Ahmès, chef des Nautoniers." *Mémoires présentés par divers savants étrangers à l'Académie* 3:1–196.

———. 1860. *Études sur le rituel funéraire des anciens égyptiens*. Paris: Bureaux de la *Revue archéologique*.

Rowell, Geoffrey. 1974. *Hell and the Victorians: A Study of the Nineteenth-Century Theological Controversies Concerning Eternal Punishment and the Future Life*. Oxford: Oxford University Press.

Rugg, Julie. 1999. "From Reason to Regulation: 1760–1850." In *Death in England: An Illustrated History*, edited by Peter C. Jupp and Claire Gittings, 202–229. Manchester: Manchester University Press.

Sacks, Kenneth S. 1990. *Diodorus Siculus and the First Century*. Princeton, NJ: Princeton University Press.

Sandys, George. 1615. *A Relation of a Journey Begun An. Dom. 1610: Four Bookes Containing a Description of the Turkish Empire, of Ægypt, of the Holy Land, of the Remote Parts of Italy, and Ilands Adioyning*. London: W. Barrett.

Sarfatti, Tamar. 2022. *The Description of Egypt from Napoleon to Champollion*. Cham: Palgrave Macmillan.

Saumarez Smith, Ferdinand. 2021. "Pagans or Patriarchs? William Stukeley's "On the Mysterys of the Antients," the Bembine Tablet, and the Religious Culture of Early English Freemasonry." *Aegyptiaca* 6:3–43.

Savary, Claude-Étienne. 1786. *Lettres sur l'Égypte, où l'on offre le parallèle des mœurs anciennes & modernes de ses habitans, où l'on décrit l'état, le commerce, l'agriculture, le gouvernement, l'ancienne religion du pays, & la descente de S. Louis à Damiette, tirée de Joinville & des auteurs arabes, avec des cartes géographiques*. 2nd ed. Paris: Onfroi.

Sawicki, Diethard. 2002. *Leben mit den Toten: Geisterglauben und die Entstehung des Spiritismus in Deutschland 1770–1900*. Paderborn: Ferdinand Schöningh.

Scalf, Foy, ed. 2017. *Book of the Dead: Becoming God in Ancient Egypt*. Chicago: Oriental Institute of the University of Chicago.

Schipper, Bernd U., ed. 2006. *Ägyptologie als Wissenschaft: Adolf Erman (1854–1937) in seiner Zeit*. Berlin: Walter de Gruyter.

Schmitz-Esser, Romedio. 2014. *Der Leichnam im Mittelalter: Einbalsamierung, Verbrennung und die kulturelle Konstruktion des toten Körpers*. Ostfildern: Jan Thorbecke.

Schwartz, Emmanuel. 2016. "Lenoir, Alexandre (25 décembre 1761, Paris–1 juin 1839, Paris)." In *Dictionnaire critique des historiens de l'art actifs en France de la Révolution à la Première Guerre mondiale*, edited by Philippe Sénéchal and Claire Barbillon. https://www.inha.fr/fr/ressources/publications/publications-numeriques/dictionnaire-critique-des-historiens-de-l-art/lenoir-alexandre.html: Institut National d'Histoire de l'Art.

Schwyzer, Philip. 2005. "Mummy Is Become Merchandise: Literature and the Anglo-Egyptian Mummy Trade in the Seventeenth Century." In *Re-orienting the Renaissance: Cultural Exchanges with the Past*, edited by Gerald MacLean, 66–87. Hampshire: Palgrave Macmillan.

———. 2017. "No Joyful Voices: The Silence of the Urns in Browne's Hydrotaphia and Contemporary Archaeology." In *The Palgrave Handbook of Early Modern Literature and Science*, edited by Howard Marchitello and Evelyn Tribble, 295–309. London: Palgrave Macmillan.

Shapin, Steven. 2010. *Never Pure: Historical Studies of Science as if It Was Produced by People with Bodies, Situated in Time, Space, Culture, and Society, and Struggling for Credibility and Authority*. Baltimore: Johns Hopkins University Press.

Shapin, Steven, and Simon Schaffer. 1985. *Leviathan and the Air-Pump: Hobbes, Boyle, and the Experimental Life*. Princeton, NJ: Princeton University Press.

Sharp, Lynn L. 2006. *Secular Spirituality: Reincarnation and Spiritism in Nineteenth-Century France*. Lanham, MD: Lexington Books.

Sharpe, Samuel. 1846. *The History of Egypt from the Earliest Times till the Conquest by the Arabs A.D. 640*. New edition. London: Edward Moxon.

———. 1863. *Egyptian Mythology and Egyptian Christianity*. London: John Russell Smith.

Shaw, Thomas. 1738. *Travels, or Observations Relating to Several Parts of Barbary and the Levant*. Oxford: Theatre.

Shearman, John. 1961. "The Chigi Chapel in S. Maria del Popolo." *Journal of the Warburg and Courtauld Institutes* 24 (3/4): 129–60.

Sheppard, Kathleen L. 2013. *The Life of Margaret Alice Murray: A Woman's Work in Archaeology*. Lanham, MD: Lexington Books.

———. 2022. *Tea on the Terrace: Hotels and Egyptologists' Social Networks, 1885–1925*. Manchester: Manchester University Press.

Shubert, Steven Blake. 2007. "Those Who (Still) Live on Earth: A Study of the Ancient Egyptian Appeal to the Living Texts." PhD diss., University of Toronto.

Sicard, Paul. 1982a. *Œuvres I: Lettres et relations inédites. Présentation et notes de Maurice Martin*. Cairo: Institut français d'archéologie orientale.

———. 1982b. *Œuvres III: Parallèle géographique de l'anciennne Égypte et de l'Égypte moderne. Présentation et notes de Serge Sauneron et Maurice Martin*. Cairo: Institut français d'archéologie orientale.

Simonetti, Elsa Giovanna. 2019. "Plutarch and the Neoplatonists: Porphyry, Proklos, Simplikios." In *Brill's Companion to the Reception of Plutarch*, edited by Sophia Xenophontos and Katerina Oikonomopoulou, 136–53. Leiden: Brill.

Simpson, William Kelly, ed. 2003. *The Literature of Ancient Egypt: An Anthology of Stories, Instructions, Stelae, Autobiographies, and Poetry*. Cairo: American University in Cairo Press.

Śliwa, Joachim. 2007. "Giovanni Nardi (c. 1580–c. 1655) and His Studies on Ancient Egypt." *Études et travaux* 21:151–60.

Smith, Andrew. 2013. "The Image of Egypt in the Platonic Tradition." In *Plato Revivied: Essays on Ancient Platonism in Honour of Dominic J. O'Meara*, edited by Filip Karfík and Euree Song, 319–25. Berlin: De Gruyter.

Smith, Malvern van Wyk. 2006. "'Would the Real James Bruce Please Stand Up?' Bruce's Travels to Discover the Sources of the Nile (1790), in Alexander Murray's edition of 1813." *English Academy Review* 23:59–83.

Smith, Mark. 2017. *Following Osiris: Perspectives on the Osirian Afterlife through the Millennia*. Oxford: Oxford University Press.

Smith, Morton. 1965. "Porphyry, Life of Pythagoras." In *Heroes and Gods: Spiritual Biographies in Antiquity*, edited by Moses Hadas and Morton Smith, 105–28. New York: Harper and Row.

Somos, Mark. 2014. "The Lost Treasures of Sethos, Enlightened Prince of Egypt (1731)." In *Athenian Legacies: European Debates on Citizenship*, edited by Paschalis M. Kitromilides, 271–314. Florence: Leo S. Olschki.

Sparn, Walter. 2007. "'Aussichten in die Ewigkeit': Jenseitsvorstellungen in der neuzeitlichen protestantischen Theologie." In *Das Jenseits: Facetten eines religiösen Begriffs*, edited by Lucian Hölscher, 12–39. Göttingen: Wallstein.

Spencer, John. 1685. *De legibus Hebræorum ritualibus et earum rationibus*. Book 3. Cambridge: John Hayes.

Sponde, Henry de. 1597. *Les cimitières sacrez*. Bordeaux: S. Millanges.

———. 1600. *Les cimitières sacrez*. 6th ed. Paris: Pierre Louys Feburier.

———. 1638. *Coemeteria sacra*. Paris: Dionysius de la Noüe.

Stadler, Martin. 2001. "War eine dramatische Aufführung eines Totengerichts Teil der ägyptischen Totenriten?" *Studien zur altägyptischen Kultur* 29:331–48.

———. 2017. "Ägyptenrezeption in der römischen Kaiserzeit." In *Platonismus und spätägyptische Religion: Plutarch und die Ägyptenrezeption in der römischen Kaiserzeit*, edited by Michael Erler and Martin Andreas Stadler, 21–42. Berlin: De Gruyter.

Stephan, Tara. 2017. "Writing the Past: Ancient Egypt through the Lens of Medieval Islamic Thought." In *Arabic Humanities, Islamic Thought: Essays in Honor of Everett K. Rowson*, edited by Joseph E. Lowry and Shawkat M. Toorawa, 256–70. Leiden: Brill.

Stephens, Walter. 2004. "When Pope Noah Ruled the Etruscans: Annius of Viterbo and His Forged *Antiquities*." *MLN* 119 (supplement): S201-23.

Stienne, Angela. 2017. "Encountering Egyptian mummies, 1753–1858." PhD diss., University of Leicester.

———. 2022. *Mummified: The Stories behind Egyptian Mummies in Museums*. Manchester: Manchester University Press.

Stocker, Arthur Frederick, and Albert Hartman Travis. 1965. *Servianorum in Vergilii carmina commentariorum editionis Harvardianae, volumen III quod in Aeneidos libros III-IV explanationes continet*. Oxford: Oxford University Press.

Stolzenberg, Daniel. 2001a. "Kircher's Egypt." In *The Great Art of Knowing: The Baroque Encyclopedia of Athanasius Kircher*, edited by Daniel Stolzenberg, 115–25. Stanford, CA: Stanford University Libraries.

———. 2001b. "Kircher among the ruins: Esoteric Knowledge and Universal History." In *The Great Art of Knowing: The Baroque Encyclopedia of Athanasius Kircher*, edited by Daniel Stolzenberg, 127–39. Stanford, CA: Stanford University Libraries.

———. 2013. *Egyptian Oedipus: Athanasius Kircher and the Secrets of Antiquity*. Chicago: University of Chicago Press.

Stuckrad, Kocku von. 2010. *Locations of Knowledge in Mediaeval and Early Modern Europe: Esoteric Discourse and Western Identities*. Leiden: Brill.

Sulimani, Iris. 2011. *Diodorus's Mythistory and the Pagan Mission: Historiography and Culture-Heroes in the First Pentad of the Bibliotheke*. Leiden: Brill.

Sutherland, Suzanne, Paula Findlen, and Iva Lelková. 2018. "Etruscan Dreams: Athanasius Kircher, Medici Patronage, and Tuscan friendships, 1633–1680." *I Tatti Studies in the Italian Renaissance* 21 (2): 299–349.

Tarlow, Sarah. 2011. *Ritual, Belief and the Dead in Early Modern Britain and Ireland*. Cambridge: Cambridge University Press.

Terrasson, Jean. 1813 [1731]. *Séthos, histoire ou vie tirée des monumens anecdotes de l'ancienne Égypte. Trad. d'un manuscrit grec*. New edition. Paris: D'Hautel.

Thévenot, Jean de. 1664. *Relation d'un voyage fait au Levant dans laquelle il est curieusement traité des estats sujets au Grand Seigneur, des mœurs, religions, forces, gouuernemens, politiques, langues, & coustumes des habitans de ce grand empire. Et des singularitez particulieres de l'Archipel, Constantinople, Terre Sainte, Egypte, pyramides, mumies, deserts d'Arabie, la Meque, et de plusieurs autres lieux de l'Asie & de l'Affrique remarquées depuis peu, & non encore décrites iusqu'a present. Outre les choses mémorables arriuées au dernier siege de Bagdat, les ceremonies faites aux receptions des ambassadeurs du Mogol: Et l'entretien de l'autheur auec celuy du Pretejan, où il est parlé des sources du Nil.* Paris: Louis Bilaine.

———. 1674. *Suite du voyage de Levant; dans laquelle apres plusieurs remarques tres-singulieres sur des particularitez de l'Egypte, de la Syrie, de la Mesopotamie, de l'Euphrate et du Tygre, il est traité de la Perse, et autres estats sujets au roy de Perse, ainsi que de sa cour, & des religions, gouvernemens, mœurs, forces, langues, sciences, arts & coûtumes des peuples de ce grand empire; et aussi des antiquitez de Tchehelminar & autres lieux vers l'ancienne Persepolis: Et particulierement de la route exacte de ce grand voyage, tant par terre en Turquie et en Perse, que par mer dans la Mediterranée, Golfe Persique et Mer des Indes.* Paris: Charles Angot.

Thevet, André. 1556. *Cosmographie de Levant.* Lyon: Jan de Tournes et Guil. Gazeau.

Thibaut-Payen, Jacqueline. 1977. *Les morts, l'église et l'état: Recherches d'histoire administrative sur la sépulture et les cimetières dans le ressort du parlement de Paris aux XVIIe et XVIIIe siècles.* Paris: Fernand Lanore.

Thompson, Jason. 1992. *Sir Gardner Wilkinson and His Circle.* Austin: University of Texas Press.

———. 1997. "Edward William Lane in Egypt." *Journal of the American Research Center in Egypt* 34:243–61.

———. 2015–18. *Wonderful Things: A History of Egyptology.* 3 vols. Cairo: American University in Cairo Press.

———. 2020. *Edward William Lane, Description of Egypt: Notes and Views in Egypt and Nubia, 1825–28.* Cairo: American University in Cairo Press.

Thorlacius, Børge. 1823. "De gamle Ægypters Forestillinger om Underverdenen og Tilstanden efter Döden." *Det skandinaviske Litteraturselskabs Skrifter* 19:165–222.

Tingle, Elizabeth. 2021. "Changing Western European Visions of Christian Afterlives, 1350–1700: Heaven, Hell, and Purgatory." In *A Companion to Death, Burial, and Remembrance in Late Medieval and Early Modern Europe, c. 1300–1700*, edited by Philip Booth and Elizabeth Tingle, 33–71. Leiden: Brill.

Todd, Richard, and Kathryn Murphy, eds. 2008. *'A Man Very Well Studyed': New Contexts for Thomas Browne.* Leiden: Brill.

Valence, Françoise de. 2008. *Jean de Thévenot, Les voyages aux Indes Orientales, contenans une description exacte de l'Indostan, des nouveaux mogols, et des autres peuples et païs des Indes Orientales, avec leurs mœurs et maximes, religions, fêtes, temples, pagodes, cimitières, commerce, et autres choses remarquables. Edition critique établie, présentée et annotée par Françoise de Valence.* Paris: Honoré Champion.

Valerianus, Joannes Pierius. 1602 [1556]. *Hieroglyphica, seu de sacris ægyptorum aliarumque gentium literis comentarii.* Lyon: Paul Frellon.

Vidal, Jean-Marie. 1929. *Henri de Sponde, recteur de Saint-Louis des français, évêque de Pamiers (1568–1643).* Rome: Établissement français/Éditions A. Picard.

Volney, Constantin-François. 1787. *Voyage en Syrie et en Égypte, pendant les années 1783, 1784, & 1785.* Paris: Volland/Desenne.

Walker, D. P. 1964. *The Decline of Hell: Seventeenth-Century Discussions of Eternal Torment.* Chicago: University of Chicago Press.

Warburton, William. 1738. *The Divine Legation of Moses Demonstrated, on the Principles of a Religious Deist, from the Omission of the Doctrine of a Future State of Reward and Punishment in the Jewish Dispensation, First Volume.* London: Fletcher Gyles.

———. 1741. *The Divine Legation of Moses Demonstrated, on the Principles of a Religious Deist, from the Omission of the Doctrine of a Future State of Reward and Punishment in the Jewish Dispensation, Second Volume.* London: Fletcher Gyles.

Wees, Hans van. 2002. "Herodotus and the Past." In *Brill's Companion to Herodotus,* edited by Egbert J. Bakker, Irene J. F. de Jong, and Hans van Wees, 321–49. Leiden: Brill.

Weir, Todd. 2008. "The Secular Beyond: Free Religious Dissent and Debates over the Afterlife in Nineteenth-Century Germany." *Church History* 77 (3): 629–58.

Weiss, Lara. 2022. *The Walking Dead at Saqqara: Strategies of Social and Religious Interaction in Practice.* Berlin: De Gruyter.

Werner, Daniel S. 2012. *Myth and Philosophy in Plato's Phaedrus.* Cambridge: Cambridge University Press.

Westrem, Scott D. 2001. *The Hereford Map: A Transciption and Translation of the Legends with Commentary.* Turnhout: Brepols.

Wettengel, Wolfgang. 2003. *Die Erzählung von den beiden Brüdern: Der Papyrus d'Orbiney und die Königsideologie der Ramessiden.* Freiburg, Schweiz/Göttingen: Universitätsverlag/Vandenhoeck und Ruprecht.

Wheeler, Michael. 1994. *Heaven, Hell, and the Victorians.* Cambridge: Cambridge University Press.

White, David A. 1989. *Myth and Metaphysics in Plato's "Phaedo."* Selinsgrove, PA: Susquehanna University Press/Associated University Presses.

Whitehouse, Helen. 1992. "Towards a Kind of Egyptology: The Graphic Documentation of Ancient Egypt, 1587–1666." In *Documentary Culture: Florence and Rome from Grand-Duke Ferdinand I to Pope Alexander VII. Papers from a colloquium held at the Villa Spelman, Florence, 1990*, edited by Elizabeth Cropper, Giovanna Perini, and Francesco Solinas, 63–79. Bologna: Nuova Alfa/Johns Hopkins University Press.

Wildish, Mark. 2018. *The Hieroglyphics of Horapollo Nilous: Hieroglyphic Semantics in Late Antiquity*. London: Routledge.

Wilkinson, John. 1971. *Egeria's Travels: Newly Translated with Supporting Documents and Notes*. London: S.P.C.K.

Wilkinson, John Gardner. 1841. *A Second Series of the Manners and Customs of the Ancient Egyptians, Including Their Religion, Agriculture, &c. Derived from a Comparison of the Paintings, Sculptures, and Monuments Still Existing, with the Accounts of Ancient Authors*. London: John Murray.

Willems, Harco. 2023. "A Geopolitical Perspective on Some Early Developments in Egyptology: Lepsius at the Second International Congress of Orientalists." *Bulletin de l'Institut français d'archéologie orientale* 123:573–606.

Wilson, John Albert. 1970. *Herodotus in Egypt*. Leiden: Nederlands Instituut voor het Nabije Oosten.

Wolloch, Nathaniel. 2007. "'Facts, or Conjectures': Antoine-Yves Goguet's historiography." *Journal of the History of Ideas* 68 (3): 429–49.

Woodward, John. 1777. "Of the Wisdom of the Antient Egyptians; a Discourse concerning Their Arts, Their Sciences, and Their Learning: Their Laws, Their Government, and Their Religion. With Occasional Reflections upon the State of Learning among the Jews; and Some Other Nations." *Archaeologia* 4:212–310.

Wurm, Julius Friedrich. 1827. *Diodor's von Sicilien historische Bibliothek, Erstes Bändchen*. Stuttgart: J. B. Metzler'schen Buchhandlung.

Young, Thomas. 1819b. "Remarks on the Probabilities of Error in Physical Observations, and on the Density of the Earth, Considered, Especially with Regard to the Reduction of Experiments on the Pendulum." *Philosophical Transactions of the Royal Society of London* 109:70–95+1–4.

———. 1824 [1819]. "Egypt." *Encyclopaedia Britannica Supplement to the Fourth, Fifth, and Sixth Editions* 4:38–74.

Žabkar, Louis V. 1968. *A Study of the Ba Concept in Ancient Egyptian Texts*. Chicago: University of Chicago Press.

Zoega, Georgius. 1797. *De origine et usu obeliscorum ad Pium Sextum pontificem maximum*. Rome: Typis Lazzarinii Typographi Cameralis.

Zographou, Gerasimoula 1995. "L'argumentation d'Hérodote concernant les emprunts faits par les Grecs à la religion égyptienne." *Kernos* 8:187–203.

Index

Page numbers in italics refer to figures.